THE MALAVIKAGNIMITRA, A SANSKRIT PLAY, BY KALIDASA

THE MALAVIKAGNIMITRA,
A SANSKRIT PLAY,
BY
KALIDASA

EDITED WITH NOTES

BY

SHANKAR P. PANDIT, M.A.,

SENIOR DAKSHINA FELLOW, DECCAN COLLEGE, &c. &c. &c.

Registered under Act XXV. of 1867.

GYAN

Published by

GYAN

Gyan Publishing House
5, Ansari Road
Daryaganj, New Delhi-110002
Phone: 011-47034999, 9811692060
E-mail: books@gyanbooks.com

Distribution Network
gyanbooks.com
India, USA, Canada, UK, Australia, France

ISBN : 978-81-212-2087-3 (PB)
First Published, 1869

2nd Impression 2021

Printed at: Gyan Press, Delhi.

The Malavikagnimitra, A Sanskrit Play,
By
Kalidasa
Edited with Notes by: Shankar P. Pandit

THE

MALAVIKAGNIMITRA,

A SANSKRIT PLAY,

BY

KALIDASA.

EDITED WITH NOTES

BY

SHANKAR P. PANDIT, M.A.,
SENIOR DAKSHINA FELLOW, DECCAN COLLEGE,
&c. &c. &c.

Bombay:
GOVERNMENT CENTRAL BOOK DEPOT.

1869.

CRITICAL NOTICE.

The present edition of the Mâlavikâgnimitra is based upon a collation of seven MSS., six of which are written in the Devanâgarî and the remaining one in the Telagu character. They are as follows :—

(1) A MS. in the office of the Secretary to the Dakshiṇâ Prize Committee and originally belonging to Mr. Ganesh Shâstrî Lele. It is altogether a recent MS., not being older than six years. It contains thirty-four and a half oblong leaves, of thick blue paper, and is written in a bold and legible hand. Its colophon is इति कालिदासविरचितमालविकाग्निमित्रनाम नाटकं समाप्तम् ॥ श्रीर्भूयाल्लेखकपाठकयोः ॥ ७ ॥ शके १७८५ रुधिरोद्गारिनामसंवत्सरे भाद्रपदशुक्ल १२ द्वादश्यां गुरुवासरे लेखनं परिपूर्णमस्तु ॥ शुभं भवतु ॥ यादृशं पुस्तकं दृष्ट्वा तादृशं लिखितं मया ॥ यदि शुद्धमशुद्धं वा मम दोषो न विद्यते ॥ १ ॥ जलाद्रक्षेत्स्थलाद्रक्षेद्रक्षेच्छिथिलबन्धनात् ॥ मूर्खहस्ते न दातव्यं एवं वदति पुस्तकं ॥ २ ॥ भग्नपृष्ठिकटिग्रीवा स्तब्धदृष्टिरधोमुखम् ॥ कष्टेन लिखितं ग्रन्थं यत्नेन परिपालयेत् ॥ ३ ॥ I have called this MS. A.

(2) Another MS., belonging to Mr. Govind Shâstrî Nirantara of Nassick, a very correct and reliable one. It ends with the couplet: सप्तसप्ताश्वसु-[कु?]-- मिते राक्षसाह्वयवत्सरे। निरन्तरोपाभिधेन गोविन्देन व्यलेखि यत् ।, and thus bearing the date S'âl. 1777, *i.e.* A.C. 1855. Besides having been copied, it seems, from a

very correct original, it contains explanatory remarks here and there in the margin of the leaves. I have called this MS. B.

(3) A third MS., a very neatly written and trustworthy copy; though bearing no date, it appears to be from 75 to 100 years old. This also belongs to a Shâstrî at Nassick. I have designated this MS. by the letter C.

(4) This also comes from Nassick. It bears the following colophon:—

मयूरेश्वरपन्तेन श्रीमद्रामतनूभुवा ।
संपादितं मालविकाग्निमित्रं नाम नाटकम् ॥

पिङ्गलोपनाम्नो धुण्डिराजस्येदं मौल्येन संपादितम् । This likewise is a very carefully copied MS., and corrected, like all the MSS. here described, *secunda manu*, with the aid of another MS. Though bearing no date, it appears equally old with the last preceding. It is accompanied by a Sanskrit translation of the Prâkṛit passages appended with a separate paging at the end. I have named this MS. D. These three MSS., B, C, D, were kindly procured for me by my friend Mr. Govind K. Sabde.

(5) Another MS., lent me by Mr. Ganesh Shâstrî Lele of Trimbakes'war. It bears the date S'âl. 1710, *i. e.* A. C. 1789, as embodied in the colophon : व्योमेन्द्वद्रिकुभिर्युक्ते कीलके शुक्रमासगे । शुक्ले शिवतिथौ चान्द्रे नाटकं लिखितमिदम् ॥ कृष्णसुतविश्वनाथेन लिखितम्. It is a very correct MS., containing 34 oblong leaves, of which the first is subsequently replaced by a different hand, marked at the end "गतपत्त्रप्रतिनिधिपत्त्रम्." In the margin of the MS. are given now and then short explanatory notes. It is a very correct and trustworthy MS. I have called it E.

(6) The sixth was kindly lent me by Mr. Pandurang Narayan, Kirloskar of Gurlhasûr, in the Belgaum Collectorate. It is an excellent MS., being written in a beautiful clear legible hand, remarkably correct, not only copied, it seems, by a conscientious and intelligent scribe, but also subsequently corrected by some one who understood the drama. The Prâkṛit

passages in it are each accompanied by a Sanskrit translation immediately following it. It ends thus :—श्रीमत्कालिदासकृतं मालविकाग्निमित्रं नाम नाटकं संपूर्णमस्तु ॥ श्रीकाशीविश्वेश्वरार्पणमस्तु ॥ शके १७२६ रक्ताक्षी नामसंवत्सरे आषाढवद्य सप्तमी भानुवासरे मुकाम शिरहटी समाप्तः ॥ ग्रन्थसंख्या ११५० ॥छ॥ The MS. is, therefore, just 65 years old. It contains forty-seven oblong leaves of a bluish kind of thick paper. I have given this the name F. The six MSS. from A to F were collated at first and the present edition prepared, with no expectation of obtaining more MSS. for collation. These six MSS. are designated "our MSS." in the Notes, critical and explanatory, accompanying the present edition. But through the kindness of Mr. Gangiah of Bangalore, I obtained, after the whole text had been put into type,

(7) An excellent MS. in the Telagu character, written on palmyra leaves, 23 in number. It is a very correct MS., almost free from error, having been copied by a Shâstrî. It is forty-three years old, as we see from the following: श्रीरामभद्रगुरुचरणारविन्दाभ्यो नमो नमः । व्ययसंवत्सरे चैत्रबहुले १३ त्रयोदशी गुरुवासरे नृसिंह्मसूरिसूनुना योगानृसिंह्मेण लिखितमिदं नाटकं स्वकीयमेव नान्यदीयम् । श्रीराम *। Though all the various readings of this MS., which I have named G, are not given in the foot-notes, the principal of them have either, wherever it seemed

* It goes on thus :—

रागाख्यवह्निमित्रं यन्नाटकं लिखितं मया ।
नृसिंह्मसूनुना योगानृसिंहेण मुदायुतम् ॥
श्रीलक्ष्मीनरसिंहभूधरजरत्कारुण्यगङ्गानदी-
पाथोबिन्दुसरो नृसिंहतनयो योगानृसिंहाभिधः ।
श्रीमत्काव्ययवंशवारिधिविधुर्वर्षे व्यये चैत्रके
श्रीमन्मालविकाग्र -[sic.]- मित्रममलं दर्शे लिलेख स्वयम् ॥

The last stanza though carved like the whole MS. is yet uninked, and seems, accordingly, to have been subsequently added. This, as well as the exigencies of the metre, would account for the mention दर्श as the date on which the MS. was written.

necessary, been adopted into the text of the present edition, or have been noticed in the Notes appended.

The seven MSS. are so characterized that they seem to belong to two families. A B C D E are certainly derived originally from one and the same source, as is proved by the fact of their reading a few passages in the same wrong way, *e. g.* शर्मिष्ठाया कृतिः for शर्मिष्ठायाः कृतिः (*p.* 22, *l.* 11), उपलभते for उपलभे (*p.* 103, *l.* 5). Of course, though originally belonging to the same source, probably D,* they have, subsequently to their genesis, been corrected, and therefore vary considerably from each other, as may be seen from the *variæ lectiones* noticed in our foot-notes. MSS. F and G, on the contrary, form a separate family by themselves. This is apparent from both of them reading certain passages in one and the same way. And yet G differs every now and then from F, a fact that seems to owe its origin to the former, or rather the source of it, having been probably corrected subsequently with the help of other MSS., though it bears no marks of correction in its present form.

As, fortunately, all the MSS. collated for the present edition were almost equally good, and as none of them exhibit a different redaction of the text, properly so called, none of them can be said to be the *basis* of the text herein given to a greater extent than another. All of them have been most minutely and carefully collated, and their differences given in the foot-notes, except such as appeared to me to have arisen from clerical errors.

The Sanskrit version (छाया) of the Prâkṛit passages, given in the present edition, though based upon the translation found in MSS. D and F, had yet to be greatly corrected by the editor, that of the MSS. in question being, as is usually the case, very inaccurate and incorrect.

---

* Thus, *e. g.*, the ते in उपलभेते in D is subsequently scratched, but not sufficiently, and hence the ते was copied into the other MSS.

One point more requires special notice; the manner, namely, that I have adopted in this edition of writing Prâkṛit conjunets containing aspirates, whether hard or soft. Thus it is usual to write the Prâkṛit forms of लक्ष्मी, पुष्प, पृष्टा as लच्छी, पुप्फ, पुच्छिदा. Editors of Sanskrit-Prâkṛit works have always, in fact, followed the same rules in writing Prâkṛit conjunets as they do in writing Sanskrit conjunet letters. And Vararuchi, also, after having enjoined, that "wherever, after performing an elision or substitution enjoined by a rule, a single consonant comes to represent a conjunct, this letter is always doubled, except in the beginning of a word" (शेषादेशयोर्द्वित्वमनादौ, *Prâkṛita-Prakâs'a* III. 50, Prof. Cowell's Edition), he states, that "wherever the single representative is an aspirate .... it is to be doubled by prefixing its own non-aspirate," (वर्गेषु युजः पूर्वः *Ibid*. III. 51). Vararuehi, therefore, clearly enjoins forms like लच्छी, पुप्फ, and पुच्छिदा, not लछ्छी, पफ्फ, पुछ्छिदा. I must accordingly explain why I have deviated from that grammarian. My authority for the deviation is the concurrent testimony of all the MSS. These have a peculiar method of writing Prâkṛit conjuncts. In Sanskrit they give all the components of a conjunct distinctly, but in Prâkṛit the presence of the first component of every eonjunet letter is merely indicated by a dot placed before it. This dot indicates that the letter before which it is placed is to be *doubled*. Thus what ought to be fully written अत्तभवं, they write अ-तभवं, *ajjăutta* is अ-जउ-त and not अज्जउत्त. And so also in the case of conjunets containing aspirates. As दि-ठा, ल-छी, पु-फ, पु-छिदा. This practice of indicating a doubling by means of a dot is not only what is found in the Devanâgarî MSS., but even the Bangalore MS., written in Telagu (that marked G), follows the same method, and that under circumstances which clearly show what importance is attached to this method of writing conjunets. For it is well known that in the Telagu character the mark for an *anusvâra*, whether this be original, as in सिंह, or substitutionary for any of the five nasals, as in नंद, is a dot put

2 P M

after that letter which has the *anusvâra* in pronunciation. But though this method is followed in respect of Sanskrit words, the dot in the Prâkṛit passages of the MS. in question always means a strengthening of the following letter by means of doubling it; and the *anusvâra* is there represented as in the Devanâgarî character by a dot put over the syllable which is to be nasalized by it. It is therefore clear from the general practice of the MSS. that the dot put before a letter in Prâkṛit conjuncts indicates that that letter is to be *doubled*. But we have the same sign put before an aspirate that we have before an unaspirate letter. I have also examined many MSS. of other Sanskrit-Prakṛit works, and I have always found the dot to be invariably used as a sign of doubling, and nowhere any the least indication that "the doubling of an aspirate is to be effected by adding before it its own non-aspirate," as taught by Vararuchi in the Sûtra वर्गेषु युजः पूर्वः, III. 51. One and the same sign being used by the MSS. to indicate *doubling*, whether of aspirate or non-aspirate letters, I have simply doubled the letter before which the MSS. put a dot, that is to say, I have not followed Vararuchi's rule about the doubling of aspirates by means of non-aspirates.

PREFACE.

The text of the Drama of Mâlavikâgnimitra was first printed at Bonn in 1840, edited by the late Otto Frederik Tullberg. That edition, however, of the Swedish scholar was, unfortunately, far from being correct. Many a passage in it is corrupt and confused; some verses are given as prose, and speeches of different characters are put into the mouth of one and the same speaker.

Then followed, in 1856, a German translation by Professor Weber. This translation was not based entirely on the unfortunately faulty edition of Dr. Tullberg; but the learned Professor, as might have been expected, took care to examine for himself into the MSS., and proposed many an emendation of the text in his notes to his translation.

But the original Sanskrit Drama, as far as I am aware, is as yet nowhere printed in a correct edition, based, as every edition of a Sanskrit work ought to be, on the collation of several trustworthy MSS. collected from different parts of India. To supply this desideratum is the principal object I have had in view in preparing the present edition.

The Drama of Mâlavikâgnimitra is a remarkable instance of how much a genuine production of a well-known poet may suffer when left to the mercies of distant posterity. The history of that play affords a most instructive illustration of the universal disfavour that is not unfrequently shown to an object that has once had the misfortune of being accidentally disfavoured by a great man. Genuine merit does not always shine forth through all clouds of misfortune. It is as frequently brought to light by an accidental glance of illustrious eyes, as thrown into obscurity by a contemptuous look of them.

Such and no other is the misfortune under which the play of "Mâlavikâ and Agnimitra" has hitherto laboured. Professor H. H. Wilson, the most eminent orientalist, was the first who brought that drama, along with many others, to the notice of European Sanskrit scholars. But in the account which he gives of this play in his Appendix to the second volume of his excellent work on the Theatre of the Hindus, that great scholar expresses himself rather unfavourably on the merits of the play, and doubts very much whether it belongs to the celebrated author of the *S'âkuntala* and the *Vikramorvas'î*. Nay he seems to have been of opinion that the play might be the production of a Kâlidâsa, who lived perhaps in the tenth or eleventh century, or even later than that.

These and other depreciatory remarks of the great orientalist on the literary merits and the pretensions to antiquity of the drama, followed by the greatly incorrect state in which the text of it was edited and published by Dr. Tullberg, has, in my humble opinion, not a little contributed to the neglect into which the play has hitherto been thrown by the public, to the fact that by some* it is regarded as a production not of that Kâlidâsa of antiquity, who has presented us with the immortal plays of the *S'âkuntala* and the *Vikramorvas'î*, but of an inferior namesake of him, who belonged to a very modern time. But how far the drama in question deserves that it should be denied the honour of coming from the hands of the celebrated author of the *S'âkuntala*, and how far he himself deserves to be deprived of the credit of writing it, seems to require some examination.

---

* Thus Dr. Hall (*Vâsavadattâ*, preface, page 15) not only believes that the play does not belong to the author of the S'âkuntala, but that it does not belong to *any* Kâlidâsa at all. He says, "I will add that the frequent omission in MSS. of this drama of the words attributing it to Kâlidâsa furnishes a strong presumption that they have been foisted into the original composition." I do not understand what words are those that Dr. Hall says are omitted in the MSS. of the play that he examined. It is difficult to see how the prologue can possibly stand without the words attributing the drama to Kâlidâsa. Indeed, the name of Kâlidâsa is twice repeated in the prologue, and unless the name of some other author is "foisted" into the text in place of that of Kâlidâsa in the MSS. of the play that Dr. Hall collated, it is impossible to suppose that they contain the prologue. None of the seven MSS. of the drama, all of them highly trustworthy, that I have collated, omit the words attributing it to Kâlidâsa, and do not furnish any "presumption that they have been foisted" into the text. It were very much to be wished that the learned editor of Vâsavadattâ had been more explicit in his note, and stated what particular words are omitted in his MSS., and how the prologue stands therein, if it does stand at all. It may not be improbable that his MSS. are not much superior to those on which Dr. Tullberg based his text of the drama.

The chief grounds on which Professor Wilson bases his doubt about the legitimacy of the Mâlavikâgnimitra as a production of the great Kâlidâsa, are: 1st, that—"There is neither the same melody in the verse nor fancy in the thoughts;" 2nd, that—"The manners described appear to be those of a degenerate state of Hindu society." Now, as to the first ground, it is not clear what is meant by "the same melody in the verse." Is it intended to be understood that the metrical portion of the drama is rough or loose? The poetry, indeed, of the Mâlavikagnimitra is as smooth and flowing as that of the S akuntala and the Vikramorvas'î. It is as little laboured and artificial as that of those two dramas. It requires as little labour to understand the one as the other. The verse in the Mâlavikâgnimitra is as regular and model-like as that in the two sister dramas of the poet. How, therefore, the latter can be said to be more melodious than the former cannot, perhaps, be very easily understood. The metres, too, are nearly the same in all the three dramas; so that if they are melodious in the S'âkuntala and the Vikramorvas'î, they are not less so in the Mâlavikâgnimitra.

But there is not "the same fancy in the thoughts" in the Mâlavikâgnimitra as in the two other dramas. This is, indeed, an objection that carries, undoubtedly, considerable weight with it. It is, doubtless, true that the play in question is not so rich in its poetry as the two other ones, and that the flights of fancy do not soar equally high in our play. Professor Weber would account for this difference by the fact that whereas the

S'âkuntala and the Vikramorvas'î have their scenes mostly in the woods and forests, and afforded their author opportunities of indulging his fancy in giving excellent descriptions of nature, and that "both rest moreover upon a mythical background, and consequently bear a more magnificent and ideal character: the Mâlavikâgnimitra portrays the life in the court of a historic prince, and consequently the bare actuality, with its self-made, and therefore, scanty concerns." Though it is perfectly true that the nature of the subjects and the places of action of the two plays may have contributed to their excellence, by enabling their author to compose them as he has done, and by making us admire them as we do, it is, nevertheless, much open to doubt whether "the life in the court of a historic prince" may have restrained a poet of Kalidasa's powers and genius in writing as excellent a drama on that subject as on the Lost Ring or the Heavenly Nymph. Considerable portions of the two dramas, whose legitimacy is unquestionable, have also their scenes in courts of princes; and if it be urged that Dushyanta and Purûravas were mythical characters, Agnimitra also, who lived according to Professor Weber himself, at least five centuries before Kâlidâsa, might have, if the latter wanted it, been invested with as much mythology as was required for dramatic excellence, if this depended on mythology. But instances are not wanting where "the bare actualities" and "the scanty concerns" of unmythical and real persons have supplied materials, even to Sanskrit poets, for dramas, whose excellence is beyond dispute.

The subject, for example, of the Mâlatîmâdhava is as unmythical as any that can be imagined.

The task of showing why one work of an author is inferior to another, why one play of a dramatist is not so rich in fancy of the thoughts or fragrance of the poetry as some other, is one that can hardly be satisfactorily performed by the author himself. Nor can we reject a work as unworthy of a celebrated poet on no other ground than that it does not possess the same excellence in regard to a point that relates to its matter or form, especially when the evidence for holding that it does belong to the same poet is overwhelmingly convincing. If the fact of the comparative excellence and the comparative inferiority of different works of one and the same author is established, all that we can do to account for the fact is necessarily of a general character, and partaking greatly of the nature of a mere conjecture. If this last is strengthened by any corroborative evidence, so as to make it probable, we can proceed no further in the investigation of the question. If, accordingly, I may be allowed to hazard a guess as to the cause of the difference between the poetical worth of the Mâlavikâgnimitra and that of either of the two other plays, the first that suggests itself to my mind is that the Mâlavikâgnimitra is the first production of Kâlidâsa, that it was written while he was yet young, and while he was yet unknown as a dramatist of note to his contemporaries, and while yet he had not made a name for himself as a poet. Such a supposition seems to be strengthened by the tone of the prologue that introduces to us the drama. The assistant (पारिपार्श्वकः) of the manager is surprised to hear his master propose that Mâlavikâgnimitra, a drama composed by Kâlidâsa, should be acted, and asks him why a drama of a living poet should be acted, at the neglect of those of the famous Bhâsa and Saumilla. If when the Mâlavikâgnimitra was composed and acted, the author had been known as a dramatist of note, and if the S'âkuntala and the Vikramorvas'î had been written and published, and acquainted the public with their author, the prologue would, in all likelihood, have been differently worded. For that prologue does not seem to introduce to the public the particular drama to which it is attached, but rather the author who wrote it.

We then come to the second objection of Professor Wilson: "The manners described appear to be those of a degenerate state of Hindu society." This is a reproach, which, I am humbly of opinion, is little deserved by the Mâlavikagnimitra in particular. If the manners described in that play are indicative of a degenerate state of Hindu society, those portrayed in the two other plays are likewise open to the same censure. Whose manners are they that are degenerate in the play? Agnimitra differs little from Dushyanta or Purûravas in the purity or otherwise of his principles. Marrying more wives than one is a privilege of a Hindu, and whether we observe the present practice, or read of ancient traditions, the privilege is especially allowed to Princes. Dushyanta has already a harem of ladies, and yet he makes love to S'akuntalâ; Purûravas likewise has more wives than one, and he does not hesitate to marry Urvas'î, a heavenly nymph that, it may be observed, in earthly language would be designated by a name by no means enviable to a woman of good character. The Mâlavikâgnimitra is no more a domestic intrigue, as it has usually been assumed, than the Vikramorvas'î. King Agnimitra's passion for Mâlavikâ is as pure, or, perhaps, more so than that of King Purûravas for Urvas'î. Agnimitra nowhere shows that he desires an unlawful gratification of his passion. We must not be misguided by the fact that Mâlavikâ was in the train of attendants of Dhâriṇî. We are nowhere told that the heroine actually served as an attendant of Dhâriṇî. Even if this had been the case, there would have been nothing of the nature of an *intrigue*, properly so called, in the king's love affairs with Mâlavikâ, as long as he wished to add his mistress formally to his harem by elevating her to the position of a queen. Indian kings were neither in ancient times, nor are they in modern times, very fastidious as to the family of every member of their harems, provided the objects of their passion are possessed of personal beauty and mental accomplishments. We need not go far in search of an illustration. The marriage of S'akuntalâ with Dushyanta, of a girl of illegitimate birth with a king of one of the most renowned dynastics of ancient India, ought to satisfy us. Nor can the play of Mâlavikâgnimitra be pronounced an household intrigue, simply because the court of the king is the scene where the events take place. The amours of

Purûravas and Urvas'î likewise have the court of that prince for their locality.

Nor can I see in the character of Mâlavikâ herself, or of Queen Dhâriṇî, or even of the light Irâvatî, of Vidûshaka, or of the professors of dancing and music, anything that can well be called "degenerate." The only thing to which objection may be taken is, perhaps, the fact that Dhâriṇî does not show quite as much indignation at the king's conduct with regard to Mâlavikâ as might be expected; as, for example, Queen Aus'înarî does in the Vikramorvas'î, or, to cite an instance from another poet, Queen Vâsavadattâ in the Ratnâvalî. But this is easily accounted for, when we remember that Dhâriṇî is an elderly lady, and that, besides, the poet has given us enough of jealousy and indignation in the character of Irâvatî, who, being still young, is evidently better suited to exhibit those passions. If Professor Wilson himself had examined into the charge of "degeneracy," as brought by him against our play, he would have seen cause to modify his estimate of its merits.

But Professor Wilson concludes from the degeneracy of manners which he imputes to the Mâlavikâgnimitra, that "it can scarcely be thought earlier than the tenth or eleventh century. It may possibly have been the production of a somewhat later day." This conclusion, based as it is, upon the alleged "degenerate state of Hindu society," is one that deserves not to be accepted without some diffidence, even if we assume for a moment the truth of the charge of degeneracy brought against the drama. For it is difficult to see why Professor Wilson thought that the alleged "degenerate manners" of the play suited the tenth or eleventh, or even a later century, any more than say the sixth or seventh, or any other century before or after the age which he so arbitrarily assigns to the genesis of the drama. The fact seems to be that the allegation is as little founded as the inference that is made to rest upon it.

The principal object, however, which I have in view here is not to examine the *pros* and *cons* of the antiquity of the drama, but the question whether it belongs to the renowned author of the S'âkuntala and the Vikramorvas'î. If a successful attempt is made to answer this question, the more general question of the age of Kâlidâsa may be left to be investigated elsewhere more appropriately.

Now, what are the means by which we can hope to prove that an extant work, the age of whose genesis is long gone by, belongs to a certain author? We have, I think, to consider the external as well the internal evidence relating to the work in question. But if the work is several centuries old, external evidence as regards such a composition is reduced merely to the form of tradition, written and oral. Oral tradition, perhaps, if it is several centuries old, loses a great deal, in fact, almost the whole of its claim to be regarded as satisfactory evidence. But if there is a written tradition, and this tradition is written in the words of the author himself, and if no one has ever doubted its correctness, we must, by all means, accept it as conclusive evidence. Now what is the nature of external evidence as regards the drama tending to show whether it does or does not belong to the author of the S'âkuntala and the Vikramorvas'î? The very prologue itself unequivocally states that the drama is a production of Kâlidâsa; and nobody has ever doubted that this Kâlidâsa is the same individual as the author who has given us the two other plays. The same kind of tradition, namely, the statement of the author introducing the play to the public, implicitly and universally believed, that fathers the S'âkuntala and the Vikramorvas'î upon Kâlidâsa, is the tradition that attributes the Mâlavikâgnimitra to him. In all the three plays KÂLIDÂSA is stated to be the author who composed them. If either of the two plays of S'âkuntala and Vikramorvas'î were to be denied to-day to be the production of the same Kâlidâsa who composed the other, laying aside internal evidence, what positive evidence should we have to show that they both belonged to one and the same Kâlidâsa? So far then as external evidence goes, there is none to show that the Mâlavikâgnimitra belongs to a different Kâlidâsa: but, on the contrary, the prologue most positively declares that the play belongs to Kâlidâsa. By external evidence, therefore, we have no grounds to suspect that the Mâlavikâgnimitra is the production of another Kâlidâsa. Traditionary external evidence has always attributed it to the same Kâlidâsa, till Professor Wilson chose to doubt the correctness of the tradition.

Turning then to internal evidence, we may observe in the outset that the prospects of success here are more hopeful than in any other means that may be used as an argument for showing that the Mâlavikâgnimitra belongs to the author of the other two great plays. The internal evidence goes so far to prove the great Kâlidâsa's authorship of the play, that even if we had not the profession of the poet himself in the prologue, we should never hesitate, after a careful perusal and comparison of the three plays, to pronounce that the Mâlavikâgnimitra comes from the same hands as the S'âkuntala and the Vikramorvas'î.

Every great writer, whether of prose or poetry, has always a settled style of composition. This is especially the case with those poets and authors who take delight in an easy and natural expression of their thoughts, and never surrender their good sense and fondness for perspicuity to a laboured and obscure style of writing. Whatever is natural and ordinary will be frequently repeated in the writings of one and the same author. And, accordingly, there are so many analogies, or, I had almost say, identities of expression, everywhere to be met with in the diction and ideas of the three dramas of S'âkuntala, Vikramorvas'î, and Mâlavikâgnimitra, that it is impossible to explain them on any other ground than that of the identity of their author. The simple occurrence of the same expressions and phrases in different works does not, it is true, necessarily show that the works come from one and the same author, but it is the repetition of those analogous expressions, phrases, and ideas with a characteristic *frequency* in each of the compositions, that is of importance in determining the identity of their author.

As regards diction the following analogies may be quoted :—अच्चाहिदं (भत्याहितम्), 'great misfortune.' Cf. note on page 82, l. 3—संभावय्, 'to honour.' Cf. note on page 47, l. 13—स्वनियोगमशून्यं कुरु, 'Go thou about thy business,' *i.e.*, 'retire, and leave us alone.' Cf. note on page 22, l. 7. —मा, with the future tense, in the sense of either the prohibitive imperative or '*lest* with the subjunctive.' Cf. note on page 21, l. 9—णिर्बन्ध:, in the sense of 'importunity.' Cf. note on page 17, l. 11—पारेदि (पारयति), in the sense of 'he can.' Cf. note on page 45, l. 5—अत्थि विसेसो (अस्ति विशेष:), 'there is some change [for the better]'. Cf. note on page 65, l. 11—पुढमो कप्पो (प्रथम: कल्प:), 'an excellent alternative.' Cf. note on page 12, l. 13 —अणुणअं गेण्हदि (अनुनयं गृह्णाति), 'allows himself to be assuaged and reconciled.' Cf. note on page 85, l. 2—पदं कृ, 'to enter upon,' 'to set foot upon.' Cf. note on page 52, l. 1—पावं, आसङ्कदि (पापमाशङ्कते), 'suspects something unfortunate.' Cf. note on page 82, l. 5—सरओओ (स्वरयोग:), 'harmony of sounds,' '*voice*.' Cf. note on page 100, l. 11—अन्तरेण with the accusative, 'as regards,' 'with reference to.' Cf. note on page 62, l. 13—शरणम्, 'the sacred abode of [Agni, &c.']. Cf. note on page 106, l. 12—सभाजइदुं , (सभाजयितुम्) 'to pay one's respects to.' Cf. note on page 113, l. 2—अनात्मज्ञ : 'foolish,' 'silly.' Cf. note on page 9, l. 1—गहीदत्था (गृहीतार्था), 'she who has understood the matter.' Cf. note on page 52, l. 5—विसंवादिदो (विसंवादित:), 'caused to be disappointed.' Cf. note on page 21, l. 10—लङ्घइस्सदि (लङ्घयिष्यति), 'will hurt,' 'will cause harm to.' Cf. note on page 77, l. 6—पकिदित्थो (प्रकृतिस्थः), 'recovered.' Cf. note on page 69, l. 2—उवआरादिक्कमं पमज्जिदुं (उपचारातिक्रमं प्रमार्ष्टुम्), 'to atone for disdaining the king's prostration.' Cf. note on page 80, ll. 5, 6.—अब्भवहार (अभ्यवहारः), 'eating,' 'dinner.' Cf. note on page 82, l. 7—वसन्दावदारसूअआणि (वसन्तावतारसूचकानि), 'indicative of the first appearance of spring.' Cf. note on page 36, l. 10—पस्सपरिवट्टिणी (पार्श्वपरिवर्तिनी), 'standing by.' Cf. note on page 95, l. 6—पर्याप्तमेतावता कामिनां, 'this that I hear is enough for lovers.' Cf. note on page 53, l. 5—एत्तिओ मे विहवो (एतावान्मे विभवः), 'thus far the flight of my genius and no further.' Cf. note on page 28, l. 7—अप्पणो छन्देण (आत्मनश्छन्देन) 'after thy own wish.' Cf. note on page 51, l. 1—विशेष, at the end of a compound, giving the notion of 'excellence' to the sense of the substantive to which it is affixed, as आकृतिविशेष शिलाविशेष. Cf. note on page 78, l. 3—विभावेमि (विभावयामि), 'I recognise,' 'I infer.' Cf. note on page 73, l. 7—अलं भवदो परिदेविदेण (अलं भवतः परिदेवितेन), 'away with your lamentation.' Cf. note on page 35, l. 7. These are some of the analogies of expression which strike at once a careful reader and comparer of the three dramas as being characteristic of one and the same author. A few more, not noticed here, may be found in the Notes. Any one that makes it his object to find such analogies from the three poems—Raghuvaṁs'a, Kumârasambhava, and the Ṛitusaṁhâra, and the three dramas of S'âkuntala, Vikramorvas'î and Mâlavikâgnimitra,—will, doubtless, be able to swell the list I have given above, by adding a great number of more similarities and identities of expression.

Let us now turn to analogies of thought. The following are a few of them :—The regret of the king that while the As'oka is blessed by the touch of Mâlavikâ's foot, he himself enjoys no such favour, and is therefore unhappy. A similar address to a bee in the S'âkuntala. Cf. note on page 53, l. 13.—The trustworthiness and the cutting sharpness of the flowery weapon of the God of Love. Cf. note on page 36, l. 5.—The withdrawing of characters from the stage, with the pretext of driving away the young deer. Cf. note on page 77, l. 6.—Comparison of the hand of a handsome woman with the S'yâmâ creeper. Cf. note on page 25, l. 4.—The gracefulness of beauty, in whatever posture and state this may be. Cf. note on page 25, l. 1.—The erection of hair through an amorous emotion compared to the sprout of a tree. Cf. note on page 61, l. 5.—The fulfilment of a Brahman's words. Cf. note on page 45, l. 6.—Description of the flower *Kurabaka*. Cf. note on page 38, l. 14.—Surprise of Nipuṇikâ that she should be supposed to have told her mistress what was untrue. Cf. note on page 79, l. 13.—The scene of Irâvatî accompanied by her attendant, Nipuṇikâ, wandering through the garden in search of the king, greatly analogous to that of Queen Aus'înarî and her attendant, *Nipuṇikâ*, in quest of King Purûravas. Cf. note on page 79, ll. 11-13.—The comparison with the thief who has been caught in the act of committing theft. Cf. note on page 57, ll. 7-9.—Sweet professions of love without love. Cf. note on page 37, l. 7.—The scornful refusal of the king's apology by Irâvatî affords him an excuse for neglecting her. Cf. note on page 60, ll. 10, 11.—The green pigeons sitting on the sloping roofs of the palace. Cf. note on page 29, l. 8.—A woman wearing the dress and bedecked just with those ornaments that she should have as the wife of a living husband. Cf. note on page 13, l. 15.—The eight forms or bodies of God (ईश). Cf. note on page 1, l. 3.—The watching for an opportunity by the king to step forward and show himself to his mistress. Cf. note on page 54, l, 6.—Vidûshaka's fear for snakes. Cf. note on page 83, l. 7.— Personification of the Vernal Beauty. Cf. notes on page 38, st. 5.—Many more analogies in thoughts may, doubtless, be added to this list from the poems and the other dramas which are allowed to belong to the Kâlidâsa of antiquity.

There are some other peculiarities of the author of the S'âkuntala and the Vikramorvas'î that make themselves felt by their conspicuous presence in the Mâlavikâgnimitra also. Thus, it is a characteristic of Kâlidâsa's writings that they all begin with a charmingly modest introduction, marked by great diffidence. The great poet never thinks that he has done well, until what he has done is pronounced good by the learned. The Raghuvaṁs'a (i. 10), and the S'âkuntala (p. 2, ll. 6, 7, आ परितोषा-द्विदुषाम्) lay down the maxim, and it is repeated in our play (p. 26, ll. 9, 10). Bhavabhûti and others, on the contrary, do not consider it at all inconsistent with modesty to give long descriptions of their genealogies and of their own attainments.* Some of them, again, Bhavabhûti, for example, are defiant, and challenge the public in their introductions. It may also be observed that the *Nândî*, or the opening and benedictory part, is characteristically short, consisting of one stanza only, in dramas that belong to Kâlidâsa, while that of other dramatists is extravagantly long, consisting oftentimes of three, four, or five stanzas, and full of metaphysical and mythological nonentities. We may add, further, that the introduction of the dramas of Kâlidâsa, as these are easy and temperate in their style, and were probably on that account intelligible to a majority of their audiences, never contains any explanation of their plots or subjects, and they always glide imperceptibly, as it were, from the reality of the stage-manager and his assistant into the scenic commencement of the play. Other authors, on the contrary, with little good taste, give a summary of the play's contents in their introductions, and end them abruptly, or, at least, so as clearly to show where the introduction ends and the play begins. We must not forget also that Kâlidâsa is more fond of the *âryâ* metre in his plays than other dramatists. This *âryâ* metre is of as frequent occurrence in the Mâlavikâgnimitra as in the S'âkuntala and the Vikramorvas'î.

These and other analogies will strike any careful reader of the three plays. The reader will in vain seek for

* See Bhavabhûti's introduction to his Mahâvîracharita or to his Mâlatîmâdhava, and also the Uttararâmacharita; also Râjas'ekhara's Viddhas'âlabhanjikâ.

similar "points of contact," as Professor Weber calls them, in works that professedly belong to different authors, unless one of them has designedly imitated in his own writings the diction, the style, the thoughts, the fancies, the modesty, and good sense of another. The conclusion that will force itself irresistibly on the mind of a reader of the three plays, that they all belong to one and the same author, can hardly be unsettled by a suggestion that the similarities may be explained on the ground of imitation. If the Mâlavikâgnimitra be the work of a person who made it his study to imitate Kalidasa, it is a most singular instance of imitation, unparalelled, probably, in the wide range of literature of ancient or modern times. What should we say of the imitating powers of a man who so transformed himself into another person that he was able to copy most faithfully every characteristic, great or small, of his master,—his style, his diction, his thoughts, his words, his taste, his good sense, his modesty, and, what is most surprising, his name itself? But when did this most unique imitator live? He could not have lived in the time of the great Kâlidâsa; nay, not even soon after him. For the imitation of a poet like Kâlidâsa, either during his lifetime or at any time subsequently, when there were critics who were yet familiar with the personal history of the great author, would surely be known by its true nature, and we should certainly have had some tradition handed down to us in one shape or another of so singular an imitator as that who composed the Mâlavikâgnimitra.

But if we should suppose that the imitation is a production of a modern age, say the time of Bhoja, when there was an unequalled activity in the cultivation of Sanskrit learning, it is impossible to think that the drama should bear no stamp whatever of the time when it was composed. For it is granted by Professor Wilson himself that it is free from all the "extravagancies of modern composition." It has none of those faults of bad taste and unnaturalness which distinguish modern Sanskrit poems and dramas.

Nor can we account for the wholesale similarities by supposing that the Mâlavikâgnimitra is an adaptation. We know of no original to which such an adaptation could be referred. And we have also to remember that adaptations, by their very nature, are devoid of all originality, of all invention. The Mâlavikâgnimitra, however, whatever its poetical merits, may fairly be allowed to be as much distinguished for the display of those qualities as the two other dramas of Kâlidâsa.

What is then the fact? What is it that caused Professor Wilson, and, through him, several other European scholars, to doubt whether the play under notice really belonged to the author of the Lost Ring? The poetical worth of the Mâlavikâgnimitra, even if not so great as that of either of the two other dramas, ought not, I think, to be reckoned as sufficient ground for holding that it belongs to a different author. All the works of a poet, even those that actually come to our hands after all the care bestowed on them by their author, are far from always being equally excellent. Every literature, whether modern or ancient, will, I think, supply instances of different works by one and the same author of world-wide fame exhibiting various powers of poesy and invention. And yet it will never do to reject the less good productions, and call them spurious, or, which is the same, attribute them to inferior hands.

Though I do not here undertake to treat the question of Kâlidâsa's age, it seems nevertheless desirable that Professor Wilson's statement that the present drama may belong to the tenth or eleventh, or even a later century, should be carefully sifted before we accept it as correct. Indeed, the great orientalist himself appears to have been, in the same summary of the drama, more than half willing to modify his statement by referring, with a candidness as great as his learning, to such of its features as would require us to assign it to a greater antiquity than the tenth or eleventh century after Christ. "The dramas," say Professor Wilson, "written in more recent periods are, invariably, as far as is yet known, mythological, and have some one of the forms or family of Vishṇu for the hero. There is no such thing as a decidedly modern drama the business of which is domestic intrigue." Whatever may be thought of the reason that he gives to account for that fact,—viz., that "such a subject, indeed, was wholly incompatible with Hindu feelings, as affected by intercourse with their Mahomedan masters, whether the effect of that intercourse was terror or imitation,"—it is perfectly correct that modern poets and dramatists seem to have written under the notion that poesy should not be debased by being made to celebrate the deeds of any hero who was not somehow or other connected with any of the incarnations of the gods; they have certainly left us no play, —with the exception, perhaps, of the Viddhas'âlabhanjikâ, that belongs to the eleventh century, of the Ratnâvalî that may be referred to the beginning of the twelfth century, and of the Mṛigânkalekhâ, which Professor Weber aptly styles "a mixture of Ratnâvalî, Urvas'î and Mâlatîmâdhava,"—that has for its subject the domestic love-affairs of an (to us) insignificant king like Agnimitra. The fact, therefore, of the subject of the present drama being very unlike any that modern writers were likely to choose to write upon, seems to point to a very much earlier period than the tenth or eleventh century as the age to which the production of the play under notice should be referred.

Again, as Professor Wilson says, the history of the hero, Agnimitra, as described in the play, is of considerable weight towards determining approximately the age when the drama must have been composed. The full history of Agnimitra or his father Pushpamitra is nowhere given in the Sanskrit works that have come down to us. The Purâṇas* mention Pushpamitra as the founder of the S'unga dynasty, but they nowhere give any more detailed account of him than that he dispossessed his master, Bṛihadratha, the last of the Maurya dynasty, of his crown, and usurped it, probably, as Professor Wilson supposes, in favour of his son. But nothing is said of Agnimitra, the hero of our

* Cf., for instance the Bhâgavata Purâṇa XII., 1. 15. Also Wilson's Vishṇu Purâṇa, (pp. 470, 471).

play, except that he succeeded his father, Pushpamitra. To suppose then that the Mâlavikâgnimitra is the production of so late a date as the tenth or eleventh century would necessitate another supposition that the history of Pushpamitra and his son, Agnimitra, which is so familiarly alluded to in the drama, existed during these ages in a far more copious form than the bare mention of the princes in the Purâṇas. Nothing, however, favours such a supposition. The only inference, therefore, that is possible is, that the play was written while the story of Pushpamitra and Agnimitra was yet fresh in the memory of men, though not quite so fresh as to make it too recent to be made the subject of a drama. This would certainly require that we should assign the piece to a time several centuries earlier than the tenth or eleventh century, since Pushpamitra founded the dynasty that immediately followed the Mauryas, and must have accordingly done so about 160 years before Christ. To suppose that the deeds of Agnimitra were chosen to be the subject of a drama at a time when nothing more was known of him than we know through the Purâṇas, would be to suppose what is not at all probable.

But, in addition to this consideration, "the style of the play," says Professor Wilson, "is very unlike that most common amongst modern writers, and most highly esteemed, being free from all jingle of sounds and from metaphorical common-place; it does not even affect anything like the uniform smoothness which seems to have preceded and ushered in the extravagancies of modern composition." Who will not be struck by the simplicity and elegance of the style of the Mâlavikâgnimitra, the total absence in it of those monstrous long compounds, which are so wearisome already in Bhavabhûti, who may belong somewhat to the beginning of the eighth century? If we had nothing else to guide us in fixing with tolerable exactness at least the century which produced the present play, the style and diction of it would alone be sufficient for assuming that it could not have been the production of any time that was not several centuries prior to the age of Bhavabhûti. In what author, again, of those ages of elaborateness and pedantry, of which the beginning is marked by the great Bhavabhûti, shall we find such a sound piece of criticism as that put into the mouth of the stage-manager (page 2, stanza 2) by the author of the Mâlavikâgnimitra? As Professor Wilson truly remarks, "it is the sentiment of a day long gone by."

There is yet another point, which, though failing against our expectations, to determine the age of the drama at present, may yet possibly reward future research. I allude to the mention in the prologue of the poets Bhâsa and Saumilla, as predecessors of Kâlidâsa. Unfortunately, Sanskrit chronology is as yet, and perhaps will be, it is difficult to say for how many ages to come, a labyrinth of uncertainties. If nothing positively is known about the time when Kâlidâsa flourished, it is equally uncertain when Bhâsa and Saumilla, his predecessors, lived! To add to the uncertainty of the ages of these latter, it does not as yet appear to be decided how we are to read their names. Dr. Tullberg chose to read, according to one MS., which is identical with that used by Professor Wilson, and which Professor Weber calls "bad in many ways," धावकसौमिल्लकविपुत्रादीनां in the prologue. Professor Weber is right in his guess that the reading *Dhâvaka* in place of *Bhâsa*[*ka*], found as it is in one single "bad" MS., is a correction "coming from a scribe who knew Dhâvaka, and not *Bhâsa*[*ka*]," the *lectio difficilior*, and must therefore, as is often the case, have substituted it for the latter. Dr. Hall (*Vâsavadattâ*, preface, page 15,) believes that he has come to the conclusion "that the poets whom it [the play] names with Bhâsaka are Râmila and Saumilla." None of the seven MSS., however, which I have collated give either *Dhâvaka*, as hinted at by Professor Wilson, and adopted by Dr. Tullberg, nor Râmila, as added by Dr. Hall. They all unanimously read Saumilla for the second, Bhâsa for the first, and except one (G.) they read simply the honorific मिश्र for the third. Now nothing is known of any of these two or three poets referred to in the prologue. Bhâsaka is nowhere mentioned as a poet. It is a mere gratuitous conjecture that Bhâsaka may be the same as the Bhâsa so much applauded in the introduction* of the Harshacharita, and mentioned by Râjas'ekhara in the verses quoted from the *S'árngadhara-paddhati*.†

---

* सूत्रधारकृतारम्भैर्नाटकैर्बहुभूमिकैः । सपताकैर्यशो लेभे भासो देवकुलैरिव, as quoted by Dr. Hall, *Vâsavadattâ*, preface, page 14.

† भासो रामिलसौमिलौ वररुचिः श्रीसाहसाङ्कः कविर्मेंघो भारविकालिदासतरला-स्कन्धः सुबन्धुश्च यः । &c., *Ibid.* page 20.

But, supposing *Bhâsa* to be the correct reading, and not *Bhásaka*, we gain nothing, as all that we know of *Bhâsa* is that he was a dramatist, and flourished before Raja-s'ekhara, as shown by the passage from the *Harshacharita*. Of *Saumilla* we know absolutely nothing at present, nor of *Kaviputra*, if that be one of the predecessors named in our prologue. It is just possible that future researches into the history of *Bhâsa* or *Saumilla*, or *Kaviputra*, none of whose works are known to exist, may throw some light on the earliest limit of age that we must assign to Kâlidâsa.

The character of "*Parivrâjikâ*" in the play appears to me of some importance in examining Professor Wilson's statement that the Mâlavikâgnimitra belongs to the tenth or eleventh, or even a later, century. As Professor Wilson says, "a Parivrâjikâ denotes an ascetic female of the Bauddha faith," and though, according to him, "there is nothing in the piece to assign the character to any particular sect," it does most likely belong to the Bauddha religion. A female ascetic, properly so called, is nowhere met with in the Brahmanical writings. A widow, who, not burning herself on the funeral pile of her dead husband, survives him, and leads a life of austerities, is, no doubt, a kind of '*Sannyâsinî*,' or '*Parivrâjikâ*'; but such a widow is neither called by the latter name, nor enjoined to assume the garments of the ascetic; nor is the 'widow Sannyâsa' ever praised as a "path fit for the virtuous" (सज्जनस्य पन्थाः : page 103, l. 10); but, on the contrary, that honour is given to the widow who burns herself with the corpse of her husband, and the 'widow Sannyâsa' is enjoined only as an alternative when the woman, under peculiar circumstances, is prevented from sacrificing herself to the flames. Nor are such garments as the Parivrâjikâ of the play assumed enjoined by the Hindu S'âstra to be worn by widows. When to this we add that the Parivrâjikâ, as the word signifies, is a wandering or itinerant mendicant, while the Hindu widow in general is never a *wandering mendicant*, it is perfectly clear that Kaus'ikî does not profess the Brahmanical religion. Further, wherever we meet with a *Parivrâjikâ* it is a Buddhistic female mendicant belonging to one or other of the sects of that religion. And when we bear in mind that though there may have been female itinerant mendicants belonging to any other sect, they are nowhere stated to have been reverentially treated in the courts of kings, it is highly probable, nay, almost certain, that Kaus'ikî was a Buddhistic mendicant. And when the religion of Buddha had already been banished from India by the end of the eighth century, it is not very natural to suppose that an author, who wrote, according to Professor Wilson, in the tenth or eleventh century, when the professors of the Brahmanical faith looked down upon the few lingerers, if these were left behind in any considerable number, from amongst their once powerful rivals, may have introduced a character in his drama professing the despised religion, and may have, moreover, made the whole court of a powerful prince pay her a most reverential homage.

Such a supposition would only be possible if the author of the Mâlavikâgnimitra had made it his object to represent by means of that play how Buddhism, that was dead in his time, had once been revered in the courts of princes. But such is not, as any one may perceive, the burden of the play; nor is it at all likely that Agnimitra might be chosen as an exemplary champion of Buddhism, even if the poet had intended to sing the former greatness of that religon, since the S'ungas, to which dynasty Agnimitra belonged, are represented to have been far from favourable to the followers of Buddha. The probability, therefore, is that the play was written, not at a time when Buddhism was despised, and had already been driven out of India, but when it was still regarded with favour, and was looked up to with reverence; and this must refer us to a time several centuries prior to the tenth or eleventh century after Christ.

In conclusion, I must confess I do not see the slightest ground for the supposition that the Mâlavikâgnimitra belongs to a different Kâlidâsa from the author of the "Lost Ring" or the "Heavenly Nymph," a supposition accidentally entertained by Professor Wilson, and unfortunately strengthened subsequently by the very incorrect state in which the public has had to read the play in Dr. Tullberg's edition. If by the present edition any success is achieved in the eyes of the cultivators of Sanskrit literature in restoring the play to its original purity, and in enabling thereby the reader to judge whether it does or does not belong to the great

Kâlidâsa, I shall regard my humble task more than sufficiently rewarded. And as for the author of the play, I hope I may be allowed to say, with the learned Professor Weber,—"So moge sich denn dies zierliche Drama auch in einen weiteren Kreise, als bisher, Freunde erwerben und zu dem wohl verdienten europäischen—[I had rather say *allgemeinen*]—Lorbeerkranze des *Kâlidâsa*, seines Verfassers, dadurch ein neues duftiges Blatt hinzugefügt werden!"

S. P. P.

Deccan College, Poona,
1st September 1869.

CORRIGENDA.

P. 34, l. 7, read the stage-direction प्रस्थिता after लहेहि in l. 6.

P. 38, l. 13, read रक्ताशोकरुचाविशेषितगुणो

P. 62, l. 15, „ पिङ्गलाक्ष्या

P. 73, l. 17, „ रत्नभाण्डं यौवनगर्वे

P. 83, l. 18, „ सर्प इति

P. 84, l. 3 English notes, right-hand column, read पुच्छिदव्वो.

॥ अथ मालविकाग्निमित्रम् ॥

एकैश्वर्यस्थितोपि प्रणतबहुफलो यः स्वयं कृत्तिवासाः
कान्तासंमिश्रदेहोप्यविषयमनसां यः पुरस्ताद्यतीनाम् ।
अष्टाभिर्यस्य कृत्स्नं जगदपि तनुभिर्बिभ्रतो नाभिमानः
सन्मार्गालोकनाय व्यपनयतु स नस्तामसीं वृत्ति-
मीशः ॥ १ ॥

मान्द्यन्ते

सूत्रधारः । नेपथ्याभिमुखमवलोक्य । मारिष इतस्तावत् ।

पारिपार्श्वकः । प्रविश्य । भाव अयमस्मि ।

सूत्र॰ । अभिहितोस्मि परिषदा कालिदासग्रथितवस्तुमालविकाग्निमित्रं नाम नाटकमस्मिन्वसन्तोत्सवे प्रयोक्तव्यमिति । तदारभ्यतां संगीतकम् ।

पारि॰ । मा तावत् । प्रथितयशसां भासकविसौमिल्लकविमिश्रादीनां प्रबन्धानतिक्रम्य वर्तमानकवेः कालिदासस्य क्रियायां कथं परिषदो बहुमानः ।

---

1 D F एकैश्वर्ये for एकैश्वर्य॰. | 4. F वः for नः.
1 m

सूत्र० । अयि विवेकविश्रान्तमभिहितम् । पश्य ।

पुराणमित्येव न साधु सर्वं
न चापि काव्यं नवमित्यवद्यम् ।
सन्तः परीक्ष्यान्यतरद्भजन्ते
मूढः परप्रत्ययनेयबुद्धिः ॥ २ ॥

पारि० । आर्यमिश्राः प्रमाणम् ।

सूत्र० । तेन हि त्वरतां भवान् ।

शिरसा प्रथमगृहीतामाज्ञामिच्छामि परिषदः कर्तुम् ।
देव्या इव धारिण्याः सेवादक्षः परिजनोयम् ॥ ३ ॥

[निष्क्रान्तौ ।

॥ प्रस्तावना ॥

। ततः प्रविशति चेटी ।

चेटी । आणत्तम्हि देवीए धारिणीए अइरप्पउत्तोवदेसं चलिअं णाम णट्टअं अन्दरेण कीरिसी मालविएत्ति णट्टाआरिअं अज्जगणदासं पुच्छिदुं । ता जाव संगीदसालं गच्छेमि । इति परिक्रामति ।

। प्रविशत्यपरा चेट्याभरणहस्ता ।

प्रथमा । अन्यां दृष्ट्वा । हेला कोमुदीए कुदो दे इअं धीरदा । जं समीवेवि आदिक्कमन्ती इदो दिट्ठिं ण देसि ।

---

१. आज्ञप्तास्मि देव्या धारिण्याचिरप्रवृत्तोपदेशं चलितं नाम नाट्यमन्तरेण कीदृशी मालविकेति नाट्याचार्यमार्यगणदासं प्रष्टुम् । तद्यावत्संगीतशालां गच्छामि ।

२. हला कौमुदिके कुतस्त इयं धीरता । यत्समीपेप्यतिक्रामन्तीतो दृष्टिं न ददासि ।

---

14. A C चलीअं; D चलीयं.—A C णाट्टअं; B D णट्ठअं.—F अन्तरेण— B C मालविअत्ति; D F मालविअत्ति.

15. A C अअ°; B D E F अ-अ°. A B C D E om. ता before जाव.

16. B D E गच्छिम्म; F गच्छामि.

17. F adds ततः before "प्रविशति."

18. A B C D E om. दे.—F धीरद.

19. B अदिक्कमन्ती.—A C न देसि.

द्वितीया । [1]अम्हो बउलावलिआ । सहि देवीए इदं सिप्पिसआसादो आणीदं सप्पमुद्दासणाहं अङ्गुलीअअं सिणिध्धं णिज्झाअन्ती तुह उवालम्भे पडिदम्हि ।

बकुलावलिका । विलोक्य । [2]ठाणे क्खु सज्जदि दिट्ठि । इमिणा अङ्गुलीअएण उब्भिण्णकिरणकेसरेण कुसुमिदो विअ दे अग्गहत्थो पडिभादि ।

कौमुदिका । [3]हला कहिं पथ्थिदासि ।

बकु० । [4]देवीए वअणेण णट्टाआरिअं अज्जगणदासं उवदेसग्गहणे कीरिसी मालविएत्ति पुछ्छिदुं ।

कौमु० । [5]सहि ईदिसव्वावारेण असंणिहिदावि दिट्ठा किल सा भट्टिणा ।

बकु० । [6]आम् । देवीए पस्संगदो सो जणो चित्ते दिट्ठो ।

---

१. अहो बकुलावलिका । सखि देव्या इदं शिल्पिसकाशात आनीतं सर्पमुद्रासनाथमङ्गुलीयकं स्निग्धं निध्यायन्ती तवोपालम्भे पतितास्मि ।

२. स्थाने खलु सज्जति दृष्टिः । अनेनाङ्गुलीयकेनोद्भिन्नकिरणकेसरेण कुसुमित इव तेऽग्रहस्तः प्रतिभाति ।

३. हला क्व प्रस्थितासि ।

४. देव्या वचनेन नाट्याचार्यमार्यगणदासमुपदेशग्रहणे कीदृशी मालविकेति प्रष्टुम् ।

५. सखि ईदृशव्यापारेणासंनिहितापि दृष्टा किल सा भर्त्रा ।

६. आम् । देव्याः पार्श्वगतोऽसौ जनश्चित्रे दृष्टः ।

---

1. A C D वहुला.°
4. A B C D E om. क्खु.
5. D त्तिय for त्तिभ.
6. B D E F पडिभाइ.
8. F मुणाहि.—A E F णट्टा.°— A C D E अ-अ°; F अय°.
9. F कीदिसी.
10. A C इदिस°; F ईरिस°.
12. E आम्म देवीए.—B पस्सगदो, D पस्संगदो, F पस्सगभो.

कौमु० । [१]कहं विअ ।

बकु० । [२]सुणाहि । चित्तसालं गदा देवी पच्चग्गवण्णराअं चित्तलेहं आअरिअस्स ओलोअन्ती चिट्ठइ । तस्सिं अन्तरे भट्टा उवट्ठिओ ।

कौमु० । [३]तदो तदो ।

बकु० । [४]तदो अ उवआराणन्दरं एकासणोववि्ठेण भट्टिणा चित्तगदाए देवीए परिअणमज्झगअं आसण्णअरं तं पेक्खिअ देवी पुच्छिदा ।

कौमु० । [५]किं विअ ।

बकु० । [६]अपुव्वरूवा इअं दारिआ तुह आसण्णा आलिहिदा किंणामहेएत्ति ।

कौमु० । [७]आकिदिविसेसेसु आदरो पदं करेइ । तदो तदो ।

---

१. कथमिव ।

२. शृणु । चित्रशालां गता देवी प्रत्यग्रवर्णरागं चित्रलेखमाचार्यस्यावलोकयन्ती तिष्ठति । तस्मिन्नन्तरे भर्तोपस्थितः ।

३. ततस्ततः ।

४. ततश्चोपचारानन्तरमेकासनोपविष्टेन भर्त्रा चित्रगताया देव्याः परिजनमध्यगतामासन्नतरां तां प्रेक्ष्य देवी पृष्टा ।

५. किमिव ।

६. अपूर्वरूपेयं दारिका तवासन्नालिखिता किंनामधेयेति ।

७. आकृतिविशेषेष्वादरः पदं करोति । ततस्ततः

---

2. A C सुणादु.—D °सालां, F °सालागदा.—A C °वणराअं.

3. B आअरीअस्स.—B C D E अन्दरे.—F तहिं for तस्सिं.

4. B वुवट्ठिदो, C D वुवट्ठिओ.

6. F °णन्तरं.

8. E om. तं before "पेक्खिअ."

10. A B C D दारीआ.—A B C D E अपुव्वा इअं.

11. B C D F °हेअत्ति.

बकु॰ । तदो अवहीरिअवअणो भट्टा संकिदो देविं पुणोपुणो अवि णिब्बन्धिदुं पवुत्तो । तदो कुमालीए वसुलच्छीए आचक्खिदं । अज्जउत्त एसा मालविएत्ति ।

कौमु॰ । सेरिसं क्खु बालभावस्स । तदो वरं कहेहि ।

बकु॰ । किं अण्णं । संपदं सविसेसं मालविआ भट्टिणो दंसणपहादो रक्खीअदि ।

कौमु॰ । हला अणुचिट्ठ अप्पणो णिओअं । अहंवि देवीए अङ्गुलीअअं उवणइस्सं ।

[इति निष्क्रान्ता ।

बकु॰ । परिक्रम्यावलोक्य च । एसो णट्टाअरिओ अज्जगणदासो संगीदसालादो णिक्कमदि । जाव अत्ताणं दंसेमि ।

गणदासः । प्रविश्य । कामं खलु सर्वस्य कुलविद्या बहुमता । न पुनरस्माकं तु नाट्यं प्रति मिथ्यागौरवम् । कुतः ।

---

१. ततोऽवधीरितवचनो भर्ता शङ्कितो देवीं पुनःपुनरपि निर्बन्धितुं प्रवृत्तः । ततः कुमार्या वसुलक्ष्म्याख्यातम् । आर्यपुत्र एषा मालविकेति ।

२. सदृशं खलु बालभावस्य । ततः परं कथय ।

३. किमन्यत् । सांप्रतं सविशेषं मालविका भर्तुर्दर्शनपथाद्रक्ष्यते ।

४. हला अनुतिष्ठस्वात्मनो नियोगम् । अहमपि देव्या अङ्गुलीयकमुपनेष्यामि ।

५. एष नाट्याचार्य आर्यगणदासः संगीतशालाया निष्क्रमते । यावदात्मानं दर्शयामि ।

---

1. A B C D E अवहिरिअणअणो.
2. A B C D E give अ for अवि. —A D णिवन्धिदुं.—D E पउत्तो. —A C कुमालिए.
3. E अचक्खिदं.—F भाउत्त for अज्जउत्त, with an explanatory note, भाउत्तो भगिनीपतिः, with also another preceding it वसुलक्ष्मीः देव्याः कनीयसी.
6. D दंसन॰.—B D E रक्खीयदि.
10. A णट्टाचारिओ, F ॰आरिओ.—D E F अ-अ॰.
11. B D E णीक्कमइ, F णिक्कमइ—A C अत्ताणं.

देवानामिदमामनन्ति मुनयः कान्तं क्रतुं चाक्षुषं
रुद्रेणेदमुमाकृतव्यतिकरे स्वाङ्गे विभक्तं द्विधा ।
त्रैगुण्योद्भवमत्र लोकचरितं नानारसं दृश्यते
नाट्यं भिन्नरुचेर्जनस्य बहुधाप्येकं समाराधनम् ॥४॥

बकु० । उपगम्य । अज्ज वन्दामि ।

गण० । भद्रे चिरं जीव ।

बकु० । अज्ज देवी पुच्छदि । अवि उवदेसग्गहणे णादिकिलिसेदि वो सिस्सा मालविएत्ति ।

गण० । विभाव्यतां देवी परमनिपुणा मेधाविनी चेति । किं बहुना ।

यद्यत्प्रयोगविषये भाविकमुपदिश्यते मया तस्यै ।
तत्तद्विशेषकरणात्प्रत्युपदिशतीव मे बाला ॥ ५ ॥

बकु० । आत्मगतम् । ओदिक्कमन्तीं विअ इरावतीं पेक्खामि । प्रकाशम् । किदत्था दाणिं वो सिस्सा । जस्सिं गुरुअणो एव्वं तुस्सदि ।

गण० । भद्रे तद्विधानामसुलभत्वात्पृच्छामि । कुतो देव्यास्तत्पात्रमानीतम् ।

---

१. आर्य वन्दे ।

२. आर्य देवी पृच्छति । अप्युपदेशग्रहणे नातिक्लिश्नाति वः शिष्या मालविकेति ।

३. अतिक्रामन्तीमिवेरावतीं प्रेक्षे । कृतार्थेदानीं वः शिष्या । यस्यां गुरुजन एवं तुष्यति ।

---

2. F स्वाङ्गैर्वि°
5. D E F अ-अ.
7. D E F अ-अ.—F णादिकिलिस्संदि.
9. F विज्ञाप्यताम् for विभाव्यताम्.
11. B उद्दिश्यते.
14. F दाणीं.—B एव्व.
16. F आयातं for आनीतम्.

बकु० । [1]अत्थि देवीए वण्णावरो भादा वीरसेणो णाम । सो भट्टिणा अन्तपालदुग्गे मन्दायणीदीरे ठ्ठाविदो । तेण सिप्पाहिआरे जोग्गा इअं दारिएत्ति भइणीए उवाअणं पेसिदा ।

गण० । आत्मगतम् । आकृतिप्रत्ययादेनामनूनवस्तुकां संभावयामि । प्रकाशम् । मया भद्रे यशस्विना भवितव्यम् । पश्य ।

पात्रविशेषन्यस्तं गुणान्तरं व्रजति शिल्पमाधातुः ।
जलमिव समुद्रशुक्तौ मुक्ताफलतां पयोदस्य ॥ ६ ॥

बकु० । [2]अह कहिं वो सिस्सा ।

गण० । इदानीमेव पञ्चाङ्गमभिनयमुपदिश्य विश्रम्यतामित्यभिहिता दीर्घिकावलोकनगवाक्षगताप्रवातमासेवमाना तिष्ठति ।

बकु० । [3]तेण हि अणुजाणादु मं अज्जो । जाव से अज्जपरितोसणिवेदणेण उच्छाहं वड्ढेमि ।

गण० । दृश्यतां सखी । अहमपि लब्धक्षणः स्वगृहं गच्छामि ।

[इति निष्क्रान्तौ ।

|| विष्कम्भकः ||

---

१. अस्ति देव्या वर्णावरो भ्राता वीरसेनो नाम । स भर्त्रान्तपालदुर्गे मन्दाकिनीतीरे स्थापितः । तेन शिल्पाधिकारे योग्येयं दारिकेति भगिन्या उपायनं प्रेषिता ।

२. अथ क्व वः शिष्या ।

३. तेन ह्यनुजानातु मामार्यः । यावदस्या आर्यपरितोषनिवेदनेनोत्साहं वर्धये ।

---

1. B वण्णाव्वरो.—B भाद्दा.
2. F मन्दाकिणीतीरे.—A B C D सिप्पाहिअरे.
4. F आकृतिविनयप्रत्ययाद्.
6. F पात्रविशेषे न्यस्तम्.
8. A C E अहवा for अह.
9. F पञ्चाङ्गाभिनयम्.
10. A E F ०गता प्रवातम्.
12. F अ०ओ.—F अ०अपरितोस'.
16. B मिश्रविष्कम्भकः, E F मिश्रविष्कम्भः.

। ततः प्रविशत्येकान्तस्थपरिजनो मन्त्रिणालेखहस्तेनान्वास्यमानो राजा ।

राजा । अनुवाचितलेखममात्यं विलोक्य । वाहतव किं प्रपद्यते वैदर्भः ।

अमात्यः । आत्मविनाशम् ।

राजा । निदेशमिदानीं श्रोतुमिच्छामि ।

अमा० । इदमिदानीमनेन प्रतिलिखितम् । पूज्येनाहमादिष्टः । पितृव्यपुत्रो भवतः कुमारो माधवसेनः प्रतिश्रुतसंबन्धो ममोपान्तिकमुपागच्छन्नन्तरा त्वदीयेनान्तपालेनावस्कन्द्य गृहीतः । स त्वया मदपेक्षया सकलत्रसोदर्यो मोचयितव्य इति । तत्र वो न विदितं यत्तुल्याभिजनेषु भूमिभरेषु राज्ञां वृत्तिः । अतो मध्यस्थः पूज्यो भवितुमर्हति । सोदर्या पुनरस्य ग्रहणविप्लवे विनष्टा । तदन्वेषणाय प्रयतिष्ये । अथावश्यमेव माधवसेनः पूज्येन मोचयितव्यः । श्रूयतामभिसंधिः ।

मौर्यसचिवं विमुञ्चति यदि पूज्यः संयतं मम श्यालम् ।
मोक्ता माधवसेनं ततोहमपि बन्धनात्सद्यः ॥ ७ ॥

इति ।

---

2. D वाहतक, corrected, it seems, from original वाहतव.

5. A B C D E प्रतिलेखितम्.

9. A B C D E omit the न after वो. —A B C तत्तुल्या.

10. A C राजसु राज्ञः for भूमिभरेषु राज्ञाम्.

16. B omits "इति."

राजा । कथम् । कार्यविनिमयेन मयि व्यवहरत्यनात्मज्ञः । वाहतव प्रकृत्यमित्रः प्रतिकूलचारी मे वैदर्भः । तद्यातव्यपक्षे स्थितस्य पूर्वसंकल्पितमुन्मूलनाय वीरसेनप्रमुखदण्डचक्रमाज्ञापय ।

अमा० । यदाज्ञापयति देवः ।

राजा । अथ वा किं भवान्मन्यते ।

अमा० । शास्त्रदृष्टमाह देवः । कुतः ।

अचिराधिष्ठितराज्यः शत्रुः प्रकृतिष्वरूढमूलत्वात् ।
नवसंरोहणशिथिलस्तरुरिव सुकरः समुद्धर्तुम् ॥ ८ ॥

राजा । तेन ह्यवितथं तन्त्रकारवचनम् । इदमेव निमित्तमादाय समुद्योज्यतां सेनापतिः ।

अमा० । तथा ।

[इति निष्क्रान्तः ।

परिजनो यथाव्यापारं राजानमभितः स्थितः

विदूषकः । प्रविश्य । आणत्तोम्हि तत्तहोदा रण्णा । गोदम चिन्तेहि दाव उवाअं जह मे जादिच्छादिट्ठपडिकिदी मालविआ पच्चक्खदंसणा भवेत्ति । मएवि तह किदं । जाव से णिवेदेमि । परिक्रामति ।

राजा । विदूषकं दृष्ट्वा । अयमपरः कार्यान्तरसचिवोस्मानुपस्थितः ।

---

१. आज्ञप्तोस्मि तत्रभवता राज्ञा । गौतम चिन्तय तावदुपायं यथा मे यदृच्छादृष्टप्रतिकृतिर्मालविका प्रत्यक्षदर्शना भवेदिति । मयापि तथा कृतम् । तावदस्य निवेदयामि ।

---

4. F °प्रमुखं.
15. B अणत्तम्हि, C अणत्तोम्हि, F आणत्तम्हि.
16. B चिन्तहि.
18. B णिवेदम्मि.

2

विदूषकः । उपसृत्य । [1]वड्ढदु भवं ।

राजा । सशिरःकम्पम् । इत आस्यताम् ।

विदूषकः । उपविष्टः ।

राजा । कच्चिदुपेयोपायदर्शने व्यापृतं ते प्रज्ञाचक्षुः ।

विदूषकः । [2]आः पओअसिद्धिं पुच्छ ।

राजा । कथमिव ।

विदूषकः । कर्णे । [3]एवं विअ ।

राजा । साधु वयस्य निपुणमुपक्रान्तम् । दुरधिगमसिद्धावप्यस्मिन्नारम्भे वयमाशंसामहे । कुतः ।

अर्थं सप्रतिबन्धं प्रभुरधिगन्तुं सहायवानेव ।
दृश्यं तमसि न पश्यति दीपेन विना सचक्षुरपि॥९॥

। नेपथ्ये ।

अलमलं बहु विकथ्य । राज्ञः समक्षमेवावयोरधरोत्तरव्यक्तिर्भविष्यति ।

राजा । सखे त्वन्नीतिपादपस्य पुष्पमुद्भिन्नम् ।

विदूषकः । [4]फलं वि देक्खिस्ससि ।

। ततः प्रविशति कञ्चुकी ।

कञ्चुकी । देव अमात्यो विज्ञापयति । अनुष्ठिता प्रभोराज्ञा ।

---

१. वर्धतां भवान् ।
२. आः प्रयोगसिद्धिं पृच्छ ।
३. एवमिव ।
४. फलमपि द्रक्ष्यसि ।

---

1. A B C वड्डदु.
5. A E आ for आः
13. ABCDE बहुविकत्थनेन.
16. A C देक्खिस्सति; F दक्खिस्ससि.
18. F reads काञ्चुकेयः and retain the same form everywhere subsequently.

एतौ पुनर्हरदत्तगणदासौ
उभावभिनयाचार्यौ परस्परजयोद्यतौ ।
त्वां द्रष्टुमिच्छतः साक्षाद्भावाविव शरीरिणौ ॥ १० ॥

राजा । प्रवेशय तौ ।

कञ्चुकी । यदाज्ञापयति देवः । इति निष्क्रम्य पुनस्ताभ्यां सह प्रविश्य । इत इतो भवन्तौ ।

हरदत्तः । राजानमवलोक्य । अहो दुरासदो राजमहिमा । तथा हि ।

न च न परिचितो न चाप्यगम्यश्
चकितमुपैमि तथापि पार्श्वमस्य ।
सलिलनिधिरिव प्रतिक्षणं मे
भवति स एव नवो नवोयमक्ष्णोः ॥ ११ ॥

गण० । महत्खलु पुरुषाधिकारमिदं ज्योतिः । तथा हि ।

द्वारे नियुक्तपुरुषानुमतप्रवेशः
सिंहासनान्तिकचरेण सहोपसर्पन् ।
तेजोभिरस्य विनिवर्तितदृष्टिपातैर्
वाक्यादृते पुनरिव प्रतिवारितोस्मि ॥ १२ ॥

कञ्चुकी । एष देवः । उपसर्पतां भवन्तौ ।

उभौ । उपेत्य । विजयतां देवः ।

राजा । स्वागतं भवद्भ्याम् । परिजनं विलोक्य । आसने तावदत्र भवतोः ।

---

3. A B C D E विवादिनौ for शरीरिणौ.

7. F विलोक्य.

8. F reads the first pâda thus: 'न च परिचितो न चापरम्यः'

10. F जलनिधि° corrected from सलिलनिधि°.

17. A E उपसर्पेताम् as an after-correction in both.

उभौ । परिजनोपनीतयोरासनयोरुपविष्टौ ।

राजा । किमिदं शिष्योपदेशकाले युगपदाचार्ययोरुपस्थानम् ।

गण० । देव श्रूयताम् । मया तीर्थादभिनयविद्या शिक्षिता । दत्तप्रयोगोस्मि । देवेन देव्या च परिगृहीतः ।

राजा । दृढं जाने ।

गण० । सोहममुना हरदत्तेन प्रधानपुरुषसमक्षमयं मे पादरजसा न तुल्य इत्यधिक्षिप्तः ।

हर० । देव अयमेव मयि प्रथमं परिवादरतः । अत्रभवतः किल मम च समुद्रपल्वलयोरिवान्तरम् । तदत्रभवानिमं मां च शास्त्रे प्रयोगे च विमृशतु । देव एव नौ विशेषज्ञः प्राश्निकश्च ।

विदूषकः । समत्थं पडिण्णादं ।

गण० । प्रथमः कल्पः । अवहितो देवः श्रोतुमर्हति ।

राजा । तिष्ठतु तावत् । पक्षपातमत्र देवी मन्यते । तत्तस्याः पण्डितकौशिक्या सहितायाः समक्षमेव न्याय्यो व्यवहारः ।

विदूषकः । सुठ्ठु भवं भणादि ।

उभौ । यद्देवाय रोचते ।

राजा । मौद्गल्य अमुं प्रस्तावं निवेद्य पण्डितकौशिक्या सार्धमाहूयतां देवी ।

---

१. समर्थं प्रतिज्ञातम् । | २. सुष्ठु भवान्भणति.

---

6. A B C D E मम for अयं मे. | 12. A C D E पडिणदं, B पडिण्णदं.

10. B विमृश्यतु, F विमर्शयतु. | 16. D भणादी, F भणदि.

कञ्चुकी । यदाज्ञापयति देवः । इति निष्क्रम्य सहपरिव्राजिकया देव्या सह पुनः प्रविश्य । इत इतो देवी धारिणी ।

देवी । परिव्राजिकां विलोक्य । [1]भअवदि हरदत्तस्स गणदासस्स अ संरम्भे कहं पेक्खसि ।

परिव्राजिका । अलं स्वपक्षावसादशङ्कया । न च पराजीयते केनचिद्गणदासः ।

देवी । [2]जइवि एव्वं तहवि राअपरिग्गहो से पहाणत्तणं उवहरइ ।

परिव्राजिका । अयि राज्ञीशब्दभाजनमात्मानमपि तावच्चिन्तयतु भवती । पश्य ।

अतिमात्रभास्वरत्वं पुष्यति भानोः परिग्रहादनलः ।
अधिगच्छति महिमानं चन्द्रोऽपि निशापरिगृहीतः ॥ १३ ॥

विदूषकः । [3]अवि हा अवि हा । उवट्ठिआ पीठमादिअं पण्डिअकोसिइं पुराकदुअ देवी ।

राजा । पश्याम्येनाम् । यैषा

मङ्गलालंकृता भाति कौशिक्या यतिवेषया ।
त्रयी विग्रहवत्येव सममध्यात्मविद्यया ॥ १४ ॥

परिव्राजिका । उपेत्य । विजयतां देवः ।

---

१. भगवति हरदत्तस्य गणदासस्य च संरम्भे कथं प्रेक्षसे ।

२. यद्यप्येवं तदपि राजपरिग्रहोऽस्य प्रभुत्वमुपहरति ।

३. अपि हा अपि हा । उपस्थिता पीठमर्दिकां पण्डितकौशिकीं पुरस्कृत्य देवी ।

---

2. F इतो देवी । इतो धारिणी देवी.
7. A C जई for जइ.
8. A अपि for अयि.
12. B D E उवट्ठिया.—B D पीठमदियं; E corrects its original पीठमदियं into पीठमद्दीयं; F पीठमद्दिअं —F पण्डिद°.
13. B °कोसिअं.—D E कोसिइं.—F पुरोकदुअ.

राजा । भगवत्यभिवादये ।

परिव्राजिका ।

महासारप्रसवयोः सदृशक्षमयोर्द्वयोः ।
धारिणीभूतधारिण्योर्भव भर्ता शरच्छतम् ॥ १९ ॥

देवी । जेदु अज्जउत्तो ।

राजा । स्वागतं देव्यै । परिव्राजिकां विलोक्य । भगवति क्रियतामासनपरिग्रहः ।

। सर्वे यथोचितमुपविशन्ति ।

राजा । भगवत्यत्रभवतोर्हरदत्तगणदासयोः परस्परेण ज्ञानसंघर्षो जातः । तदत्रभवत्या प्राश्निकपदमध्यासितव्यम् ।

परिव्राजिका । सस्मितम् । अलमलमुपालम्भेन । पत्तने विद्यमानेपि ग्रामे रत्नपरीक्षा ।

राजा । मामैवम् । पण्डितकौशिकी खलु भवती । पक्षपातिनावनयोर्हरदत्तगणदासयोरहं देवी च ।

उभौ । सम्यगाह देवः । मध्यस्था भवती नौ गुणदोषतः परिच्छेत्तुमर्हति ।

राजा । तेन हि प्रस्तूयतां विवादवस्तु ।

परिव्राजिका । देव प्रयोगप्रधानं हि नाट्यशास्त्रम् । किमत्र वाग्व्यवहारेण ।

राजा । कथं देवी मन्यते ।

---

१. जयत्वार्यपुत्रः ।

---

5. D E अ-अ°.
12. E रत्नपरीक्षणम्.
20. B omits "देवी मन्यते."

देवी । [1]जइ मं पुच्छसि एदाणं विवादो एव्व ण मे रुच्चइ ।

गण० । न मां देवी समानविद्यतः परिभवनीयमनुमन्तुमर्हति ।

विदूषकः । [2]देवि देक्खामो उरब्भसंवादं । किं मुहा वेअणदाणेण ।

देवी । [3]णं कलहप्पिओसि ।

विदूषकः । [4]मा चण्डि । अण्णोण्णकलहिदाणं मत्तहत्थीणं एकतरस्सिं अणिज्जिदे कुदो उवसमो ।

राजा । ननु स्वाङ्गसौष्ठवाभिनयमुभयोर्दृष्टवती भवती ।

परि० । अथ किम् ।

राजा । तदिदानीमतः किमाभ्यां प्रत्याययितव्यम् ।

परि० । एतदेव वक्तुकामास्मि ।

शिष्टा क्रिया कस्यचिदात्मसंस्था
संक्रान्तिरन्यस्य विशेषयुक्ता ।
यस्योभयं साधु स शिक्षकाणां
धुरि प्रतिष्ठापयितव्य एव ॥ १६ ॥

---

१. यदि मां पृच्छसि, एतयोर्विवाद एव न मे रोचते ।

२. देवि पश्याम उरभ्रसंवादम् । किं मुधा वेतनदानेन ।

३. ननु कलहप्रियोऽसि ।

४. मा चण्डि । अन्योन्यकलहितयोर्मत्तहस्तिनोरेकतरस्मिन्ननिर्जिते कुत उपशमः ।

---

1. B येव्व.
2. B °विद्यातः.—F परिहीनम् for परिभवनीयम्.
3. F दख्खामो.
6. A °कलिहदाणं.

विदूषकः । [1]सुदं अज्जेहिं भअवदीए वअणं । एस पिण्डिदत्थो [2]उवदेसदंसणेण णिण्णओ त्ति ।

हर॰ । परमुचितं नः ।

गण॰ । देव एवं स्थितमेव ।

देवी । [3]जदा उण अमेहाविणी सिस्सा उवदेसं मलिणएइ तदा आअरिअस्स दोसो णं ।

राजा । देवि एवमुपपद्यते ।

गण॰ । विनेतुरद्रव्यपरिग्रह एव बुद्धिलाघवं प्रकाशयति ।

देवी । कहं दाणिं । गणदासं विलोक्य । जनान्तिकम् । अलं एअस्स अज्जउत्तस्स उच्छाहकालणं मणोरहं पूरिअ । विरम णिरत्थआदो आरम्भादो ।

---

१. श्रुतमार्याभ्यां भगवत्या वचनम् । एष पिण्डितार्थ उपदेशदर्शनेन निर्णय इति ।

२. यदा पुनरमेधाविनी शिष्योपदेशं मलिनयति तदाचार्यस्य दोषो ननु ।

३. कथमिदानीम् । अलमेतस्यार्यपुत्रस्योत्साहकारणं मनोरथं पूरयित्वा । विरम निरर्थकादारम्भात् ।

---

1. D अय्येहिं.
2. A B C D E उवदेसदंसणे अ णिणओ त्ति.
3. D परमसुचितं for परमुचितं.
5. A B C D अम्मेहाविणी.
7. F एवमापतति.
8. F अद्रव्यपात्रपरिग्रहः, with the following explanation in the margin: 'द्रव्यं गुणानामाधारे भेषजे योगवित्तयोरिति यादवः ।' अयोग्यपात्रस्वीकारः ।
9. The MS all read thus: गणदासं विलोक्य । जनान्तिकम् । कहं [F जह] दाणिं । &c. The reading given in our edition is that of Tulberg's.
10. D E F अ-अ°.

विदूषकः । [1]सुट्ठु होदी भणादि । भो गणदास संगीतओवदेसं आरहिअ किं सरस्सइउवाअणमोदआइं खादअमाणस्स सुलहणिग्गहेण विवादेण ।

गण० । सत्यमयमेवार्थो देवीवचनस्य । श्रूयतामवसरप्राप्तम् ।

लब्धास्पदोस्मीति विवादभीरोस्
तितिक्षमाणस्य परेण निन्दाम् ।
यस्यागमः केवलजीविकैव
तं ज्ञानपण्यं वणिजं वदन्ति ॥ १७ ॥

विदूषकः । [2]अइरोवणीदा वो सिस्सा । ता अवरिणिट्ठिदस्स उवदेसस्स अण्णअं पआसणम् ।

गण० । अत एव निर्बन्धः ।

देवी । [3]तेण हि दुवेवि भअवदीए उवदेसं दंसह ।

परि० । नैतन्न्याय्यम् । सर्वज्ञस्याप्येकाकिनो निर्णयाभ्युपगमो दोषाय ।

---

१. सुष्ठु भवती भणति । भो गणदास संगीतकोपदेशमारभ्य किं सरस्वत्युपायनमोदकान्खादतः सुलभनिग्रहेण विवादेन ।

२. अचिरोपनीता वः शिष्या । तदपरिनिष्ठितस्योपदेशस्यान्याय्यं प्रकाशनम् ।

३. तेन हि द्वावपि भगवत्या उपदेशं दर्शयतम् ।

---

1. B D E संगीतयोव°.
2. A C D सरस्साहि° (सरस्सदि ?). —A B C D उवाभणं मोद,° E उवाभणं मोदअं.

4. A सत्यमेवायमेवार्थः.—F °प्राप्तमिदम्.
9. A B C E अचिर°, D अपरि.°
10. A C E आणअं; D अणअं.

देवी । जनान्तिकम् । ¹मूढे परिव्वाजिए किं जागतिंवि मं सुत्तं विअ करेसि । इति सासूयं परावर्तते ।

राजा । देवीं परिव्राजिकायै दर्शयति ।

परि० । विलोक्य ।

अनिमित्तमिन्दुवदने किमत्रभवतः पराङ्मुखी भवसि ।
प्रभवन्त्योपि हि भर्तृषु कारणकोपाः कुटुम्बिन्यः ॥१८॥

विदूषकः । ²ण सकारणं एव्व । अप्पणो पक्खो रक्खिदव्वोत्ति । गणदासं विलोक्य । दिट्ठिआ कोवव्वाएण देवीए परित्तादो भवं । सुसिक्खिओवि सव्वो उवदेसेण णिवुणो होइ ।

गण० । देवि श्रूयताम् । एवं जनो गृह्णाति । तदिदानीं

विवादे दर्शयिष्यन्तं क्रियासंक्रान्तिमात्मनः ।
यदि मां नानुजानासि परित्यक्तोस्म्यहं त्वया ॥ १९ ॥

आसनादुत्तिष्ठति ।

देवी । स्वगतम् । ³का गई । प्रकाशम् । पहवदि अज्जो सिस्सजणस्स ।

---

१. मूढे परिव्राजिके किं जाग्रतीमपि मां सुप्तामिव करोषि ।

२. ननु सकारणमेव । आत्मनः पक्षो रक्षितव्य इति । दिष्ट्या कोपव्याजेन देव्या परित्रातो भवान् । सुशिक्षितोपि सर्व उपदेशेन निपुणो भवति ।

३. का गतिः । प्रभवत्यार्यः शिष्यजनस्य ।

---

1. F omits मं.
7. C एव्वं.—B आप्पणो.
8 C कोविवएण, A B D E कोवो-वाएण.
9. A सुसुखिओ, B D E सुसुक्खियो.
14. D F अ-भो for अज्जो.

गण० । चिरमपदे शङ्कितोऽस्मि । राजानं विलोक्य । अनुज्ञातं देव्या । तदाज्ञापयतु देवः । कस्मिन्नभिनयवस्तुन्युपदेशं दर्शयिष्यामि ।

राजा । यदादिशति भगवती ।

परि० । किमपि देव्या मनसि वर्तते । तच्छङ्कितास्मि ।

देवी । भण विस्सधं । णं प्पहविस्सं अत्तणो परिअणस्स ।

राजा । मम चेति ब्रूहि ।

देवी । भअवदि भण दाणिं ।

परि० । देव चतुष्पदोद्भवं चलितमुदाहरन्ति । तत्रैकार्थसंश्रयमुभयोः प्रयोगं पश्यामः । तावता ज्ञायत एव तत्रभवतोरुपदेशान्तरम् ।

उभौ । यदाज्ञापयति भगवती ।

विदूषकः । तेण हि दुवे वि गदुअ पेक्खाघरए संगीदरअणं करिअ अत्तभवदो दूदं विसज्जेह ।

---

१. भण विश्रब्धम् । ननु प्रभविष्याम्यात्मनः परिजनस्य ।

२. भगवति भणेदानीम् ।

३. तेन हि द्वावपि गत्वा प्रेक्षागृहे संगीतरचनां कृत्वात्रभवते दूतं विसर्जयतम् ।

---

2. A B C D E अभिनय°.

9. The MSS: प्पहविस्ससि, except F.

13. F वग्गा (*i. e.* वर्गौ) for गदुअ.

14. F अत्तभवन्दो (=अत्रभवन्तो.)—A B C D E विसइजेहि.

अह वा मिअङ्गसद्दो एव्व णो उट्ठावइस्सदि ।

हरि० । तथा । इत्युत्तिष्ठति ।

गण० । देवीमवलोकयति ।

देवी । ²ण हि विअअपच्चत्थिणी अहं अज्जस्स ण होमि ।

उभौ । प्रस्थितौ ।

परि० । इतस्तावदाचार्यौ ।

उभौ । परिवृत्य । इमौ स्वः ।

परि । निर्णयाधिकारे ब्रवीमि । सर्वाङ्गसौष्ठवाभिव्यक्तये विगतनेपथ्ययोः पात्रयोः प्रवेशोस्तु ।

उभौ । नेदमप्यावयोरुपदेश्यम् ।

[निष्क्रान्तौ ।

देवी । राजानं विलोक्य । ³जइ इदरेसु राजकज्जेसुवि एव्वं उवाअणिउणदा अज्जउत्तस्स णं सोहणं भवे ।

राजा । देवि

अलमन्यथा गृहीत्वा न खलु मनस्विनि मया प्रयुक्तमिदम् ।
प्रायः समानविद्याः परस्परयशःपुरोभागाः ॥ २० ॥

। नेपथ्ये मृदङ्गशब्दः ।

सर्वे । कर्णं ददति ।

---

१. अथ वा मृदङ्गशब्द एव न उत्थापयिष्यति ।

२. न हि विजयप्रत्यर्थिन्यहमार्यस्य न भवामि ।

३. यदीतरेषु राजकार्येष्वप्येवमुपायनिपुणतार्यपुत्रस्य ननु शोभनं भवेत् ।

---

4. E F अ-भस्स.— A B C D E read thus : ण हि विअअपिच्चत्थिणी अहं अज्जस्स । विजई होहि.

9. F विरलनेपथ्ययोः

12. B जई.—A एवं.

13. D E F अ-अ°.—F सोभणं.

परि० । हन्त प्रवृत्तं संगीतकम् । तथा ह्येषा

जीमूतस्तनिताविशङ्किभिर्मयूरैर्
उद्ग्रीवैरनुरसितस्य पुष्करस्य ।
निर्ह्रादिन्युपहितमध्यमस्वरोत्था
मायूरी मदयति मार्जना मनांसि ॥ २१ ॥

राजा । देवि सामायिका भवामः ।

देवी । आत्मगतम् । ¹अहो अविणओ अज्जउत्तस्स ।

सर्वे । उत्तिष्ठन्ति ।

विदूषकः । अपवार्य । ²भो धीरं गच्छ । मा क्खु अत्तहोदी धारिणी विसंवादइस्सदि ।

राजा ।

धैर्यावलम्बिनमपि त्वरयति मां मुरजवाद्यनादोयम् ।
अवतरतः सिद्धिपथं शब्दः स्वमनोरथस्येव ॥ २२ ॥

[इति निष्क्रान्ताः सर्वे ।

॥ इति प्रथमोऽङ्कः ॥

---

१. अहो अविनय आर्यपुत्रस्य ।

२. भो धीरं गच्छ । मा खल्वत्रभवती धारिणी विसंवादयिष्यति ।

---

1. E संगीतम्.
4. A D E निहृादिन्युप०.
6. A B C D F सामवायिका:
7. D E F अ=भ.°
12. A B D E तुमं for मा.

[ततः प्रविशति संगीतरचनायां कृतायामासनस्थः सवयस्यो राजा परिव्राजिका धारिणी विभवतश्च परिवारः ।

राजा । भगवति अत्रभवतोराचार्ययोः कतरस्य प्रथममुपदेशं द्रक्ष्यामः ।

परि० । ननु समानेपि ज्ञानवृद्धभावे वयोधिकत्वाद्गणदासः पुरस्कारमर्हति ।

राजा । तेन हि मौद्गल्य एवमेवात्रभवतोरावेद्य स्वनियोगमशून्यं कुरु ।

कञ्चुकी । यदाज्ञापयति देवः ।

[इति निष्क्रान्तः ।

गण० । प्रविश्य । देव शर्मिष्ठायाः कृतिर्लयमध्या चतुष्पदा । तस्याश्चतुर्थवस्तुकप्रयोगमेकमनाः श्रोतुमर्हति देवः ।

राजा । आचार्य बहुमानादवहितोस्मि ।

[निष्क्रान्तो गणदासः ।

राजा । जनान्तिकम् । वयस्य

नेपथ्यपरिगतायाश्चक्षुर्दर्शनसमुत्सुकं तस्याः ।
संहर्तुमधीरतया व्यवसितमिव मे तिरस्करिणीम् ॥१॥

विदूषकः । अपवार्य । हो उवत्थिअं णअणमहु । संणिहिदं मक्खिअं च । ता अप्पमत्तो दाणिं पेक्ख ।

[ततः प्रविशत्याचार्यप्रत्यवेक्ष्यमाणाङ्गसौष्ठवा मालविका ।

---

१. भो उपस्थितं नयनमधु । संनिहिता मक्षिका च । तदप्रमत्त इदानीं पश्य ।

---

2. D परीवारः.

16. F °परिणतायाः

18. A C होउ and B D E होदु for "हो".—B णयणमहू, E F णयणमहु.

20. A B C प्रत्यवेक्षमाणा.

विदूषकः । जनान्तिकम् । [1]पेक्खदु भवं । ण हु से पडिच्छन्दादो परिहीअदि महुरदा ।

राजा । जनान्तिकम् । वयस्य

चित्रगतायामस्यां कान्तिविसंवादशङ्कि मे हृदयम् ।
संप्रति शिथिलसमाधिं मन्ये येनेयमालिखिता ॥ २ ॥

गण० । वत्से मुक्तसाध्वसा सत्त्वस्था भव ।

राजा । आत्मगतम् । अहो सर्वास्ववस्थास्वनवद्यता रूपस्य ।

दीर्घाक्षं शरदिन्दुकान्तिवदनं बाहू नतावंसयोः
संक्षिप्तं निबिडोन्नतस्तनमुरः पार्श्वे प्रमृष्टे इव ।
मध्यः पाणिमितो नितम्बि जघनं पादावरालाङ्गुली
छन्दो नर्तयितुर्यथैव मनसः श्लिष्टं तथास्या वपुः ॥३॥

मालविका । उपवहनं कृत्वा चतुष्पदं वस्तु गायति ।

[2]दुल्लहो पिओ तस्सिं भव हिअअ णिरासं ।
अम्हो अपङ्गओ मे पप्फुरइ किंपि वामो ॥ ४ ॥

---

१. पश्यतु भवान् । न खल्वस्याः प्रतिच्छन्दात्परिहीयते मधुरता ।

२. दुर्लभः प्रियस्तस्मिन्भव हृदय निराशम् । अम्ब हे अपाङ्गको मे प्रस्फुरति किमपि वामः ।

---

2. A B C DE पडिहीअदि.

6. B C D E मुग्धसाध्वसा.

7. A B C D E सर्वावस्थासु.

11. A C D मनसश्लिष्टं (मनसः श्लिष्टं ?); B मनसः श्लिष्टं, corrected from मनसश्लि°; E मनसा श्लिष्टं also corrected from मनसश्लिष्टं.

12. F कपोतकं कृत्वा.

13. D E पियो.—B D E हियय.

14. B D E अपङ्गयो.—F किंवि.—F वामओ.

एसो सो चिरदिट्ठो कहं उवणइदव्वो ।
णाह मं पराहीणं तुइ गणअ सतिण्हं ॥ ८ ॥

इति यथारसमभिनयति ।

विदूषकः । जनान्तिकम् । [२]भो चउप्पदं वथ्थुअं दुवारं कदुअ तुइ उवक्खित्तो विअ अप्पा तत्तहोदीए ।

राजा । सखे एवमावयोर्हृदयम् । अनया खलु

जनमिममनुरक्तं विद्धि नाथेति गेये
वचनमभिनयन्त्या स्वाङ्गनिर्देशपूर्वम् ।
प्रणयगतिमदृष्ट्वा धारिणीसंनिकर्षाद्
अहमिव सुकुमारप्रार्थनाव्याजमुक्तः ॥ ९ ॥

मालविका । गीतान्ते गन्तुमिच्छति।

विदूषकः । [३]होदि चिट्ठ । किंवि विसुमरिदं कमभेदेण । तं पुच्छिस्सं दाव ।

गण॰ । वत्से स्थीयताम् । उपदेशविशुद्धौ यास्यसि ।

मालविका । निवृत्य स्थिता ।

---

१ एषोसौ चिरदृष्टः कथमुपनेतव्यः । नाथ मां पराधीनां त्वयि गणय सतृष्णाम् ।
२. भो चतुष्पदं वस्तुकं द्वारं कृत्वा त्वय्युपक्षिप्त इवात्मा तत्रभवत्या ।
३. भवति तिष्ठस्व । किमपि विस्मृतं क्रमभेदेन तत्प्रक्ष्यामि तावत् ।

---

3. A omits the whole of "इति यथारसमभिनयति."
5. D E उवक्खित्तो.
6 A om. "सखे".
12. B D किमपि. A C E किंपि.—C D °भेदेन.—A omits "तं" before "पुच्छिस्सं".—B D E कम्मभेदेण (=कर्मभेदेन.)
14. A °विशुद्धा, F °शुद्धौ.
15. B निवृत्य.

राजा । आत्मगतम् । अहो सर्वास्ववस्थासु चारुता शोभां पुष्यति । तथा हि

वामं संधिस्तिमितवलयं न्यस्य हस्तं नितम्बे
कृत्वा श्यामाविटपसदृशं स्रस्तमुक्तं द्वितीयम् ।
पादाङ्गुष्ठालुलितकुसुमे कुट्टिमे पातिताक्षं
नृत्तादस्याः स्थितमतितरां कान्तमृज्वायतार्धम् ॥७॥

देवी । [१]णं गोदमवअणंपि अज्जो हिअए करेदि ।

गण० । देवि मैवम् । देवप्रत्ययात्संभाव्यते सूक्ष्मदर्शिता गौतमस्य । पश्य ।

मन्दोप्यमन्दतामेति संसर्गेण विपश्चितः ।
पङ्कच्छिदः फलस्येव निकषेणाविलं पयः ॥ ८ ॥

विदूषकं विलोक्य । शृणुमो विवक्षितमार्यस्य ।

विदूषकः । गणदासं विलोक्य । [२]सक्खिणीं दाव पुच्छ । पच्छा जो मये कमभेदो लक्खिदो त्तं भणिस्सं ।

गण० । भगवति यथादृष्टमभिधीयतां दोषो वा गुणो वा ।

---

१. ननु गौतमवचनमप्यार्यो हृदये करोति ।

२. साक्षिणीं तावत्पृच्छ । पश्चाद्यो मया क्रमभेदो लक्षितस्तं भणिष्यामि ।

---

1. A B C D E सर्वावस्थासु.— F शोभान्तरम्.
11. A B C D E निकर्षेण.
13. A B C D E भिक्खुणीं for "सक्खिणीं."
14. D E तं.
15. A B C D E यथादर्शनम् for "यथादृष्टम्"

परि० । यथाशास्त्रं सर्वमनवद्यम् । कुतः ।

अङ्गैरन्तर्निहितवचनैः सूचितः सम्यगर्थः
पादन्यासो लयमनुगतस्तन्मयत्वं रसेषु ।
शाखायोनिर्मृदुरभिनयस्तद्विकल्पानुवृत्तौ
भावो भावं नुदति विषयाद्रागबन्धः स एव ॥ ९ ॥

गण० । देवः कथं मन्यते ।

राजा । गणदास वयं स्वपक्षशिथिलाभिमानाः संवृत्ताः ।

गण० । अथ नर्तयितास्मि ।

उपदेशं विदुः शुद्धं सन्तस्तमुपदेशिनः ।
श्यामायते न युष्मासु यः काञ्चनमिवाग्निषु ॥ १० ॥

देवी । [१]दिट्ठिआ परीक्खकाराहणेण अज्जो वड्ढइ ।

गण० । देवीपरिग्रहश्च मे वृद्धिहेतुः । विदूषकं विलोक्य । गौतम वदेदानीं यत्ते मनसि वर्तते ।

विदूषकः । [२]पुढमोवदेसदंसणे पुढमं बम्हणस्स पूआ इच्छिदव्वा । सा उण वो विसुमारिदा ।

---

१. दिष्ट्या परीक्षकाराधनेनार्यो वर्धते ।

२. प्रथमोपदेशदर्शने प्रथमं ब्राह्मणस्य पूजेष्टव्या । तस्याः पुनर्यूयं विस्मृतवन्तः ।

---

8. F अद्य for "अथ."

11. A B परिक्खराहणेण. — D E F अ-ओ.—A B C D E परिक्ख°.

14. A पढमो°—B D E पूआ.

15. Our MSS. सा ण वोपलक्खिदा (= सा न व उपलक्षिता). We according to G.

परि० । अहो प्रयोगाभ्यन्तरः प्राश्निकः ।

सर्वे । प्रहसिताः ।

। मालविका च स्मितं करोति ।

राजा । आत्मगतम् । आप्तसारश्चक्षुषा स्वविषयः । यदनेन

स्मयमानमायताक्ष्याः किंचिदभिव्यक्तदशनशोभि मुखम् ।
असमग्रलक्ष्यकेसरमुच्छ्वसदिव पङ्कजं दृष्टम् ॥ ११ ॥

गण० । महाब्राह्मण न खलु नेपथ्यसंगीतकमिदम् । अन्यथा कथं त्वामर्चनीयं नार्चयिष्यामः ।

विदूषकः । [1]मए णाम मुध्धचादएण विअ सुक्खघणगज्जिदे अन्तरिक्खे जलपाणं इच्छिदं ।

परि० । एवमेव ।

विदूषकः । [2]तेण हि पण्डिदपरिदोसपच्चआ मूढाजादी । जइ तत्तहोदीए सोभणं गण्हिदं तदो इमं पारितोसिअं पअच्छामि । इति राज्ञो हस्तात्कटकमाकर्षति ।

---

१. मया नाम मुग्धचातकेनेव शुष्कघनगर्जितेन्तरिक्षे जलपानमिष्टम् ।

२. तेन हि पण्डितपरितोषप्रत्यया मूढजातिः । यद्यत्रभवत्या शोभनं गृहीतं तदिदं पारितोषिकं प्रयच्छामि ।

---

1. F प्रयोगाभ्यन्तरप्रा°.
7. B F नैपथ्य°.
8. F दक्षणीयं for "अर्चनीयं."
9. B °चादयेण.—E सुक्कघण°.
12. F पण्डिअ°.—E °परिनोस°.
13. F भणिदं for "गण्हिदं."—E F अत्तहोदीए.—B तदा for "तदो."
14. B F om. "इति;" C E om. the whole stage-direction beginning from "इति."

देवी । [1]चिट्ठ । गुणन्तरं अआणन्तो किंति तुमं आहरणं देसि ।

विदूषकः । [2]परकीअंति करिअ ।

देवी । आचार्यौ विलोक्य । [3]अज्ज गणदास णं दंसिदोवदेसा वो सिस्सा ।

गण० । वत्से प्रतिष्ठस्वेदानीम् ।

[मालविका सहाचार्येण निष्क्रान्ता ।

विदूषकः । जनान्तिकम् । राजानं विलोक्य । [4]एत्तिओ मे विहवो भवन्तं सेविदुं ।

राजा । जनान्तिकम् । अलमलं परिच्छेदेन । अद्य हि

भाग्यास्तमयमिवाक्ष्णोर्हृदयस्य महोत्सवावसानमिव ।
द्वारपिधानमिव धृतेर्मन्ये तस्यास्तिरस्करिणीम् ॥ १२ ॥

विदूषकः । [5]साहु तुमं दरिद्दादुरो विअ वेज्जेण उवणीअमाणं ओसहं इच्छसि ।

हरदत्तः । प्रविश्य । देव मदीयमिदानीमवलोकयितुं प्रयोगं क्रियतां प्रसादः ।

---

१. तिष्ठ । गुणान्तरमजानन्किमिति त्वमाभरणं ददासि ।

२. परकीयमिति कृत्वा.

३. आर्य गणदास ननु दर्शितोपदेशा वः शिष्या ।

४. एतावान्मे विभवो भवन्तं सेवितुम् ।

५. साधु त्वं दारिद्र्यातुर इव वैद्येनोपनीयमानमौषधमिच्छसि ।

---

1. C अभणन्तो.—A B C D E अहिणन्देसि for "आहरणं देसि."

2. A परकरयंति; B परे केरयंति; E corrects its परकेरयंति into पक्खोयंति; C D परकेरयंति

3. D E F अ॰अ.—A B C D E om. णं.

7. C अत्तिओ; D यत्तिओ, E येत्तिओ.

11. F तिरस्करणम्.

15. F adds इति after "क्रियताम्."

राजा । आत्मगतम् । अवसितो दर्शनार्थः । प्रकाशम् । दाक्षिण्यमवलम्ब्य हरदत्त पर्युत्सुका एव वयम् ।

हर० । अनुगृहीतोस्मि ।

॥ नेपथ्ये ॥

वैतालिकः । जयतु देवः । उपारूढो मध्यमह्नः सविता । तथा हि ।

पत्रच्छायासु हंसा मुकुलितनयना दीर्घिकापद्मिनीनां
सौधान्यत्यर्थतापाद्वलभिपरिचयद्वेषिपारावतानि ।
बिन्दूत्क्षेपान्पिपासुः परिपतति शिखी भ्रान्तिमद्वारियन्त्रं
सर्वैरुस्रैः समग्रैस्त्वमिव नृपगुणैर्दीप्यते सप्तसप्तिः ॥१३॥

विदूषकः । ¹अवि हा अवि हा । ण्हाणभोअणवेला संवुत्ता अत्तहोदो । उइदवेलादिक्कमे चिइस्सआ दोसं उदाहरन्ति ।

राजा । हरदत्त किं भणसि ।

हर० । नास्त्यवकाशो मद्वचनस्य ।

राजा । हरदत्तं विलोक्य । तेन हि त्वदीयमुपदेशं श्वो वयं द्रक्ष्यामः । विश्राम्यतु भवान् ।

हर० । यदाज्ञापयति देवः ।

[इति निष्क्रान्तः ।

---

१. अपि हा अपि हा । स्नानभोजनवेला संवृत्तात्रभवतः । उचितवेलातिक्रमे चिकित्सका दोषमुदाहरन्ति ।

---

5. C उपारूढो मध्यः सविता.
11. A C do not repeat "अवि हा."
—E अत्तहोदे.
12. B C D E चिइस्सया.
16. B D विश्रम्यतु.

देवी । णिवुत्तेदु अज्जउत्तो मज्झणविहिं ।

विदूषकः । [2]होदि विसेसेण पाणभोअणं तुवरेदु ।

परि० । उत्थाय । स्वस्ति भवते ।

[सपरिजनया देव्या सह निष्क्रान्ता ।

विदूषकः । [3]भो ण केवलं रूवे सिप्पेवि अद्दुदीआ मालविआ ।

राजा ।

अव्याजसुन्दरीं तां विज्ञानेन ललितेन योजयता ।
परिकल्पितो विधात्रा बाणः कामस्य विषदिग्धः ॥१४॥

किं बहुना । चिन्तयितव्योस्मि ।

विदूषकः ।[4]भवदावि अहं । दिढं विपणिकन्दू विअ मे उदरम्भन्तरं ढज्जइ ।

राजा । एवमेव । भवान्सुहृदर्थे त्वरताम् ।

---

१. निर्वर्तयत्वार्यपुत्रो मध्याह्नविधिम् ।

२. भवति विशेषेण पानभोजनं त्वर्यताम् ।

३. भो न केवलं रूपे शिल्पेप्यद्वितीया मालविका ।

४. भवताप्यहम् । दृढं विपणिकन्दुरिव म उदराभ्यन्तरं दह्यते ।

---

1. A C णिवुत्तोदु; B D णिवत्तेदु, F णिव्वददु.—D E F अ-अ°.

5. A C D E F सिप्पे अ for "सिप्पेवि."

12. B ढढज्जई.

13. A B C D E त्वरते.

विदूषकः । गेहीदक्खणोम्हि । किं दु मेहोवरुध्धजोण्हा विअ परा-
हीणदंसणा तत्तभोदी । भवंवि सूणोपरिचरो विहंगमो
विअ आमिसलोलुवो भीरुओ अ अच्चादुरो भविअ क-
ज्जसिध्धिं पथ्थयन्तो मे रुच्चइ ।

राजा । सखे कथं नातुरो भविष्यामि । यदा

सर्वान्तःपुरवनिताव्यापारप्रतिनिवृत्तहृदयस्य ।
सा वामलोचना मे स्नेहस्यैकायनीभूता ॥ १९ ॥

[इति निष्क्रान्तौ ।

॥ इति द्वितीयोऽङ्कः ॥

---

१. गृहीतक्षणोऽस्मि । किं तु मेघोपरुद्धज्योत्स्नेव पराधीनदर्शना तत्रभवती । भवानपि सूनोपरिचरो विहंगम इवामिषलोलुपो भीरुकश्चात्यातुरो भूत्वा कार्यसिद्धिं प्रार्थयन्मे रोचते ।

---

1. A B C D E गहिदक्खिणो.— B °जोन्हा.–A B C D E मेहाव-रुध्ध°.

6. B C °व्यापारं.

8. B इति निष्क्रान्ताः सर्वे ; E निष्क्रान्ताः सर्वे.

। ततः प्रविशति परिव्राजिकायाः परिचारिका ।

परिचारिका । [1]आणत्तम्हि भअवदीए । जहा समाधिमदिए देवस्स सभाअणथ्थं बीजपूरअं गेण्हिअ आअच्छेत्ति । ता जाव प्पमदवणपालिअं महुअरिअं अण्णेस्सामि । परिक्रम्यावलोक्य च । एसा तवणीआसोअं ओलोअन्ती महुअरिआ चिट्ठइ । जाव णं संभावेमि ।

। ततः प्रविशत्युद्यानपालिका ।

प्रथमा । उपसृत्य । [2]महुअरिए अवि सुहो दे उज्जाणव्वणव्वावारो ।

द्वितीया । [3]अम्हो समाहिमदिआ । सहि साअदं दे ।

समाधिमतिका । [4]हला भअवदी आणवेदि । अरित्तपाणिणा अम्हारिसजणेण अथ्थपइ दक्खिदव्वो । ता बीजपूरएण सुस्सूसिदुं इच्छामित्ति ।

---

१. आज्ञप्तास्मि भगवत्या । यथा समाधिमतिके देवस्य सभाजनार्थं बीजपूरकं गृहीत्वागच्छेति । तत्तावत्प्रमदवनपालिकां मधुकरिकामन्वेष्यामि । एषा तपनीयाशोकमालोकयन्ती मधुकरिका तिष्ठति । तावदिमां संभावयामि ।

२. मधुकरिके अपि सुखस्त उद्यानवनव्यापारः ।

३. अहो समाधिमतिका । सखि स्वागतं ते ।

४. हला भगवत्याज्ञापयति । अरिक्तपाणिनास्मादृशजनेनार्थपतिर्द्रष्टव्यः । तद्बीजपूरकेण शुश्रूषितुमिच्छामीति ।

---

2. B अणत्तंम्हि, A C D E अणत्तम्हि.– F om. 'जहा समाधिमदिए.'

4. B महुआरिआं.–A B C D E अण्णेसामि.

5. A मधुअरिआ; B महुआरिआ.

6. A चिठ्ठई.—B संभवेमि.

8. F सुविहिदो (=सुविहितः) for "सुहो." —B ०वणवाव्वारो.—F om. ०व्वण०.

9. F समाहुदिआ (= समाभृतिका) here and everywhere else throughout the work.

10. A आणव्वेदि.

11. B अम्मोरिस०.—B अथ्थपई.—E देक्खि०.

मधुकरिका । [1]णं संणिहिदं बीजपूरअं । कहेहि दुवेणं संगीदओवदेसणिमित्तं अण्णोण्णसंघरिसिदाणं णट्टाअरिआणं उवदेसं देक्खिअ कदरो भअवदीए पसंसिदोत्ति ।

समाधि० । [2]दुवेवि किल आअमिणो पओअणिउणा अ । किं दु सिस्सागुणविसेसेण गणदासो उण्णमिदोवदेसो ।

मधु० । [3]अह मालविआगअं कोलीणं किंति सुणीअदि ।

समाधि० । [4]बलियं खु साहिलासो तस्सिं भट्टा । केवलं देवीए धारिणीए चित्तं रक्खिदुं अहिलासदंसणे पहुत्तणं ण दंसेदि ।

---

१. ननु संनिहितं बीजपूरकम् । कथय द्वयोः संगीतकोपदेशनिमित्तमन्योन्यसंघर्षिणोर्नाट्याचार्ययोरुपदेशं दृष्ट्वा कतरो भगवत्या प्रशंसित इति ।

२. द्वावपि किलागमिनौ प्रयोगनिपुणौ च । किं तु शिष्यागुणविशेषेण गणदास उन्नमितोपदेशः ।

३. अथ मालविकागतं कौलीनं किमिति श्रूयते ।

४. बलवत्खलु साभिलाषस्तस्यां भर्ता । केवलं देव्या धारिण्याश्चित्तं रक्षितुमभिलाषदर्शने प्रभुतां न दर्शयति ।

---

1. B C मधुकारिका.
2. A °संघरिसिन्दाणं
3. F णट्टाचारिआणं.—D E देक्खिय.—
   A वसंसिदोत्ति
4. F पओग°.
5. F गणदासे उंण्णमिदो उवदेसो.
6. A B C D E किंपि.— for "किंति"
   A B C D E read thus :—.
   "मधु० । अह मालविआगअं कोलीणं किंपि सुणीअदि । मालविआए किल साहिलासो भट्टा केवलं देवीए धारिणीए चित्तं रक्खिदुं अहिलासदंसणे पहुत्तणं ण दंसेदि ।"
   समाधि० । बलियं खु साहिलासो तस्सिं भट्टा । . . . . . . मं ।
7. A C देविए.
8. B धारणीए.—F अहिलासं ण दंसेदि.

मालविआवि इमेसु दिअहेसु अणुभूदमुत्ता विअ मालदीमाला मिलायमाणा लक्खीअदि। अदो वरं ण आणे। विसज्जेहि मं।

मधु०। [1]एअं साहावलम्बिणं बीजपूरअं गेण्ह।

समाधि०। नाट्येन गृहीत्वा। [2]हला तुमंवि इदो विपुलदरं साहुजणसुस्सूसाए फलं लहेहि।

मधु०। प्रस्थिता। [3]सहि समं जेव्व गच्छामो। अहंवि इमस्स चिराअमाणकुसुमुग्गमस्स तवणीआसोअस्स दोहलणिमित्तं देवीए विण्णवेमि।

समाधि०। [4]जुज्जइ। अहिआरो क्खु तुह।

[इति निष्क्रान्ते।

। प्रवेशकः।

मालविकाप्येतेषु दिवसेष्वनुभूतमुक्तेव मालतीमाला म्लायमाना लक्ष्यते। अतः परं न जाने। विसर्जय माम्।

१. एतच्छाखावलम्बि बीजपूरकं गृहाण।

२. हला त्वमपीतो विपुलतरं साधुजनशुश्रूषायाः फलं लभस्व।

३. सखि सममेव गच्छावः। अहमप्येतस्य चिरायमाणकुसुमोद्गमस्य तपनीयाशोकस्य दोहदनिमित्तं देव्यै विज्ञापयामि।

४. युज्यते। अधिकारः खलु तव।

---

2. A B C D E जाणे for " आणे."
3. B मां.
4. A E साहावलम्बिदं.
5. F om. इदो, and reads पेसलतरं for " विपुलदरं."
6. A C सुस्सुसाए.
7. A B C ज्जेव, F एव्व.
8. D तवणी आहोअस्स.
9. A C देविए विणवेमि. E also reads विणवेमि.
10. B तुह for "तुह."—F om क्खु.

। ततः प्रविशति काममानावस्थो राजा विदूषकश्च ।

राजा । आत्मानं विलोक्य ।

शरीरं क्षामं स्यादसति दयितालिङ्गनसुखे
भवेत्सास्रं चक्षुः क्षणमपि न सा दृश्यत इति ।
तया सारङ्गाक्ष्या त्वमसि न कदाचिद्विरहितं
प्रसक्ते निर्वाणे हृदय परितापं वहसि किम् ॥ १ ॥

विदूषकः । [1]अलं भवदो धीरदं उज्झिअ परिदेविएण । दिट्ठा क्खु मए तत्तहोदीए मालविआए प्पिअसही बउलावलिआ । सुणाविदा अ तं अथ्थं भवदा जो संदिट्ठो ।

राजा । ततः किमुक्तवती ।

विदूषकः । [2]विण्णवेहि भट्टारं । अणुगहीदाम्हि इमिणा णिओएण । किं दु सा तवास्सिणी देवीए अहिअदरं रक्खिअमाणा णाअरक्खिदो मणी विअ ण सुहं समासादइदव्वा । तहवि घडइस्संति ।

---

१. अलं भवतो धीरतामुज्झित्वा परिदेवितेन । दृष्टा खलु मया तत्रभवत्या मालविकायाः प्रियसखी बकुलावलिका । श्राविता च तमर्थं भवता यः संदिष्टः ।

२. विज्ञापय भर्तारम् । अनुगृहीतास्म्यनेन नियोगेन । किं तु सा तपस्विनी देव्याधिकतरं रक्ष्यमाणा नागरक्षितो मणिरिव न सुखं समासादयितव्या । तथापि घटिष्य इति ।

---

7. B उइझीअ.
8. A C D पिअ°.
11. A विणवेहि.—A B C D E अणुगेण्हिदम्हि.
12. F सादरं for "अहिअदरं."
13. A C D णाअरखिओ.—A B C D वीअ.—A B C D E read विअ मणी, and add अहं णिहं रण्णा (= अहर्निशम्, राज्ञा)
14. D समासादयिदव्वा.—B पटईस्सं°.

राजा। भगवन्संकल्पयोने प्रतिबन्धवत्स्वापि विषयेष्वभिनिवेश्य तथा प्रहरसि यथा जनोयं कालान्तरक्षमो न भवति । सविस्मयम् ।

क्व रुजा हृदयप्रमाथिनी क्व च ते विश्वसनीयमायुधम्।
मृदुतीक्ष्णतरं यदुच्यते तदिदं मन्मथ दृश्यते त्वयि॥२॥

विदूषकः। णं भणामि तास्सिं साहणिज्जे कज्जे किदो उवाओवक्खेवोत्ति । ता पज्जवत्थावेदु अत्ताणं तत्तभवं ।

राजा। अथेमं दिवसशेषमुचितव्यापारपराङ्मुखेन चेतसा क्व नु खलु यापयामि ।

विदूषकः। णं भवं अज्ज एव्व वसन्दपुढमावदारसूअआणि रत्तकुरबआणि उवाअणं पेसिअ णववसन्तावदारावदेसेण इरावदीए णिउणिआमुहेण पत्थिदो । इच्छामि अज्जउत्तेण सह डोलाहिरोहणं अणुहोदुंति । भवदावि से पडिण्णादं । ता पमदवणं जेव्व गच्छम्ह ।

---

१. ननु भणामि तस्मिन्साधनीये कार्ये कृत उपायोपक्षेप इति । तत्पर्यवस्थापयत्वात्मानं तत्रभवान् ।

२. ननु भवानद्यैव वसन्तप्रथमावतारसूचकानि रक्तकुरबकाण्युपायने प्रेष्य नववसन्तावतारापदेशेनेरावत्या निपुणिकामुखेन प्रार्थितः । इच्छाम्यार्यपुत्रेण सह दोलाधिरोहणमनुभवितुमिति । भवताप्यस्यै प्रतिज्ञातम् । तत्प्रमदवनमेव गच्छावः ।

---

1. A B C D E प्रतिबन्धवस्तुष्वपि.
6. D उवाआवक्खेवो corrected from उवाओवक्खेवो.
9. F om. नु.
10. B D° सुअआणि.
11. A B C D °कुरवयाणि.—B पेसोअ.
12. A C D णिउणीआ°.—Our MSS इच्छेअं. We with G.
13. D E F अ..अ°.—A B C D भवदापि.
14. A पडिणादं—A B C जेव.—B D E F गच्छह.

राजा । न क्षममिदम् ।

विदूषकः । [1]कहं विअ ।

राजा । वयस्य निसर्गनिपुणाः स्त्रियः । कथं मामन्यसंक्रान्तहृदयमुपलालयन्तमपि ते सखी न लक्षयिष्यति । अतः पश्यामि

उचितः प्रणयो वरं विहन्तुं बहवः खण्डनहेतवो हि दृष्टाः ।
उपचारविधिर्मनस्विनीनां न तु पूर्वाभ्यधिकोपि भावशून्यः ॥ ३ ॥

विदूषकः । [2]णारुहदि भवं अन्तेउरपडिट्ठिदं दाक्खिण्णं एक्कपदे पिट्ठदो कादुं ।

राजा । विचिन्त्य । तेन हि प्रमदवनमार्गमादेशय ।

विदूषकः । [3]इदो इदो भवं ।

। उभौ परिक्रामतः ।

विदूषकः । [4]वसन्दो किल एदाहिं पवणचलिदाहिं पल्लवङ्गुलीहिं तुवरेदि विअ भवन्तं एदं पमदवणं पविसेत्ति ।

---

१. कथमिव ।

२. नार्हति भवानन्तःपुरप्रतिष्ठितं दाक्षिण्यमेकपदे पृष्ठतः कर्तुम् ।

३. इत इतो भवान् ।

४. वसन्तः किलैताभिः पवनचलिताभिः पल्लवाङ्गुलीभिस्त्वरयतीव भवन्तमेतत्प्रमदवनं प्रविशेति ।

---

7. A B C E ननु for "नत्तु."

9. A D नारुहदि.—E °प्पडिट्ठिदं.—A B C D E add जणं after दक्खिणं which they read for "दक्खिण्णं."

15. A B C D E तुवरावेदि.—B °प्पविसेति.

राजा । स्पर्शं निरूप्य । अभिजातः किल वसन्तः ।

सखे पश्य

आमत्तानां श्रवणसुभगैः कूजितैः कोकिलानां
सानुक्रोशं मनसिजरुजः सह्यतां पृच्छतेव ।
अङ्गे चूतप्रसवसुरभिर्दक्षिणो मारुतो मे
सान्द्रस्पर्शः करतल इव व्यापृतो माधवेन ॥ ४ ॥

विदूषकः । [1]पविस णिवुदिलाहाअ ।

। उभौ प्रविशतः ।

विदूषकः । [2]भो वअस्स अवधाणेण दाव दिट्ठिं देहि । एदं खु भवन्तं विलोहइदुकामाए पमदवणलच्छीए जुवईवेसलज्जाइत्तअं वसन्तकुसुमणेवत्थअं गहिअं ।

राजा । ननु विस्मयादवलोकयामि ।

रक्ताशोकरुचा विशेषितगुणो बिम्बाधरालक्तकः
प्रत्याख्यातविशेषकं कुरबकं श्यामावदातारुणम् ।
आक्रान्ता तिलकक्रियापि तिलकैर्लीनद्विरेफाञ्जनैः
सावज्ञेव मुखप्रसाधनविधौ श्रीर्माधवी योषिताम् ॥५॥

---

१. प्रविश्य निर्वृतिलाभाय ।

२. भो वयस्य अवधानेन तावद्दृष्टिं देहि । एतत्खलु भवन्तं विलोभयितुकामया प्रमदवनलक्ष्म्या युवतिवेषलज्जयितृकं वसन्तकुसुमनेपथ्यं गृहीतम् ।

---

1. F reads रूपयित्वा, and never puts नि before रूपम् used in stage-directions occurring subsequently.

4. B सह्यते.

7. AC णिउ°.

9. A E वयस्य.—B अवहाणेण.

10. A B C D E भवन्तं विभ लोहइदुकामाए.

11. A B C D E °लज्जावइत्तअं.—A B C D E गाहिअं.

। उभावुद्यानशोभां निर्वर्णयतः ।

। ततः प्रविशति पर्युत्सुका मालविका ।

मालविका । [१]अणभिण्णादहिअअं भट्टारं अभिलसन्दी अप्पणोवि दाव लज्जेमि । कुदो विहवो सिणिध्धअणस्स वुत्तन्तं आचक्खिदुं । ण आणे अप्पडिआरगुरुअं वेअणं केत्तिअं कालं मअणो मं णइस्सदित्ति । कतिचित्पदानि गत्वा । कहिं णु पथ्थिदम्हि । विचिन्त्य । आम् संदिट्ठम्हि देवीए । गोदमचावलादो डोलापरिभट्टा ण सक्कुणोमि अहं चलणे चालइदुं । तुमं दाव तवणीआसोअस्स दोहलं णिव्वत्तेहि । जादि सो पञ्चरत्तब्भन्तरे कुसुमं दंसेइ तदोहं— । अन्तरा निःश्वस्य । अहिलासपूरइत्तअं पसादं दाइस्सांति । दाव णिओअभूमिं पुढमं गदा होमि । जाव अणुपदं मह चलणालंकारहथ्थाए बउलावलिआए आअन्तव्वं परिदेविस्सं दाव विस्सध्धं मुहुत्तअं ।

१. अनभिज्ञातहृदयं भर्तारमभिलषन्त्यात्मनोपि तावल्लज्जे । कुतो विभवः स्निग्धजनस्य वृत्तान्तमाख्यातुम् । न जानेऽपरिहारगुर्वीं वेदनां कियन्तं कालं मदनो मां नेष्यतीति । क्व नु प्रस्थितास्मि । आम् संदिष्टास्मि देव्या । गौतमचापलाद्दोलापरिभ्रष्टा न शक्नोम्यहं चरणौ चालयितुम् । त्वं तावत्तपनीयाशोकस्य दोहदं निर्वर्तय । यदि स पञ्चरात्राभ्यन्तरे कुसुमं दर्शयति तदाहम्—अभिलाषपूरकं प्रसादं दास्यामीति । तावन्नियोगभूमिं प्रथमं गता भवामि । यावदनुपदं मम चरणालंकारहस्तया बकुलावलिकयागन्तव्यं परिदेविष्ये तावद्विश्रब्धं मुहूर्तकम् ।

1. A C वर्णयतः.
3. F अणहिण्णादं°.—B भट्टारअं—A B °लसन्ति.
4. A B C D E add सहो between "सिणिध्ध" and "अणस्स."
5. B D E आअक्खिदुं.—D अपडियार°; E अपडिहार.°
10. A C D णिवत्तेहि; E णिवट्टेहि.
11. F पदं पसादे for पसादं.
14. B इयन्तव्वं; C D इअन्तव्वं—A B C परिदेविस्सं.— A B C D वीसध्धं.

परिक्रामति ।

विदूषकः । [1]ही ही इअं सीधुपाणुव्वेजिअस्स मच्छण्डिआ उवणदा ।

राजा । अयि किमेतत् ।

विदूषकः । [2]एसा क्खु णादिपज्जत्तवेसा उस्सुअवण्णा विअ एआइणी मालविआ अदूरे वट्टइ ।

राजा । सहर्षम् । कथं मालविका ।

विदूषकः । [3]अह इं ।

राजा । शक्यमिदानीं जीवितमवलम्बितुम् ।

त्वदुपलभ्य समीपगतां प्रियां
हृदयमुच्छ्वसितं मम विक्लवम् ।
तरुवृतां पथिकस्य जलार्थिनः
सरितमारसितादिव सारसात् ॥ ६ ॥

अथ क्व तत्रभवती ।

विदूषकः । [4]एसा णं तरुराइमज्झादो णिक्कन्दा इदो ज्जेव्व आअच्छदि ।

राजा । वयस्य पश्याम्येनाम् ।

---

१. ही ही इयं सीधुपानोद्वेजितस्य मत्स्यण्डिकोपनता ।
२. एषा खलु नातिपर्याप्तवेषोत्सुकवर्णेवैकाकिनी मालविकादूरे तिष्ठति ।
३. अथ किम् ।
४. एषा ननु तरुराजिमध्यान्निष्क्रान्तेत एवागच्छति ।

---

2. A C D मत्सण्डिआ.
15. F णिग्गदा.—D जेव्व.
16. D E F आअच्छइ.
17. A om. " वयस्य."

विपुलं नितम्बबिम्बे मध्ये क्षामं समुन्नतं कुचयोः ।
अत्यायतं नयनयोर्मम जीवितमेतदायाति ॥ ७ ॥

सखे पूर्वस्मादवस्थान्तरमारूढा तत्रभवती । तथा हि ।

शरकाण्डपाण्डुगण्डस्थलेयमाभाति परिमिताभरणा ।
माधवपरिणतपत्रा कतिपयकुसुमेव कुन्दलता ॥ ८ ॥

विदूषकः । [1]एसावि भवं विअ मअणवाहिणा परिमिट्ठा भविस्सदि ।

राजा । सौहार्दमेवं पश्यति ।

मालविका । [2]अअं सो ललिअदोहलापेख्खी अगहीदकुसुमणेवथ्थो उक्कण्ठिदं मं अणुकरेइ असोओ । जाव से पछ्छाअसीअले सिलापट्टे णिसण्णा भविअ अत्ताणं विणोदेमि ।

विदूषकः । [3]सुदं भवदा उक्कण्ठिदम्हित्ति तत्तहोदीए मन्तिदं ।

राजा । नैतावता भवन्तं प्रसन्नतर्कं मन्ये । कुतः

वोढा कुरबकरजसां किसलयपुटभेदसीकरानुगतः ।
अनिमित्तोत्कण्ठामपि जनयति मनसो मलयवातः ॥ ९ ॥

मालविका । उपविष्टा ।

---

१. एषापि भवानिव मदनव्याधिना परिमृष्टा भविष्यति ।

२. अयं स ललितदोहदापेक्ष्यगृहीतकुसुमनेपथ्य उत्कण्ठितां मामनुकरोत्यशोकः । तावदस्य प्रच्छायशीतले शिलापट्टे निषण्णा भूत्वात्मानं विनोदयामि ।

३. श्रुतं भवतोत्कण्ठितास्मीत्यत्रभवत्या मन्त्रितम् ।

---

9. A C D °दोहलापेखो.—B अगहीद°.—A C D E °णेवछ्छो.

10. B °करेदि.

11. F पछ्छाय°.

13. A तत्तहोदिए.

14. F नैतावता [भवतः ?] प्रसन्नतर्कता [मन्ये.

राजा । वयस्य इतस्तावदावां लतान्तरितौ भवावः ।

विदूषकः । [1]इरावदीं विअ दूरे समत्थेमि ।

राजा । न हि कमलिनीं दृष्ट्वा ग्राहमवेक्षते मतंगजः । विलोकयन्स्थितः ।

मालविका । [2]हिअअ णिप्फलादो मणोरहादो विरम । किं मं आआसअसि ।

विदूषकः । राजानमवेक्षते ।

राजा । प्रिये पश्य वामतां स्नेहस्य ।

औत्सुक्यहेतुं विवृणोषि न त्वं
तत्त्वावबोधैकरसो न तर्कः ।
तथापि रम्भोरु करोमि लक्ष्यम्
आत्मानमेषां परिदेवितानाम् ॥ १० ॥

विदूषकः । [3]संपदं भअदो णिस्संसओ भविस्सदि । एसा अप्पिअमअणसंदेसा विवित्ते णं बउलावलिआ उवट्ठिदा ।

राजा । अपि स्मरेदस्मदभ्यर्थनाम् ।

---

१. इरावतीमिव दूरे समर्थयामि ।

२. हृदय निष्फलान्मनोरथाद्विरम । किं मामायासयसि ।

३. सांप्रतं भवतो निःसंशयो भविष्यति । एषार्पितमदनसंदेशा विविक्ते ननु बकुलावलिकोपस्थिता ।

---

2. B समथ्येम्हि.

5. F णिरवलम्बादो for "णिप्फलादो."—A C अआसअसि.

8. A B C D E read आत्मगतम् before "प्रिये पश्य" &c.

13. E F भवदो.—E णिःसंसयो; F णिःसंसअं.—A C add त्ति after "भविस्सदि." [उपट्ठिआ.

14. F एआ (=एका) for "णं."—E

16. A C अयि for "अपि."

विदूषकः । [1]किं दाणिं एसा दासीए सुदा दाव तुह गुरुअं संदेसं विसुमरेदि । अहंवि दाणिं एदं ण विसुमरेमि ।

। प्रविश्य चरणालंकारहस्ता बकुलावलिका ।

बकुलावलिका । [2]अवि सुहं सहीए ।

मालविका । [3]अम्हो बउलावलिआ उवट्ठिआ । सहि साागदं दे । उवविस ।

बकुलावलिका । [4]हला तुमं दाणिं दोहलकरणजोग्गदाए णिउत्ता । ता एक्कं दे चलणं उवणेहि । जाव णं सालत्तअं सणेउरं करेमि ।

मालविका । आत्मगतम् । [5]हिअअ अलं सुहिददाए अअं विहवो उवट्ठिदोत्ति । कहं दाणिं अत्ताणं मोएअं । अह वा एदं एव्व मह मिच्चुमण्डणं भविस्सदि ।

---

१ किमिदानीमेषा दास्याः सुता तावत्तव गुरुं संदेशं विस्मरति । अहमपीदानीमेतं न विस्मरामि ।

२. अपि सुखं सख्याः ।

३. अहो वकुलावलिकोपस्थिता । सखि स्वागतं ते । उपविश ।

४. हला त्वमिदानीं दोहदकरणयोग्यतया नियुक्ता । तदेकं ते चरणमुपनय । तावदेतं सालक्तकं सनूपुरं करोमि ।

५. हृदय अलं सुखिततयायं विभव उपस्थित इति । कथमिदानीमात्मानं मोचयेयम् । अथ वैतदेव मम मृत्युमण्डनं भविष्यति ।

---

1. A C दाणीं.—F om. "तुह."
2. F om. "एदं."
4. A C D सहिए.
5. A C E उवट्ठिआ; B उवट्ठिदा.—B स्सागदं.
6. A C D E उपविस.
7. B दाणीं.—F दोहलकरणे जोग्गदाए.
8. F सालत्तअणेउरं.

बकुलावलिका । [१]किं विआरेसि । उस्सुआ क्खु इमस्स तवणीआसोअस्स कुसुमसमुग्गमे देवी ।

राजा । कथमशोकदोहदनिमित्तोयमारम्भः ।

विदूषकः । [२]किं खु ण जाणासि अकालणादो देवी इमं अन्तेउरणेवथ्थेण ण संजोअइस्सदित्ति ।

मालविका । पादमुपहरति । [३]हला मरिसेहि दाणिं ।

बकुलावलिका । [४]अयि सरीरंसि मे । नाट्येन चरणसंस्कारमारभते ।

राजा ।

चरणान्तनिवेशितां प्रियायाः
सरसां पश्य वयस्य रागरेखाम् ।
प्रथमामिव पल्लवप्रसूतिं
हरदग्धस्य मनोभवद्रुमस्य ॥ ११ ॥

विदूषकः । [५]चलणाणुरूवो क्खु तत्तहोदीए अहिआरो उवक्खित्तो ।

राजा । सम्यगभिहितं भवता ।

---

१. किं विचारयसि । उत्सुका खल्वस्य तपनीयाशोकस्य कुसुमसमुद्गमे देवी ।

२. किं खलु न जानास्यकारणाद्देवीमामन्तःपुरनेपथ्येन न संयोजयिष्यतीति ।

३. हला मर्षयेदानीम् ।

४. अयि शरीरमसि मे ।

५. चरणानुरूपः खलु तत्रभवत्या अधिकार उपक्षिप्तः ।

---

1. D E विचिआरेसि.—D F उस्सिआ.
2. A C कुसुमग्गमे.
4. A B C D E insert णु after "किं" and before "क्खु."
5. B D E संजोभइस्सिदित्ति.
6. A B C D E दाणीं.
7. Our MSS चरणमलंकरोति. We according to G.
13. A चलणाणुरूपो.—A C अभिहारो.

नवकिसलयरागेणाग्रपादेन बाला
स्फुरितनखरुचा द्वौ हन्तुमर्हत्यनेन।
अकुसुमितमशोकं दोहलापेक्षया वा
प्रणिहितशिरसं वा कान्तमार्द्रापराधम् ॥ १२ ॥

विदूषकः। [1]पारइस्सासि अत्तहोदीए अवरध्धुं।

राजा। परिगृहीतं वचः सिद्धिदर्शिनो ब्राह्मणस्य।

। ततः प्रविशत्युन्मत्तवेषेरावती चेटी च।

इरावती। [2]हञ्जे णिउणिए सुणामि बहुसो मदो किल इत्थिआजणस्स विसेसमण्डणंति। अवि सच्चो लोअवादो।

निपुणिका। [3]पुढमं लोअवादो एव्व। अज्ज सच्चो संवुत्तो।

इरावती। [4]अलं सिणेहभणिदेण। कुदो दाणिं अवगदं डोलाघरअं पुढमं गदो भट्टेत्ति।

नपुणिका। [5]भट्टिणीए अखण्डिदादो पणआदो।

इरावती। [6]अलं सेवाए। मज्झत्थदं गेण्हिअ भणाहि।

---

१. पारयिष्यस्यत्रभवत्या अपराद्धुम्।
२. हञ्जे निपुणिके शृणोमि बहुशो मदः किल स्त्रीजनस्य विशेषमण्डनमिति। अपि सत्यो लोकवादः।
३. प्रथमं लोकवाद एव। अद्य सत्यः संवृत्तः।
४. अलं स्नेहभणितेन। कुत इदानीमवगतं दोलागृहं प्रथमं गतो भर्तेति।
५. भट्टिन्या अखण्डितात्प्रणयात्।
६. अलं सेवया। मध्यस्थतां गृहीत्वा भण।

---

8. A हञ्ज.
9. F अअं for "अवि."
11. D संउत्तो.
12. B दाणीं.— A B C D E वुत्तन्तो आगमिदो for "अवगदं."
14. B पणगादो; E पणअदो.

निपुणिका । [1]वसन्दोवाअणलोलुवेण अज्जगोदमेण कहिदं । तुवरदु भट्टिणी ।

इरावती । अवस्थासदृशं परिक्रम्य । [2]हला मदेण मिलाअमाणं अत्ताणं अज्जउत्तदंसणे हिअअं तुवरेदि । चलणा उण ण मग्गे पसरन्दि ।

निपुणिका । [3]णं पत्तम्ह डोलाघरअं ।

इरावती । [4]णिउणिए ण उण एत्थ अज्जउत्तो दीसइ ।

निपुणिका । [5]ओलोएदु । भट्टिणीए परिहासणिमित्तं कहिंवि गुम्मे गूढेण भट्टिणा होदव्वं । अम्हेवि इमं पिअङ्गुलदा-परिक्खित्तं असोअसिलापट्टअं पविस्सम्ह ।

---

१. वसन्तोपायनलोलुपेनार्यगौतमेन कथितम् । त्वरतां भट्टिनी ।

२. हला मदेन म्लायन्तमात्मानमार्यपुत्रदर्शने हृदयं त्वरते । चरणौ पुनर्न मार्गे प्रसरतः ।

३. ननु प्राप्ते स्वो दोलागृहकम् ।

४. निपुणिके न पुनरत्रार्यपुत्रो दृश्यते ।

५. अवलोक्यताम् । भट्टिन्याः परिहासनिमित्तं कुत्रापि गुल्मे गूढेन भर्त्रा भवितव्यम् । आवामपीमं प्रियंगुलतापरिक्षिप्तमशोकशिलापट्टकं प्रविशावः ।

---

1. D E F अ-अ°.
2. A तुवराइदु; C तुवरइदु corrected from an original तुवराइदु.
4. A आत्ताणं.—D E F अ-अ°.
5. A E have each their original ओसज्जन्ति corrected into ओसप्पन्ति; B C D ओसज्जन्नि (= अवसज्जन्ति).
6. B पतम्ह.
7. A C एथ्थं.—D E F अ-अ°.—F दिसइ.
8. A C आलोयदु.
9. E गूढे for "गूढेण."
10. A B C °परिक्खित्ते. — B प-विसम्ह.

इरावती । तथा करोति ।

निपुणिका । परिक्रम्य विलोक्य । [1]ओलोअदु भट्टिणी । चुदङ्कुरं विचिण्णन्दीणं अम्हाणं पिपीलिआदंसणं।

इरावती । [2]किं विअ एदं ।

निपुणिका । [3]एसा असोअपाअवच्छाआअं मालविआए बउलावलिआ चलणालंकारं णिव्वट्टेइ ।

इरावती । शङ्कां रूपयित्वा । [4]अभूमि इअं मालविआए । किं तक्केसि ।

निपुणिका । [5]तक्केमि डोलापरिब्भट्टचलणाए देवीए असोअदोहलाहिआरे मालविआ णिउत्तेत्ति । अण्णहा कहं देवी सअं धारिदं एदं णेउरजुअलं परिअणस्स अब्भणुजाणिस्सदि ।

इरावती । [6]महदी क्खु से संभावणा ।

---

१. अवलोकयतु भट्टिनी । चूताङ्कुरं विचिन्वत्योरावयोः पिपीलिकादंशनम् ।

२. किमिवैतत् ।

३. एषाशोकपादपच्छायायां मालविकाया बकुलावलिका चरणालंकारं निर्वर्तयति ।

४. अभूमिरियं मालविकायाः । किं तर्कयसि ।

५ तर्कयामि दोलापरिभ्रष्टचरणया देव्याशोकदोहदाधिकारे मालविका नियुक्तेति । अन्यथा कथं देवी स्वयं धारितमेतन्नूपुरयुगुलं परिजनस्याभ्यनुज्ञास्यति ।

६. महती खल्वस्याः संभावना ।

---

2. B आलोअदु.

3. A C D विचिण्णन्दाणं ; B विचिणन्दोणं; F विउण्णन्तीणं.— A पिपोलआ° ; B पिप्पलिआ° ; C पिपालआ° (पिपीलआ°?); F पिपोलीआ°.

6. A C णिवट्टइ ; D णिवट्टेइ ; E णिवट्टेइ.

8. C तक्कसि.

10. E णिउत्तेति.

11. B D E धारीदं.—A अरोअण्णस्स ; B अरीअणस्स.—B D अब्भणु°.

13. A C मे for "से."

निपुणिका । [1]किं ण अण्णेसीअदि भट्टा ।

इरावती । [2]हञ्जे मे चलणा अग्गदो ण पवट्टन्ति । मणो मह विआरेदि । आसङ्किदस्स दाव अन्तं गमिस्सं ।

मालविका निर्वर्ण्य । आत्मगतम् । ठाणे क्खु कादरं मे हिअअं ।

बकुलावलिका । चरणं दर्शयन्ती । [3]अवि रोआदि दे अअं चलणराअरेहाविण्णासो ।

मालविका । [4]हला अत्तणो चलणंगदंति लज्जेमि पसंसिदुं । कहेहि केण सिप्पसाहणकलाअं अहिविणीदासि ।

बकुलावलिका । [5]एत्थ क्खु भट्टिणो सिस्सम्हि ।

विदूषकः । [6]तुवरेहि दाणिं गुरुदक्खिणाए ।

मालविका । [7]दिट्ठिआ ण गव्विदासि ।

---

१. किं नान्विष्यते भर्ता ।

२. हञ्जे मे चरणावग्रतो न प्रवर्तेते । मनो मम विक्रियते । आशङ्कितस्य तावदन्तं गमिष्यामि । स्थाने खलु कातरं मे हृदयम् ।

३. अपि रोचते तेयं चरणरागरेखाविन्यासः ।

४. हला आत्मनश्चरणगतमिति लज्जे प्रशंसितुम् । कथय केन शिल्पसाधनकलायामभिविनीतासि ।

५. अत्र खलु भर्तुः शिष्यास्मि ।

६. त्वरस्वेदानीं गुरुदक्षिणायै ।

७. दिष्ट्या न गर्वितासि ।

---

1. B अण्णेसिअदि.
3. A C D E F मम for "मह."
5. A अपि for "अवि."—C अअं दे instead of "दे अअं."—A adds another दे after "अअं."
6. A C °रेहविणासो.
7. A चलणगदं.
8. A B C D E °कला.
9. B एत्थं—A C om. "क्खु."
10. F inserts दाव before "दाणिं."
11. A C D गव्विदासी ; B गव्विदासो.

बकुलावलिका । [1]उवदेसाणुरूवे चलणे लम्भिअ दाणिं गव्विदा भविस्सं । रागं विलोक्य । आत्मगतम् । सिध्धं मे दोच्चं । प्रकाशम् । सहि एकस्स दे चलणस्स अवसिदो राअणिक्खेवो । केवलं मुहमारुदो लम्भइदव्वो । अह वा पवादो एव्व अअं पएसो ।

राजा । सखे पश्य पश्य ।

आर्द्रालक्तकमस्याश्चरणं मुखमारुतेन वीजयितुम् ।
प्रतिपन्नः प्रथमतरः संप्रति सेवावकाशो मे ॥ १३ ॥

विदूषकः । [2]कुदो दे अणुसओ । चिरं भवदा एदं अणुहोदव्वं अचिरेण ।

बकुलावलिका । [3]अरुणसदपत्तं विअ सोहदि दे चलणो । सव्वहा भट्टिणो अङ्कपरिवट्टिणी होहि ।

इरावती । निपुणिकामुखमवेक्षते ।

राजा । ममेयमाशीः ।

मालविका । [4]हला अवचणीअं मन्तेसि ।

बकुलावलिका । [5]मन्तिदव्वं एव्व मए मन्तिदं ।

---

१. उपदेशानुरूपौ चरणौ लब्ध्वेदानीं गर्विता भविष्यामि । सिद्धं मे दौत्यम् । सखि एकस्य ते चरणस्यावसितो रागनिक्षेपः । केवलं मुखमारुतो लम्भयितव्यः । अथ वा प्रवात एवायं प्रदेशः ।

२. कुतस्तेनुशयः । चिरं भवतैतदनुभवितव्यमचिरेण ।

३. अरुणशतपत्त्रमिव शोभते ते चरणः । सर्वथा भर्तुरङ्कपरिवर्तिनी भव ।

४. हला अवचनीयं मन्त्रयसि ।

५. मन्त्रयितव्यमेव मया मन्त्रितम् ।

---

3. A B C एक्कस्स.

5. B पवेसो (पदेसो ?).

7. F वीजयतः.

10. Our MSS. कमेण (=क्रमेण) for "अचिरेण." We according to G.

मालविका । [1]पिआ क्खु अहं तुह ।

बकुलावलिका । [2]ण केवलं मह ।

मालविका । [3]कस्स वा अण्णस्स ।

बकुलावलिका । [4]गुणेसु अहिणिवेसिणो भट्टिणोवि ।

मालविका । [5]अलीअं मन्तेसि । एदं एव्व मइ णत्थि ।

बकुलावलिका । [6]सच्चं तुइ णत्थि । भट्टिणो किसेसु ईसिपरिपण्डरेसु अङ्गेसु दीसइ ।

निपुणिका । [7]पुढमं भणिदं विअ हदासाए उत्तरं ।

बकुलावलिका । [8]अणुराओ अणुराएण पडिक्खिदव्वोत्ति सुजणचरिदं पमाणीकरेहि ।

---

१. प्रिया खल्वहं तव ।

२. न केवलं मम ।

३. कस्य वान्यस्य ।

४. गुणेष्वभिनिवेशिनो भर्तुरपि ।

५. अलीकं मन्त्रयसि । एतदेव मयि नास्ति ।

६. सत्यं त्वयि नास्ति । भर्तुः कृशेष्वीषत्परिपाण्डुरेष्वङ्गेषु दृश्यते ।

७. प्रथमं भणितमिव हताशाया उत्तरम् ।

८. अनुरागोनुरागेण परीक्षितव्य इति सुजनचरितं प्रमाणीकुरु ।

---

1. A तुव for "तुह."
2. A C D E मम for "मह."
5. E has एदे एवं (एव्व ?) मइ ण होन्दि for "एदं &c.; A B C also एदे for "एदं."—A C मई.
6. E ण होन्दि for "णत्थि."—B इसि°.—E दीसन्दि.
8. B C D put the speech "पुढमं" &c. in the mouth of Nipuṇikâ; A and E also originally assigned it to the same character, but they afterwards correct themselves so as to give it to Mâlavikâ.— F पुडमभणिदं विअ.
9. F पडिच्छिदव्वो (= परिच्छेत्तव्यः)
10. A पमाणि°.

मालविका । किं अप्पणो छन्देण मन्तेसि ।

बकुलावलिका । णं हि । भट्टिणो एदाइं पणअमआइं अक्खराइं बिम्बन्तरिदाइं ।

मालविका । हला देविं विचिन्तिअ ण मे हिअअस्स पहविस्सं ।

बकुलावलिका । मुध्धे भमरसंबध्धोत्ति वसन्दावदारसव्वस्सो ण चूदपल्लवो किं ओदंसइदव्वो ।

मालविका । तुमं दाव दुज्जादे मे अच्चन्तसाहाइणी होहि ।

बकुलावलिका । [६]विमद्दसुरही बउलावलिआ क्खु अहं ।

राजा । साधु बकुलावलिके साधु ।

भावज्ञानानन्तरं प्रस्तुतेन
प्रत्याख्याने दत्तयुक्तोत्तरेण ।
वाक्येनेयं स्थापिता स्वे निदेशे
स्थाने प्राणाः कामिनां दूत्यधीनाः ॥ १४ ॥

---

१. किमात्मनश्छन्देन मन्त्रयसि ।

२. न हि । भर्तुरेतानि प्रणयमयान्यक्षराणि बिम्बान्तरितानि ।

३. हला देवीं विचिन्त्य न मे हृदयस्य प्रभविष्यामि ।

४. मुग्धे भ्रमरसंबद्ध इति वसन्तावतारसर्वस्वो न चूतपल्लवः किमवतंसयितव्यः ।

५. त्वं तावद्दुर्जाते मेऽत्यन्तसाहाय्यकारिणी भव ।

६. विमर्दसुरभिर्बकुलावलिका खल्वहम् ।

---

1. D छन्देन.
2. A B C D एदाईं.
4. B विचिन्तीअ; C विचिन्दिअ.
5. Our MSS. भमरसंपादोत्ति. We with G.—A C D E °सव्वस्सं.
7. A B C D °साहाहिणी.
8. A B C D E °सुरहि.

इरावती। हञ्जे पेक्ख। कारिदं एव्व बउलावलिआए मालविआए पदं।

निपुणिका। [2]भट्टिणी णिव्विआरस्सवि उस्सुअत्तणज्जणओ उवदेसो।

इरावती। [3]ठाणे क्खु सङ्किदं मे हिअअं। गहीदत्था अणन्तरं चिन्तइस्सं।

बकुलावलिका। [4]एसो दे दुदीओवि समत्तपडिकम्मो चलणो। जाव दुवेवि सणेउरा करेमि। नाट्येन नूपुरयुगुलमामुच्य। हला उट्ठेहि। अणुचिट्ठ देवीए दाणिं असोअविआसइत्तअं णिओअं।

। उभे उत्तिष्ठतः।

इरावती। [5]सुदो देवीए णिओओत्ति। होदु दाणिं।

बकुलावलिका। एसो उवारूढराओ उवभोअक्खमो दे पुरदो वट्टइ।

---

१. हञ्जे प्रेक्षस्व। कारितमेव बकुलावलिकया मालविकया पदम्।

२. भट्टिनि निर्विकारस्याप्यौत्सुक्यजनक उपदेशः।

३. स्थाने खलु शङ्कितं मे हृदयम्। गृहीतार्थानन्तरं चिन्तयिष्यामि।

४. एष ते द्वितीयोपि समाप्तप्रतिकर्मा चरणः। तावद्द्वावपि सनूपुरौ करोमि। हला उत्तिष्ठ। अनुतिष्ठ देव्या इदानीमशोकविकाशयितृकं नियोगम्।

५. श्रुतो देव्या नियोग इति। भवत्विदानीम्।

६. एष उपारूढराग उपभोगक्षमस्ते पुरतो वर्तते।

---

1. A B C D देक्ख for "पेक्ख."

3. F भट्टिणि.—A निव्वि°.—A B C D E omit °त्तण°.

5. B ट्ठाणे.—A C E गहिद°.

7. D E दुदीयो°.

8. E °युगल°.

9. A C दाणीं; F omits it altogether.

11. B तिष्ठतः.

मालविका । सहर्षम् । [1]किं भट्टा ।

बकुलावलिका । सस्मितम् । [2]ण दाव भट्टा । एसो असोअसाहावलम्बी पल्लवगुच्छो । ओदंसेहि णं ।

विदूषकः । [3]अवि सुदं भवदा ।

राजा । पर्याप्तमेतावता कामिनाम् ।

अनादरोत्कण्ठितयोः प्रसिध्यता
समागमेनापि रतिर्न मां प्रति ।
परस्परप्राप्तिनिराशयोर्वरं
शरीरनाशोऽपि समानुरागयोः ॥ १५ ॥

मालविका । रचितपल्लवावतंसा सलीलमशोकताडनाय पादं प्रहिणोति ।

राजा । वयस्य पश्य ।

आदाय कर्णकिसलयमस्मादियमत्र चरणमर्पयति ।
उभयोः सदृशविनिमयादात्मानं वञ्चितं मन्ये ॥ १६ ॥

बकुलावलिका । [4]हला णत्थि दे दोसो अगुणो अअं असोओ जइ कुसुमसमुब्भेदमन्थरो भवे । जो ईरिसं चलणसक्कारं लहेइ ।

---

१. किं भर्ता ।

२. न तावद्भर्ता । एषोऽशोकशाखावलम्बी पल्लवगुच्छः । अवतंसयैनम् ।

३. अपि श्रुतं भवता ।

४. हला नास्ति ते दोषः अगुणोऽयमशोको यदि कुसुमसमुद्भेदमन्थरो भवेत् । ईदृशं चरणसत्कारं लभते ।

---

4. E omits "अवि."

9. A F समानरागयोः

10. Our MSS. भशोकाय. We according to G.

11. F omits पश्य.

15. A C जई.—F °मन्धरो.

16. A B C D E लहेयि.

राजा ।

अनेन तनुमध्यया मुखरनूपुराराविणा
नवाम्बुरुहकोमलेन चरणेन संभावितः ।
अशोक यदि सद्य एव कुसुमैर्न संपत्स्यसे
वृथा वहसि दोहलं ललितकामिसाधारणम् ॥ १६ ॥

सखे वचनावसरपूर्वकं प्रवेष्टुमिच्छामि ।

विदूषकः । [1]एहि णं परिहासइस्सं ।

। उभौ प्रवेशं कुरुतः ।

निपुणिका । [2]भट्टिणी भट्टा एत्थ पविस्सदि ।

इरावती । [3]एदं मम पुढमं चिन्तिदं हिअएण ।

विदूषकः । उपसृत्य । [4]होदि ण जुत्तं णाम अत्तहोदो पिअवअस्सो असोओ वामपादेण ताडेदुं ।

उभे ससंभ्रमम् । [5]अम्हो भट्टा ।

विदूषकः । [6]बउलावलिए तुए गहीदथ्थाए अत्तहोदी ईरिसं अविणअं करन्ती किस ण वारिदा ।

मालविका । भयं निरूपयति ।

---

१. एह्येनां परिहासयिष्यामि ।

२. भट्टिनि भर्तात्र प्रविशति ।

३. इदं मम प्रथमं चिन्तितं हृदयेन ।

४. भवति न युक्तं नामात्रभवतः प्रियवयस्योऽशोको वामपादेन ताडयितुम् ।

५. अहो भर्ता ।

६. बकुलावलिके त्वया गृहीतार्थयात्रभवतीदृशमविनयं कुर्वन्ती कथं न वारिता ।

---

7. B परिहासईस्सं.

9. F भट्टिणि.—F अथ्थ for "एथ्थ."

10. Our MSS. इदं मालविआए for "एदं मम." We according to G.—F पुडमं.

11. A B C D E insert एदं before "ण जुत्तं."

14. A B C D E गहिद°.—A C ईरिसं.

15. F किं सा for "किस."

निपुणिका । [1]भट्टिणी देक्खव किं पवुत्तं अज्जगोदमेण ।

इरावती । [2]कहं स बम्हबन्धू अण्णहा जीविस्सादि ।

बकुलावलिका । [3]अज्ज देवीए एसा णिओअं अणुचिट्ठइ । एदस्सिं अदिक्कमे परवदी इअं । पसीददु भट्टा । आत्मना समभेना प्रणिपातयति ।

राजा । यद्येवमनपराधः । भद्रे उत्तिष्ठ । हस्तेन गृहीत्वोत्थापयति ।

विदूषकः । [4]जुज्जइ । देवी एत्थ माणइदव्वा ।

राजा ।

किसलयमृदोर्विलासिनि कठिने निहितस्य पादपस्कन्धे ।
चरणस्य न ते बाधा संप्रति वामस्य वामोरु ॥ १७ ॥

मालविका । लज्जते ।

इरावती । सासूयम् । [5]अम्हो णवणीदकप्पहिअओ अज्जउत्तो ।

---

१. भट्टिनि पश्य किं प्रवृत्तमार्यगौतमेन ।

२. कथं स ब्रह्मबन्धुरन्यथा जीविष्यति ।

३. आर्य देव्या एषा नियोगमनुतिष्ठति । एतस्मिन्नतिक्रमे परवतीयम् । प्रसीदतु भर्ता ।

४. युज्यते । देव्यत्र मानयितव्या ।

५. अहो नवनीतकल्पहृदय आर्यपुत्रः ।

---

1. E F भट्टिणि.—F दक्खव.—D E अ॰अ°.—B पउत्तं.—F पउंत्तं, translated by प्रयुक्तम्.
2. B जोविसदि ; D E जविस्सिदि.
3. D E F अ॰अ.—B अणुचिट्ठई.

7. F अत्थ for "एत्थ."
10. F वामोरु वामस्य.
11. C लज्जति.
12. Our MSS. omit सासूयम्. We according to G. — F omits

मालविका । [1]बउलावलिए एहि । अणुट्ठिदं अत्तणो णिओअं देवीए णिवेदेम्ह ।

बकुलावलिका । [2]तेण विण्णवेहि भट्टारं विसज्जेहिन्ति ।

राजा । भद्रे यास्यसि । मम तावदुत्पन्नावसरमर्थित्वं श्रूयताम् ।

बकुलावलिका । [3]अवहिदा सुणाहि । आणवेदु भट्टा ।

राजा ।

धृतिपुष्पमयमपि जनो बध्नाति न तादृशं चिरात्प्रभृति ।
स्पर्शामृतेन पूरय दोहलमस्याप्यनन्यरुचेः ॥ १८ ॥

इरावती । सहसोपसृत्य । [4]पुरेहि पुरेहि । णं असोओ कुसुमं दंसेदि । अअं उण ण केवलं पुप्फइ फलइ अ ।

। सर्वे इरावतीं दृष्ट्वा संभ्रान्ताः ।

राजा । जनान्तिकम् । वयस्य का प्रतिपत्तिरत्र ।

विदूषकः । [5]किं अण्णं । जङ्घाबलं एव्व ।

---

१. बकुलावलिके एहि । अनुष्ठितमात्मनो नियोगं देव्यै निवेदयावः ।
२. तेन विज्ञापय भर्तारं विसृजेति ।
३. अवहिता शृणु । आज्ञापयतु भर्ता ।
४. पूरय पूरय । नन्वशोकः कुसुमं दर्शयति । अयं पुनर्न केवलं पुष्प्यति फलति च ।
५. किमन्यत् । जङ्घाबलमेव ।

---

2. B C D णिवेदेम.
3. A विण्णवेहि.—E विसज्जहिन्ति.
4. B has 'भद्रे यास्यसि मा तावत्.'
9. B ण्णं for "णं."—A B C E do not repeat "पुरेहि;" F पूरेहि पूरेहि.—F translates णं by एनम् in its छाया.
10. F दंसेइ.
12. F omits अत्र.
13. A अणं.—Our MSS. जङ्घावलम्वणं. We according to G.

इरावती । [1]बउलावलिए साहु तुए उपक्कन्तं । मालविए तुमं दाव अज्जउत्तं सफलपत्थणं करेहि ।

उभे । [2]पसीददु भट्टिणी । का अम्हे भट्टिणो प्पणअप्पसङ्गस्स ।

[निष्क्रान्ते ।

इरावती । [3]अहो अविस्ससणीआ पुरुसा । मए क्खु अत्तणो वञ्चणावअणं पमाणीकरिअ वाहजणगीदरत्ताए हरिणीए विअ असङ्किताए एदं ण विण्णादं ।

विदूषकः । जनान्तिकम् [4]पडिओजेहि किंपि । कम्मगहीदेण कुम्भिलएण "संधिच्छेअसिक्खकोम्हि"त्ति एत्थ वत्तव्वं होदि ।

राजा । सुन्दरि मालविकायां न मे कश्चिदर्थः । मया त्वं चिरायसीति कथंचिदात्मा विनोदितः ।

---

१. वकुलावलिके साधु त्वयोपक्रान्तम् । मालविके त्वं तावदार्यपुत्रं सफलप्रार्थनं कुरु ।

२. प्रसीदतु भट्टिनी । के आवां भर्तुः प्रणयप्रसङ्गस्य ।

३. अहो अविश्वसनीयाः पुरुषाः । मया खल्वात्मनो वञ्चनावचनं प्रमाणीकृत्य व्याधजनगीतरक्तया हरिण्येवाशङ्कितयेदं न विज्ञातम् ।

४. प्रतियोजय किमपि । कर्मगृहीतेन कुम्भिलकेन "संधिच्छेदशिक्षकोस्मी"त्यत्र वक्तव्यं भवति ।

---

1. B तए for "तुए."
2. D E F अ-अ°.
3. A D E पणअ°.—F पणअपडिग्गहस्स.
5. E पुरिसा.
6. A E पमाणी°.—B °करीअ.
7. F omits "असङ्किताए."
8. F पडियोजेहि किंवि.—A B C D E °गहिदेण.—F takes कम्म with पडियोजेहि किंवि, and explains its translation कर्म by "मृषोद्यमित्यर्थः". But this is hardly possible. कम्मगहीदेण = by (a thief) caught in the act.
12. B कथं कथंचिन्.

इरावती । [1]विस्ससणीओसि । मए ण विण्णादं एतारिसं विणोदवथ्थु अज्जउत्तेण उवलध्धंति । अण्णहा दुख्खतरं एव्वं ण करेमि ।

विदूषकः । [2]मा दाव अत्तहोदी अत्तहोदो दख्खिण्णस्स उवरोहं भणादु । समापत्तिदिट्ठेण देवीए परिजणेण संकहावि जइ अवराही ठावीअदि एथ्थ तुमं एव्व प्पमाणं ।

इरावती । [3]णं संकहा णाम होदु । केत्तिअं कालं अत्ताणं आआसइस्सं । रुष्टा प्रस्थिता ।

राजा । अनुसरन् । प्रसीदतु भवती ।

इरावती । रशनासंदितचरणा व्रजत्येव ।

राजा । सुन्दरि न शोभते प्रणयिजननिरपेक्षता ।

इरावती । [4]सठ अविस्ससणीअहिअओसि ।

---

१. विश्वसनीयोसि । मया न विज्ञातमेतादृशं विनोदवस्त्वार्यपुत्रेणोपलब्धमिति । अन्यथा दुःखतरमेवं न करोमि ।

२. मा तावदत्रभवत्यत्रभवतो दाक्षिण्यस्योपरोधं भणतु । समापत्तिदृष्टेन देव्याः परिजनेन संकथापि यद्यपराधी स्थाप्यतेत्र त्वमेव प्रमाणम् ।

३. ननु संकथा नाम भवतु । कियन्तं कालमात्मानमायासयिष्यामि ।

४. शठ अविश्वसनीयहृदयोसि ।

---

1. A विणादं.
2. D E F अ–अ°.
3. A B C D E एव्व for "एव्वं".
4. F अवराहं (= अपराधं) for "उवरोहं."
5. A B C जई.
6. F अवराहे.—D E पमाणं.
7. A संकह णाम.
10. F °संदानितचरणा.
12. A सट.—A C अविस्ससणीडज°; B has विस्ससणीडज° corrected from अविस्ससणीडज°.

राजा ।

शठ इति मयि तावदस्तु ते
परिचयवत्यवधीरणा प्रिये ।
चरणपतितया न चण्डतां
विसृजसि मेखलयापि याचिता ॥ १९ ॥

इरावती । [१]इअंपि हदासा तुमं एव्व अणुसरदि । रशनामादाय राजानं ताडयितुमिच्छति ।

राजा । एषा

बाष्पासारा हेमकाञ्चीगुणेन
श्रोणीबिम्बादव्यपेक्षाच्च्युतेन ।
चण्डी चण्डं हन्तुमभ्युद्यता मां
विद्युद्दाम्ना मेघराजीव विन्ध्यम् ॥ २० ॥

इरावती । [२]किं मं भूओवि अवरध्धं करेसि । इति सरशनहस्तमालम्बते ।

राजा ।

अपराधिनि मयि दण्डं संहरसि किमुद्यतं कुटिलकेशि ।
वर्धयसि विलसितं त्वं दासजनायात्र कुप्यसि च ॥२१॥

आत्मगतम् । नूनमिदानीमनुज्ञातम् । पादयोः पतति ।

---

१. इयमपि हताशा त्वामेवानुसरति ।
२. किं मां भूयोऽप्यपराद्धां करोषि ।

---

6. F इअवि.
10. A B C D E अभ्युपेक्षा°.
11. E अभ्युद्यना.
13. A मां for "मं."— A B C D E भूओवि.—F अवरध्धं, translated in its छाया by अवरोधं.

इरावती । [1]ण हु इमे मालविआए चलणा जे दे परिसदोहलं पूरइस्सन्दि ।

[ससखी निष्क्रान्ता ।

विदूषकः । [2]भो उट्ठेहि उट्ठेहि । किदप्पसादोसि ।

राजा । उत्थायेरावतीमपश्यन् । कथं गतैव प्रिया ।

विदूषकः । [3]दिट्ठिआ इमस्स अविणअस्स अप्पसादिदा गदा । ता वअं सिग्घं अवक्कमाम जाव अङ्गारओ रासिं विअ सा अणुवक्कं ण करेइ ।

राजा । अहो मनसिजवैषम्यम् ।

मन्ये प्रियाहृतमनास्तस्याः प्रणिपातलङ्घनं सेवाम् ।
एवं हि प्रणयवती सा शक्यमुपेक्षितुं कुपिता ॥२२॥

॥ इति परिक्रम्य निष्क्रान्ताः सर्वे ॥

॥ इति तृतीयोऽङ्कः ॥

---

१. न खल्विमौ मालविकायाश्चरणौ यौ ते स्पर्शदोहदं पूरयिष्यतः ।
२. भो उत्तिष्ठोत्तिष्ठ । कृतप्रसादोसि ।
३. दिष्ट्यैतस्याविनयस्याप्रसादिता गता । तदावां शीघ्रमपक्रमावो यावदङ्गारको राशिमिव सानुवक्रं न करोति ।

---

1. F हरिसदोहलं.
2. A C E पूरइस्सदि.
4. F omits "भो."
6. D E अविणयस्स.—A B C D अप्पसादिदा.
7. F दाव सिग्घं for "ता वअं सिग्घं."

। ततः प्रविशति पर्युत्सुको राजा प्रतीहारी च ।

राजा । आत्मगतम् ।

तामाश्रित्य श्रुतिपथगतामास्थया लब्धमूलः
संप्राप्तायां नयनविषयं रूढरागप्रवालः ।
हस्तस्पर्शैर्मुकुलित इव व्यक्तरोमोद्गतत्वात्
कुर्यात्क्लान्तं मनसिजतरुर्मां रसज्ञं फलस्य ॥१॥

प्रकाशम् । सखे गौतम ।

प्रतीहारी । [१]जेदु भट्टा । असंणिहिदो गोदमो ।

राजा । आत्मगतम् । अये मालविकावृत्तान्तज्ञानाय प्रेषितः ।

विदूषकः । प्रविश्य । [२]जेदु भवं ।

राजा । जयसेने जानीहि क्व देवी धारिणी कथं वा सरुजचरणत्वाद्विनोद्यत इति ।

प्रतीहारी । [३]जं देवो आणवेदि ।

[इति निष्क्रान्ता ।

राजा । सखे को वृत्तान्तस्ते सख्यास्तत्रभवत्याः ।

विदूषकः । [४]जो बिडालगहीदाए परहुदिआए ।

राजा । सविषादम् । कथमिव ।

---

१. जयतु भर्ता । असंनिहितो गौतमः ।

२. जयतु भवान् ।

३. यद्देव आज्ञापयति ।

४. यो विडालगृहीतायाः परभृतिकायाः ।

---

5. B D F °रोमोद्गमत्वात्.

8. B भट्टो.

16. A B C D E °गहिदाए.

विदूषकः । [1]सा क्खु तवस्सिणी ताए पिङ्गलच्छीए सारभण्ड-भूमिघरए मिच्चुमुहे विअ णिक्खित्ता ।

राजा । ननु मत्संपर्कमुपलभ्य ।

विदूषकः । [2]अह इं ।

राजा । गौतम क एवं विमुखोऽस्माकं येन चण्डी कृता देवी ।

विदूषकः । [3]सुणादु भवं । परिव्वाजिआ मे कहेइ । हिओ किल तत्तहोदी इरावदी रुजाविहत्थचलणं देविं सुहं पुच्छिदुं आअदा । तदो सा देवीए पुच्छिदा । किं ण लक्खिदो जणो वल्लहोत्ति । ताए उत्तं । मन्दो वो उवआरो । जं दे परिअणस्स वल्लहत्तणं तं ण जाणासित्ति ।

राजा । भो निर्भेदादृतेऽपि मालविकायामयमुपन्यासः शङ्कयति ।

विदूषकः । [4]तदो ताए अणुणिब्बन्धिज्जमाणाए भवदो अविणअं अन्तरेण परिगहीदत्था किदा देवी ।

---

१. सा खलु तपस्विनी तया पिङ्गलाक्ष्या सारभाण्डभूमिगृहे मृत्युमुख इव निक्षिप्ता ।

२. अथ किम् ।

३. शृणोतु भवान् । परिव्राजिका मे कथयति । ह्यः किल तत्रभवतीरावती रुजाविहस्तचरणां देवीं सुखं प्रष्टुमागता । ततः सा देव्या पृष्टा । किं न लक्षितो जनो वल्लभ इति । तयोक्तम् । मन्दो व उपचारः । यत्ते परिजनस्य वल्लभत्वं तन्न जानासीति ।

४. ततस्तयानुनिर्बध्यमानया भवतोऽविनयमन्तरेण परिगृहीतार्था कृता देवी ।

---

3. F उपलभ्यते.
4. A C ई for "इं."
6. F पडिव्वाजिआ.
7. A ततहोदो·—A देवीसुहं; C देविं- [सुहं·
9. F omits "वो."
10. A णं for "ण."
13. A B C D E अणुवन्धिज्ज°.
14. A B C D E परिगहिद°.

राजा | अहो दीर्घरोषता तत्रभवत्याः | अतः परं कथय |

विदूषकः | [1]अदो वरं किं | मालविआ बउलावलिआ अ णिअलवदीओ अदिट्ठसूज्जपादं पादालवासं णाअकण्णआ विअ अणुहोन्ति |

राजा | कष्टम् |

मधुररवा परभृतिका भ्रमरी च विबुद्धचूतसङ्गिन्यौ |
कोटरमकालवृष्ट्या प्रबलपुरोवातया गमिते || २ ||

वयस्य अप्यत्रोपक्रमस्य कस्याचिद्गतिः स्यात् |

विदूषकः | [2]कहं भविस्सदि | जं सारभण्डवाउदा माहविआ देवीए संदिट्ठा मह अङ्गुलीअमुद्दं अदेक्खिअ ण मोत्तव्वा तुए हदासा मालविएत्ति |

राजा | निःश्वस्य | सखे किमत्र प्रतिकर्तव्यम् |

विदूषकः | विचिन्त्य | [3]अत्थि अथ्थ उवाओ |

राजा | क इव |

---

१. अतः परं किम् | मालविका बकुलावलिका च निगडवत्यावदृष्टसूर्यपादं पातालवासं नागकन्यके इवानुभवतः |

२. कथं भविष्यति | यत्सारभाण्डव्यापृता माधविका देव्या संदिष्टा ममाङ्गुलीयमुद्रामदृष्ट्वा न मोक्तव्या त्वया हताशा मालविकेति |

३. अस्त्यत्रोपायः |

---

1. B अत्रभवत्यां for "तत्रभवत्याः."
3. A B C D E °सुज्ज.°
6. F मधुरस्वरापरभृतिः as the first pâda.
8. F वयस्य अप्यस्य कस्यचिदुपक्रमस्य &c.
10. A C D E F मम for "मह."—F अदक्खिअ.
13. E एथ्थ. But it seems to have originally read अथ्थ.—F अत्थि एव उवाओ (= अस्त्येवोपायः).

विदूषकः । सदृष्टिक्षेपम् । [1]कोवि अदिट्ठो सुणादि । ता कण्णे दे कहेमि । उपश्लिष्य कर्णे । एव्वं विअ ।

राजा । सष्ठु चिन्तितं प्रयुज्यतां सिद्धये ।

प्रतीहारी । प्रविश्य । [2]देव पवादसअणे देवी णिसण्णा रत्तचन्दणधारिणा परिअणहथ्थगहीदेण चलणेण भअवदीए परिव्वाजिआए कहाहिं विणोदिअमाणा चिठ्ठइ ।

राजा । अस्मत्प्रवेशयोग्योयमवसरः ।

विदूषकः । [3]ता गछ्छदु भवं । अहंवि देविं देख्खिदुं अरित्तपाणि भविस्सं ।

राजा । जयसेनायास्तावत्संवेद्य गच्छ ।

विदूषकः । कर्णे । [4]होदि एव्वं विअ ।

[इति निष्क्रान्तः ।

राजा । जयसेने प्रवातशयनमार्गमादेशय ।

प्रतीहारी । [5]इदो इदो ।

। ततः प्रविष्टा शयनस्था देवी परिव्राजिका विभवतश्च परिवारः ।

---

१. कोप्यदृष्टः शृणोति । तत्कर्णे ते कथयामि । एवमिव ।

२. देव प्रवातशयने देवी निषण्णा रक्तचन्दनधारिणा परिजनहस्तगृहीतेन चरणेन भगवत्या परिव्राजिकया कथाभिर्विनोद्यमाना तिष्ठति ।

३. तद्गच्छतु भवान् । अहमपि देवीं प्रेक्षितुमरिक्तपाणिर्भवामि ।

४. भवति एवमिव ।

५. इत इतः ।

---

4. B पादसअणे.—A C णिस्सण्णा.

5. A B C D E °गहिदेण.

8. B गछ्छदु.—F देवीं दख्खिदुं.—D F °पाणो.

10. F संपाद्य for "संवेद्य."

11. B omits "होदि".—A C E F एवं.

14. D does not repeat "इदो."

15. B परीवारः.

देवी । [1]भअवदि अदिरमणिज्जं कहावत्थु । तदो तदो ।

परिव्राजिका । सदृष्टिक्षेपम् । अतःपरं पुनः कथयिष्यामि । अत्रभवानीश्वरः संप्राप्तः ।

देवी । [2]अम्हो अज्जउत्तो । इत्युत्थातुमिच्छति ।

राजा । अलमलमुपचारयन्त्रणया ।

अनुचितनूपुरविरहं नार्हसि तपनीयपीठकालम्बि ।
चरणं रुजापरीतं कलभाषिणि मां च पीडयितुम् ॥३॥

परिव्राजिका । विजयतां देवः ।

देवी । [3]जेदु अज्जउत्तो ।

राजा । परिव्राजिकां प्रणम्योपविश्य । देवि अपि सह्या वेदना ।

देवी । [4]अत्थि मे दाणिं विसेसो ।

। ततः प्रविशति यज्ञोपवीतबद्धाङ्गुष्ठः
संभ्रान्तो विदूषकः ।

विदूषकः । [5]अवि हा अवि हा । सप्पेण संदट्ठोम्हि ।

। सर्वे विषण्णाः ।

राजा । कष्टम् । क्व भवान्परिभ्रान्तः ।

---

१. भगवति अतिरमणीयं कथावस्तु । ततस्ततः ।

२. अहो आर्यपुत्रः ।

३. जयत्वार्यपुत्रः ।

४. अस्ति म इदानीं विशेषः ।

५. अपि हा अपि हा । सर्पेण संदष्टोस्मि ।

---

1. C रमाणज्जं; F रमणीज्जं.
4. D E F अ-अ°.
6. A B C E नार्हति.
9. E अ-अ°.
11. F omits "दाणिं" altogether.
14. E omits the repeated "अवि हा."

विदूषकः । देविं देक्खिस्संति आआरपुप्फग्गहणकालणादो प्पमदवणं गदोम्हि । परित्ताअदु परित्ताअदु ।

देवी । [2]हद्धि हद्धि । अहं एव्व बम्हणस्स जीविदसंसए णिमित्तं जादा ।

विदूषकः । [3]तहिं असोअत्थवअस्स कालणादो मए प्पसारिदे अग्गहत्थे कोडरणिग्गदेण कालेण सप्परूविणा दट्ठो । णं एदाइं दुव्वे दन्तपदाइं । इति दंशं दर्शयति ।

परिव्राजिका । तेन हि दंशच्छेदः पूर्वकर्मेति श्रूयते । स तावदस्य क्रियताम् ।

छेदो दंशस्य दाहो वा क्षतेर्वा रक्तमोक्षणम् ।
एतानि दष्टमात्राणामायुषः प्रतिपत्तयः ॥ ४ ॥

राजा । संप्रति विषवैद्यानां कर्म । जयसेने क्षिप्रमानीयतां ध्रुवसिद्धिः ।

प्रतीहारी । [4]जं देवो आणवेदि ।

[इति निष्क्रान्ता ।

विदूषकः । [5]अहो पावेण मिच्चुणा गहीदोम्हि ।

---

१. देवीं द्रक्ष्यामीत्याचारपुष्पग्रहणकारणात् [i. e. °ग्रहणाय]प्रमदवनं गतोऽस्मि । परित्रायतां परित्रायताम् ।

२. हा धिक् हा धिक् । अहमेव ब्राह्मणस्य जीवितसंशये निमित्तं जाता ।

३. तत्राशोकस्तवकस्य कारणात् [i.e. अशोकस्तबकाय] मया प्रसारितेऽग्रहस्ते कोटरनिर्गतेन कालेन सर्परूपिणा दष्टः । नन्वेते द्वे दन्तपदे ।

४. यद्देव आज्ञापयति ।

५. अहो पापेन मृत्युना गृहीतोऽस्मि ।

---

1. F देवीं दक्खिदुं,त.
2. A C D E पमद°.
3. F जीविदसंसअणिमित्तं.
5. B आसोअत्थवयस्स; D असोअ°.
6. F हत्थे for "अग्गहत्थे".—F सव्वरूविणा.
10. Our MSS., and even G, make the couplet "छेदो" &c. a part of the following speech of the king. We with Tullberg.
14. A C अण्णवेदि.
16. A C मिच्चुणा; F मित्थुणा.—A B C D E गहिदो.

राजा। मा कातरो भूः। अविषः कदाचिद्दंशो भवेत्।

विदूषकः। [1]कहं ण भाइस्सं। सिमिसिमाअन्ति मे अङ्गाइं।

विषवेगं निरूपयति।

देवी। उपसृत्य। [2]ही ही असुहं दंसिदं विआरेण। हला अवलम्बह णं।

परिजनः। ससंभ्रममवलम्बते।

विदूषकः। राजानमवलोक्य। [3]भो भवदो बालत्तणादोवि पिअवअस्सोम्हि। तं विआरिअ मुध्धाए मे जणणीए ओअक्खेमं वहेहि।

राजा। मा भैषीः। अचिरात्त्वां वैद्यश्चिकित्सते। स्थिरो भव।

प्रविश्य प्रतीहारी।

प्रतीहारी। [4]देव धुवसिध्धी विण्णवेदि। इह ज्जेव आणीअदु गोदमोत्ति।

राजा। तेन हि वर्षवरपरिगृहीतमेनं तत्रभवतः सकाशं प्रापय।

प्रतीहारी। [5]तह।

---

१. कथं न भेष्यामि। सिमिसिमायन्ति मेऽङ्गानि।

२. हा हा। असुखं दर्शितं विकारेण। हला अवलम्बध्वमेनम्।

३. भो भवतो बाल्यादपि प्रियवयस्योऽस्मि। तद्विचार्य मुग्धाया मे जनन्या योगक्षेमं वहस्व।

४. देव ध्रुवसिद्धिर्विज्ञापयति। इहैवानीयतां गौतम इति।

५. तथा।

---

1. F अविपोपि.
2. A C भाइस्सं.
3. D रूपयति.
4. Our MSS. अहिअं दंसिदं विअ विआरेण for "असुहं" &c. We according to G.
8. E बुध्धाए.
12. A विणवेदि.—F इह एव्व.—A B C आणीयदु.
14. E वर्षभर°.

विदूषकः । देवीं विलोक्य । [1]भोदी जीवेअं वा ण वा जं मए अत्तभवन्तं सेवमाणेण दे अवरध्धं तं सव्वं अवराहं मरिसेहि ।

देवी । [2]दीहाऊ होहि ।

[निष्क्रान्तो विदूषकः प्रतीहारी च ।

राजा । प्रकृतिभीरुस्तपस्वी । ध्रुवसिद्धेरपि यथाथनाम्नः सिद्धिं न मन्यते ।

प्रतीहारी । प्रविश्य । [3]जेदु भट्टा । धुवसिध्धी विण्णवेदि उदकुम्भविहाणे सप्पमुद्दिअं कंपि अण्णेसीअदुत्ति ।

देवी । [4]इदं सप्पमुद्दिअं अङ्गुलीअअं । पच्छा मह हत्थे देहि णं । इति प्रयच्छति ।

राजा । जयसेने कर्मसिद्धावाशु प्रतिपत्तिमानय ।

प्रतीहारी । [5]जं देवो आणवेदि ।

[इति निष्क्रान्ता ।

परिव्राजिका । यथा मे हृदयमाचष्टे तथा निर्विषो गौतमः ।

राजा । भूयादेवम् ।

---

१. भवति जीवेयं वा न वा यन्मयात्रभवन्तं सेवमानेन तेपराद्धं तं सर्वमपराधं मर्षय ।

२, दीर्घायुर्भव ।

३. जयतु भर्ता । ध्रुवसिद्धिर्विज्ञापयति । उदकुम्भपिधाने सर्पमुद्रिका काम्यन्विष्यतामिति ।

४. इदं सर्पमुद्रीयमङ्गुलीयकम् । पश्चान्मम हस्ते देह्येतत् ।

५. यद्देव आज्ञापयति ।

---

1. A C भोदि.—F reads thus: जं मए अत्तभवन्तं सेवमाणेण दे अवरध्धं तं सव्वं अवराहं मरिसेहि । होदि जीवेअं वा ण वा.

2. A तस्सव्वं ; B त्तं सव्वं.—B मरिस्सेहि.

7. Our MSS. सिद्धिं मन्ये. We with Tullberg.

8. A C ध्रुवसिध्धि ; B ध्धुवसिध्धी ; D ध्रुवसिद्धी.—A विणवेदि.

10. B सप्पमुद्दीअं ; C °मुद्दीअं.—E F मम for "मह."

11. B D E omit "इति."

प्रतीहारी । प्रविश्य । [१]जेदु भट्टा । णिवुत्तविसवेओ गोदमो पकिदिट्ठिदो एव्व संवुत्तो ।

देवी । [२]दिट्ठिआ वअणीआदो मुत्तम्हि ।

प्रतीहारी । [३]एसो अमच्चो वाहदवो विण्णवेदि । राअकज्जं बहु मन्तिदव्वं । ता दंसणेण अणुग्गहीदुं इच्छामित्ति ।

देवी । [४]गच्छदु अज्जउत्तो कज्जसिध्धीए ।

राजा । देवि आतपाक्रान्तोयमुद्देशः । शीतक्रिया चास्य प्रशस्ता । तदन्यत्र नीयतां शयनीयम् ।

देवी । [५]बालिआ अज्जउत्तवअणं अणुचिट्ठह ।

परिजनः । [६]तह ।

[इति निष्क्रान्ता देवी परिव्राजिका परिजनश्च ।

राजा । जयसेने गूढपथेन प्रमदवनं प्रापय ।

प्रतीहारी । [७]इदो इदो देवो ।

राजा । जयसेने ननु समाप्तकृत्यो गौतमः ।

---

१. जयतु भर्ता । निवृत्तविषवेगो गौतमः प्रकृतिस्थ एव संवृत्तः ।

२ दिष्ट्या वचनीयान्मुक्तास्मि ।

३. एषोमात्यो वाहतवो विज्ञापयति । राजकार्यं बहु मन्त्रितव्यम् । तद्दर्शनेनानुग्रहीतुम् [i. e. दर्शनानुग्रहम्] इच्छामीति ।

४. गच्छत्वार्यपुत्रः कार्यसिद्ध्यै ।

५. बालिका आर्यपुत्रवचनमनुतिष्ठत ।

६. तथा ।

७. इत इतो देवः ।

---

1. F निव्वुत्तविस°.
4. B C D वाहदव्वो.—B राजकज्जं.
5. A C अणुगहिदुं.
6. D E F अ-अ.°
9. B बालिअ; F बालिसा (= बालिशाः).—D E F अ-अ°.

प्रतीहारी । [1]अह इं ।

राजा ।

इष्टाधिगमनिमित्तं प्रयोगमेकान्तसाधुमपि मत्वा ।
संदिग्धमेव सिद्धौ कातरमाशङ्कते चेतः ॥ ८ ॥

। प्रविश्य विदूषकः ।

विदूषकः । [2]जेदु जेदु भवं । सिध्धाइं मे मङ्गलकज्जाइं ।

राजा । जयसेने त्वमपि नियोगमशून्यं कुरु ।

प्रतीहारी । [3]जं देवो आणवेदि ।

[इति निष्क्रान्ता ।

राजा । वयस्य क्षुद्रा माधविका । न किंचिद्विचारितमनया ।

विदूषकः । [4]देवीए अङ्गुलीअमुद्दं देक्खिअ कहं विआरीअदि ।

राजा । न खलु मुद्रामधिकृत्य ब्रवीमि । तयोर्बद्धयोः किंनिमित्तोयं मोक्षः । किं देव्याः परिजनमतिक्रम्य भवान्संदिष्ट" इत्येवमनया प्रष्टव्यम् ।

---

१. अथ किम् ।

२. जयतु जयतु भवान् । सिद्धानि मे मङ्गलकार्याणि ।

३. यद्देव आज्ञापयति ।

४. देव्या अङ्गुलीयमुद्रां दृष्ट्वा कथं विचार्यते ।

---

6. A D E F do not repeat "जेदु."—A C D E °कम्माइ.

10. F reads thus : वयस्य क्षुद्रमाधविका न किंचिद्विचारितमनया ।

11. B अङ्गुलि°.—B देक्खीअ ; F दक्खिअ.

विदूषकः । [1]णं पुच्छिदोम्हि । पच्चुप्पण्णबुध्धिणा मए कहिदं । देव्वचिन्तएहिं राआ भणिओ । सोवसग्गं वो णख्खत्तं । ता सव्वबन्धणमोख्खो करिअदुत्ति । तं सुणिअ देवीए धारिणीए इरावदीचित्तं रख्खन्तीए राआ किल मोएदित्ति तुमं एव्व मोएहित्ति अहं संदिट्ठोम्हि । तदो जुज्जइत्ति ताए संपादिओ अथ्थो ।

राजा । विदूषकं परिष्वज्य । सखे प्रियोहं तव ।

न हि बुद्धिगुणेनैव सुहृदामर्थदर्शनम् ।
कार्यसिद्धिपथः सूक्ष्मः स्नेहेनाप्युपलभ्यते ॥ ६ ॥

विदूषकः । [2]तुवरदु भवं । समुद्दघरए ससहिं मालविअं ठाविअ भवन्तं पच्चुग्गदोम्हि ।

राजा । अहमेनां संभावयामि । गच्छाग्रतः ।

विदूषकः । [3]एदु भवं । एदं समुद्दघरअं ।

---

१. ननु पृष्टोस्मि । प्रत्युत्पन्नबुद्धिना मया कथितम् । दैवचिन्तकै राजा भणितः । सोपसर्गं वो नक्षत्रम् । तत्सर्वबन्धनमोक्षः क्रियतामिति । तच्छ्रुत्वा देव्या धारिण्येरावतीचित्तं रक्षन्त्या राजा किल मोचयतीति त्वमेव मोचयेत्यहं संदिष्टोस्मि । ततो युज्यत इति तया संपादितोर्थः ।

२. त्वरतां भवान् । समुद्रगृहे ससखीं मालविकां स्थापयित्वा भवन्तं प्रत्युद्गतोस्मि ।

३. एतु भवान् । एतत्समुद्रगृहम् ।

---

1. B पच्चुपण्ण°; F पच्चुत्तरपच्चुप्पण्णबुध्धिणा (= प्रत्युत्तरप्रत्युत्पन्नबुद्धिना.)
3. A B C सुणीअ.
4. A राओ.
5. A B C D E omit "एव्व" after "तुमं."
9. B F उपलक्ष्यते.
10. E तुवरेदु.

राजा । साशङ्कम् । एषा कुसुमावचयव्यग्रहस्ता सख्यास्त इरावत्याः परिचारिका चन्द्रिका समागच्छति । इतस्तावदावां भित्तिगूढौ भवावः ।

विदूषकः । [1]कुम्भिलएहिं कामुएहिं अ पलिहलणीआ चन्दिआ ।

। उभौ यथोक्तं कुरुतः ।

राजा । गौतम कथं नु ते सखी मां प्रतिपालयति । एह्येनां गवाक्षमाश्रित्य विलोकयावः ।

। इति विलोकयन्तौ स्थितौ ।

। ततः प्रविशति मालविका बकुलावलिका च ।

बकुलावलिका । [2]हला पणम भट्टारं जो पस्सदो पिट्ठदो देक्खीअदि ।

राजा । मन्ये प्रतिकृतिं मे दर्शयति ।

मालविका । सहर्षम् । [3]णमो दे । द्वारमवलोक्य सविषादम् । कहिं भट्टा । हला विप्पलम्भेसि मं ।

---

१. कुम्भीलकैः कामुकैश्च परिहरणीया चान्द्रिका ।

२. हला प्रणम भर्तारं यः पार्श्वतः पृष्ठतो दृश्यते ।

३. नमस्ते । क्व भर्ता । हला विप्रलभसे माम् ।

---

1. Our MSS., and even G, कुसुमापचय.° We with Tullberg.
3. B °गूढं.
4. F पडिहलणीआ.
7. F omits "नु."
8. F reads प्रतिपालयावः अवलोकयावः (the latter most likely intended to be an explanation of the former) in place of our "विलोकयावः"
9. B D E omit "इति."
11. A C D E पणम.—A C देखी°; F दक्खिअदि.
14. B आलोक्य.

राजा । सखे हर्षविषादाभ्यामत्रभवत्याः प्रीतोस्मि ।

सूर्योदये भवति या सूर्यास्तमये च पुण्डरीकस्य ।
वदनेन सुवदनायास्ते समवस्थे क्षणादूढ ॥ ७ ॥

बकुलावलिका । [1]णं एसो चित्तगओ भट्टा ।

उभे । प्रणिपत्य । [2]जेदु भट्टा ।

मालविका । [3]हला तदा संमुहट्ठिदा अहं भट्टिणो रूवदंसणेण तह ण वितिण्हम्हि जह अज्ज । विभाविदो चित्तगददंसणो एव्व भट्टा ।

विदूषकः । [4]सुदं भवदा । अत्तहोदीए दिट्ठो जह चित्ते ण तह दिट्ठो भवंति मन्तिदं । मुधा दाणिं मञ्जूसा विअ रअणभण्डं जोव्वणगव्वं वहेसि ।

---

१. नन्वेष चित्रगतो भर्ता ।

२. जयतु भर्ता ।

३. हला तदा संमुखस्थिताहं भर्तू रूपदर्शनेन तथा न वितृष्णास्मि यथाद्य । विभावितश्चित्रगतदर्शन एव भर्ता ।

४. श्रुतं भवता । अत्रभवत्या दृष्टो यथा चित्रे न तथा दृष्टो भवानिति मन्त्रितम् । मुधेदानीं मञ्जूषेव रत्नभाण्डं यौवनगर्वं वहसि ।

---

3. F reads the fourth pâda thus: ते समवस्थे क्षणादुपारूढे, thus turning the ârya into a gîti.

6. Our MSS. ससंभमं उक्कण्ठआ for "संमुहट्ठिदा." We with G. — A B C D E omit "तदा."

7. A B C D E omit "ण."—B C संभाविदो.

8. F omits "एव्व."

9. Our MSS. अत्तहोदीए [F अत्तहोदी] चित्ते जह दिट्ठो भवं तह अदिट्ठोत्ति मन्तेदि. We according to G.

11. E जोब्वण°.

राजा । सखे कुतूहलवानपि निसर्गशालीनः स्त्रीजनः । पश्य ।

काल्स्न्र्येन निर्वर्णयितुं च रूपम्
इच्छन्ति तत्पूर्वसमागतानाम् ।
न च प्रियेष्वायतलोचनानां
समग्रपातीनि विलोचनानि ॥ ८ ॥

मालविका । [1]का एसा ईसिपरिउत्तवअणा भट्टिणा सिणिध्धाए दिट्ठीए णिज्झाइअदि ।

बकुलावलिका । [2]णं इअं पस्सगदा इरावदी ।

मालविका । [3]सहि अदक्खिणो विअ मे पडिभाइ । जो सव्वं देवीजणं उज्झिअ एदाए मुहे बध्धलक्खो ।

बकुलावलिका । आत्मगतम् । [4]चित्तगदं भट्टारं परमत्थं गेण्हिअ असूएदि । होदु । कीलिस्सं दाव एदाए । प्रकाशम् । भट्टिणो वल्लहा एसा ।

मालविका । [5]तदो किं दाणिं अत्ताणं आआसेमि । सासूयं परावर्तते ।

---

१. कैषेषत्परिवृत्तवदना भर्त्रा स्निग्धया दृष्ट्या निध्यायते ।
२. नन्वियं पार्श्वगतेरावती ।
३. सखि अदक्षिण इव मे प्रतिभाति । यः सर्वं देवीजनमुज्झित्वैतस्या मुखे बद्धलक्षः ।
४. चित्रगतं भर्तारं परमार्थं गृहीत्वासूयति । भवतु । क्रीडिष्यामि तावदेतया । भर्तुर्वल्लभैषा ।
५. ततः किमिदानीमात्मानमायासयामि ।

---

2. A B C D E हि for "च."
4. A B C D E प्रियेष्या°.
6. D ईसीपरि°.—B D दिट्ठिए.
8. A C पस्संगदा.—D E इरावई.
9. A B C अदक्खिणो.—E पइभाइ.
10. B उज्झोअ.
11. F परमत्थदो.—A C गिण्हिअ.
12. A C असूआदि.—B C कीलिसं.
14. B दाणीं.

राजा । पश्य सखे ते सख्या मुखम् ।

भ्रूभङ्गभिन्नतिलकं स्फुरिताधरोष्ठं
सासूयमाननमितः परिवर्तयन्त्या ।
कान्तापराधकुपितेष्वनया विनेतुः
संदर्शितेव ललिताभिनयस्य शिक्षा ॥ ९ ॥

विदूषकः । [1]अणुणअसज्जो दाणिं होहि ।

मालविका । [2]अज्जगोदमोवि एत्थ एव्व सेवेदि णं । पुनः स्थानान्तराभिमुखी भवितुमिच्छति ।

बकुलावलिका । मालविकां रुद्ध्वा । [3]ण हु कुविदा दाणिं तुमं ।

मालविका । [4]जइ चिरं कुविदं मण्णेसि एसो पच्चाणीअदि कोवो ।

राजा । उपेत्य ।

कुप्यसि कुवलयनयने चित्रार्पितचेष्टया किमेवमयि ।
ननु तव साक्षादयमहमनन्यसाधारणो दासः ॥ १० ॥

बकुलावलिका । [5]जेदु भट्टा ।

मालविका । आत्मगतम् । [6]कहं चित्तगदो भट्टा मए असूइदो । सव्रीडवदनाञ्जलिं करोति ।

---

१. अनुनयसज्ज इदानीं भव ।
२. आर्यगौतमोऽप्यत्रैव सेवत एनम् ।
३. न खलु कुपितेदानीं त्वम् ।
४. यदि चिरं कुपितां मन्यसे एष प्रत्यानीयते कोपः ।
५. जयतु भर्ता ।
६. कथं चित्रगतो भर्ता मयासूयितः ।

---

3. B C °वर्तयन्त्याः.
7. D E अ—अ°.—Our MSS. अज्जगोदमो एत्थ ण सेवेदि. We with G.
9. E णं हि; AB C D हि for "हु."
10. A F कुविदा.
12. A omits "उपेत्य."

राजा । मदनकातर्यं निरूपयति ।

विदूषकः । [1]किं भवं उदासीणा विअ ।

राजा । अविश्वसनीयत्वात्सख्यास्ते ।

विदूषकः । [2]मा दाव अत्तहोदीअं तुह अविस्सासो ।

राजा । श्रूयताम् ।

पथि नयनयोः स्थित्वा स्वप्ने तिरोभवति क्षणात्
सरति सहसा बाह्वोर्मध्यं गताप्यबला सती ।
मनसिजरुजा क्लिष्टस्यैवं समागममायया
कथमिव सखे विश्रब्धं स्यादिमां प्रति मे मनः ॥ ११ ॥

बकुलावलिका । [3]सहि बहुसो किल भट्टा विप्पलध्धो । दाव एथ्थ विस्ससणिज्जो अप्पा करीअदु ।

मालविका । [4]सहि मम उण मन्दभाआए सिविणअसमाअमो- वि भट्टिणो दुल्लहो आसी ।

बकुलावलिका । [5]भट्टा देहि से उत्तरं ।

---

१. किं भवानुदासीन इव ।

२. मा तावदत्रभवत्यां तवाविश्वासः ।

३. सखि बहुशः किल भर्ता विप्रलब्धः । तावदत्र विश्वसनीय आत्मा क्रियताम् ।

४. सखि मम पुनर्मन्दभाग्यायाः स्वप्नसमागमोऽपि भर्तुर्दुर्लभ आसीत् ।

५. भर्तर्देह्यस्या उत्तरम् ।

---

2. A उदासिणो.

4. F अत्तहोदिअं.

6. G स्थित्वा स्थित्वा for "स्थित्वा स्वप्ने."

9. E F विस्रब्धं.

11. F अथ्थ.—D E आप्पा; F अत्ता.

12. B मन्दहाआए.— F सिविणसमा- गमो.

13. A C D E F आसि.

14. B C D भट्टा अ देहि &c.

राजा ।

उत्तरेण किमात्मैव पञ्चबाणाग्निसाक्षिकम् ।
तव सख्यै मया दत्तो न सेव्यः सेविता रहः ॥ १२॥

बकुलावलिका । [1]अणुग्गहीदम्हि ।

विदूषकः । परिक्रम्य ससंभ्रमम् । [2]बउलावलिए एसो बालासोअरुक्खस्स पल्लवाणि हरिणो लङ्घिदुं आअच्छइ । ता एहि णिवारेम णं ।

बकुलावलिका । [3]तह । प्रस्थिता ।

राजा । एवमस्मद्रक्षणेऽवहितेन भवितव्यम ।

विदूषकः । [4]एदंवि गोदमो णं संदिस्सीअदि ।

बकुलावलिका । [5]अज्जगोदम अहं अप्पआसे चिट्ठामि । तुमं दुवाररक्खओ होहि ।

विदूषकः । [6]जुज्जइ ।

---

१. अनुगृहीतास्मि ।

२. बकुलावलिके एष बालाशोकवृक्षस्य पल्लवान्हरिणो लङ्घितुमागच्छति । तदेहि निवारयाव एनम् ।

३. तथा ।

४. एतदपि गौतमो ननु संदिश्यते ।

५. आर्यगौतम अहमप्रकाशे तिष्ठामि । त्वं द्वाररक्षको भव ।

६. युज्यते ।

---

4. ACDE अणुगहि°; B अणुग्गहि°.
5. ABCDE एस for "एसो."
6. Our MSS. पल्लवा. We with G.

10. F एवंवि.—A B C D E omit "णं"
11. EF अ–अ°.
13. D जुज्जइ; E जुज्जई.

[निष्क्रान्ता बकुलावलिका ।

विदूषकः । [1]इमं दाव फलिअत्थलं आस्सिदो होमि । तथा कृत्वा । अहो सुहप्परिसदा सिलाविसेसस्स । निद्रायते ।

मालविका । ससाध्वसं तिष्ठति ।

राजा ।

विसृज सुन्दरि संगमसाध्वसं
ननु चिरात्प्रभृति प्रणयोन्मुखे ।
परिगृहाण गते सहकारतां
त्वमतिमुक्तलताचरितं मयि ॥ १३ ॥

मालविका । [2]देवीए भएण अत्तणोवि प्पिअं कादुं ण पारेमि ।

राजा । अयि न भेतव्यं न भेतव्यम् ।

मालविका । [3]जो ण भाएदि सो मए भट्टिणीदंसणे दिट्ठसमवत्थो भट्टा ।

राजा ।

दाक्षिण्यं नाम बिम्बोष्ठि बैम्बिकानां कुलव्रतम् ।
तन्मे दीर्घाक्षि ये प्राणास्ते त्वदाशानिबन्धनाः ॥ १४ ॥

---

१. इदं तावत्स्फटिकस्थलमाश्रितो भवामि । अहो सुखस्पर्शता शिलाविशेषस्य ।
२. देव्या भयेनात्मनोपि प्रियं कर्तुं न पारयामि ।
३. यो न बिभेति स मया भट्टिनीदर्शने दृष्टसमवस्थो भर्ता ।

---

1. E inserts इति before "निष्क्रान्ता" &c.
3. A C सुहेपरिस°; E has °प्फंसदा as a marginal gloss on °परिसदा.
10. A D E पिअं
11. A B C D अपि for "अयि."
12. B °दंसणो; F °दस्सणे.—F दिट्ठो समवत्थो भट्टा.

तदयमनुगृह्यतां चिरानुरक्तो जनः । इति संश्लेषमभिनयति ।

मालविका । नाट्येन परिहरति ।

राजा । आत्मगतम् । रमणीयः खलु नवाङ्गनानां मदनविषयव्यापारः । एषा हि

हस्तं कम्पवती रुणद्धि रशनाव्यापारलोलाङ्गुलिं
हस्तौ स्वौ नयति स्तनावरणतामालिङ्ग्यमाना बलात् ।
पातुं पक्ष्मलचक्षुरुन्नमयतः साचीकरोत्याननं.
व्याजेनाप्यभिलाषपूरणसुखं निर्वर्तयत्येव मे ॥ १४ ॥

। ततः प्रविशतीरावती निपुणिका च ।

इरावती । [1]हञ्जे णिउणिए सच्चं तुह चन्दिआए संदिट्ठं समुद्दघरालिन्दए अज्जगोदमो एआई दिट्ठोत्ति ।

निपुणिका । [2]किं अण्णहा भट्टिणीए विण्णाविदं ।

इरावती । [3]तेण हि तहिं एव्व गच्छामो संसआदो णिम्मुत्तं अज्जउत्तस्स पिअवअस्सं पिअं पुच्छिदुं । च –

---

१. हञ्जे निपुणिके सत्यं तव चन्द्रिकया संदिष्टं समुद्रगृहालिन्द आर्यगौतम एकाकी दृष्ट इति ।

२. किमन्यथा भट्टिन्यै विज्ञापितम् ।

३. तेन हि तत्रैव गच्छावः संशयान्निर्मुक्तमार्यपुत्रस्य प्रियवयस्यं प्रियं प्रष्टुम् । च—

---

1. A B C D E omit " अयम्."
3. F मदनविषयावतारः.
5. A B C D E कम्पयती (कम्पयेत ?) —A B C D E °लोलांशुकम्.
7. F °नेत्रमुन्नमयतः.
12. Our MSS. °घरए. We with G. D E F अ-अ°.
13. F अलीअं for " अण्णहा."
15. A B C D E अ for " च."— None of our MSS. read

निपुणिका । [१]सावसेसं विअ भट्टिणीए वअणं ।

इरावती । [२]अण्णं च चित्तगदं अज्जउत्तं पसादेदुं ।

निपुणिका । [३]अह दाणिं भट्टा एव्व किं ण पच्चणुणीअदि ।

इरावती । [४]मुध्धे जारिसो चित्तगदो तारिसो एव्व अण्णसंकन्तहिअओ अज्जउत्तो । केवलं उवआरादिक्कमं पमज्जिदुं अम्हाणं आरम्भो ।

निपुणिका । [५]इदो भट्टिणी । इति परिक्रामतः ।

। प्रविश्य चेटी ।

चेटी । [६]जेदु भट्टिणी । देवी भणादि । एसो ण मे मच्छुरस्स कालो ।

---

१. सावशेषमिव भट्टिन्या वचनम् ।

२. अन्यच्च चित्रगतमार्यपुत्रं प्रसादयितुम् ।

३. अथेदानीं भर्तैव किं न प्रत्यनुनीयते ।

४. मुग्धे यादृशश्चित्रगतस्तादृश एवान्यसंक्रान्तहृदय आर्यपुत्रः । केवलमुपचारातिक्रमं प्रमार्ष्टुमस्माकमारम्भः ।

५. इतो भट्टिनी ।

६. जयतु भट्टिनी । देवी भणति । एष न मे मत्सरस्य कालः ।

---

in this passage णिम्मुत्तुं or मुत्तुं, the latter of which is read by Dr. Tullberg. Supposing it were possible for मुत्तुं to be the Prâkṛit form of the infinitive, the omission of a word like अत्ताणं as its object would speak much against that reading. G has altogether a different version. It reads "संसभादो मुत्तंसं । दंसवुत्तन्तं अ-अउत्तस्स पिअवअस्सं पुच्छिदुं अ ।" But मुत्तंसं for मोक्ष्ये or मुक्ता भविष्यामि is at least very suspicious. See our Notes.

2. D E F अ-अ°.—G reads चित्तगदं भट्टारं पसादेदुं अ for "अण्णं च" &c.

3. G reads कहं for "किं" and puts it before "भट्टा."

4 F जादिसो for "जारिसो."

5. D E F अ-अ°.—A B C पमजिदुं; F पमज्जिअदुं.

7. B D E omit "इति."

तुह बहुमाणं वढ्ढिदुं वअस्सिआए सह णिअलबन्धणे किदा मालविआ । जइ अणुमण्णेसि अज्जउत्तस्स पिअं कादुं तह करेमि । जं तुह इछिदं तं भणाहि-त्ति ।

इरावती । [1]णाअरिए विण्णवेहि भट्टिणीं । का वअं भट्टिणीं णिओजेदुं । परिअणणिग्गहेण मइ दंसिदो अणुग्गहो । कस्स वा अण्णस्स प्पसादेण अअं जणो वढ्ढदित्ति भणाहि ।

चेटी । [2]तह ।

[इति निष्क्रान्ता ।

निपुणिका । परिक्रम्यावलोक्य च । [3]भट्टिणी एस दुवारुछ्ङ्गे समुद्द-

---

तव बहुमानं वर्धयितुं वयस्यया सह निगडबन्धने कृता मालविका । यद्यनुमन्यसे, आर्यपुत्रस्य प्रियं कर्तुं,तथा करोमि । यत्तवेष्टं तद्भणेति ।

१. नागरिके विज्ञापय भट्टिनीम् । का वयं भट्टिनीं नियोजयितुम् । परिजननिग्रहेण मयि दर्शितोनुग्रहः । कस्य वान्यस्य प्रसादेनायं जनो वर्धत इति भण ।

२. तथा ।

३. भर्ट्टिन एष द्वारोत्सङ्गे समुद्रगृहस्य विपणिगतो वृषभ इव विश्रब्ध आर्यगौतम आसीन एव निद्रायते ।

---

1. A B C वट्टिदुं; E वड्टिदुं.
2. A B C D E मण्णेमि for "अणुमण्णेसि."—D E अ-भ°.—F reads as follows, after "मालविआ" । जइ अणुमण्णसि अ-अउत्तंति तुह किदे विण्णावइस्सं ॥ एवं कज्जं । तह करेमि ॥ जं तुह इछिदं तं मे भणाहित्ति ॥
6. F णिओएदुं.—Our MSS. insert वि (= अपि) after °ग्गहेण. We with G.—F दस्सिदो.
7. A B C पसादेण.—B C वट्टिदित्ति; D वड्ढदित्ति.

11

घरस्स विपणिगओ वुसहो विअ विस्सध्धो अज्जगोदमो आसीणो एव्व णिद्दाअदि ।

इरावती । [1]अच्चाहिदं । ण क्खु सावसेसो विसवेओ भवे ।

निपुणिका । [2]पसण्णमुहो दीसइ । अवि अ धुवसिध्धिणा चिइस्सिदो । ता से असङ्कणीअं पावं ।

विदूषकः । उत्स्वप्नायते । [3]होदि मालविए– ।

निपुणिका । [4]सुदं भट्टिणीए । कस्स एसो अत्तणीणो । अब्भवहारसंवादापेक्खी हदासो ओदरिओ इदो ससक्कारं सोत्थिवाअणमोदएहिं कुक्खिं भरिअ संपदं मालविअं उस्सिविणावेदि ।

---

१. अत्याहितम । न खलु सावशेषो विषवेगो भवेत् ।

२. प्रसन्नमुखो दृश्यते । अपि च ध्रुवसिद्धिना चिकित्सित ः । तदरयाशङ्कनीयं पापम् ।

३. भवति मालविके— ।

४. श्रुतं भट्टिन्या । कस्यैष आत्मनीनः । अभ्यवहारसंवादापेक्षो हताश औदरिक इतः ससत्कारं स्वस्तिवायनमोदकैः कुक्षिं पूरयित्वा सांप्रतं मालविकामुत्स्वप्नायते ।

---

1. E विपणिठाओ, F विपणिणिलयो, for "विपणिगओ."—A B C D E om. "वुसहो" after "विपणिगओ." — F omits "विस्सध्धो."—D E F अ–अ°.
2. B D णिद्दायदि ; E णिदायदि.
3. F सावसेसविसो भवे.—B D णं खु.—F अच्चहिदं.
5. A B C D असक्कणीअं ; E असंकणीअं.
6. A C D E होदी.
7. A C अभवहार°
8. B ओदरीओ.—A B C D ससकारं; F सव्वकालं for "ससक्कारं."
10. A B C उस्सिविणं आइवेदि ; E उस्सिविणआइवेदि.

विदूषकः । [1]इरावदिं अदिक्कमन्दी होहि ।

निपुणिका । [2]सुदं अच्चाहिदं । भुअंगभीरुअं बम्हबन्धुं इमिणा भुअंगमकुडिलेण अत्तणो दण्डकट्ठेण तम्भन्तरिदा भाअआमि ।

इरावती । [3]अरुहदि किल किदवो उवद्दवस्स ।

निपुणिका । विदूषकस्योपरि दण्डकाष्ठं पातयति ।

विदूषकः । सहसा प्रतिबुध्य । [4]अवि हा अवि हा । णं दव्वीकरो मे उवरि पडिदो ।

राजा । सहसोपसृत्य । सखे न भेतव्यं न भेतव्यम् ।

मालविका । अनुसृत्य । [5]भट्टा मा दाव सहसा णिक्कम । सप्पोत्ति भणादि ।

इरावती । [6]हद्धि हद्धि । भट्टा इदो एव्व धावइ ।

---

१. इरावतीमातिक्रामन्ती भव ।

२. श्रुतमत्याहितम् । भुजंगभीरुकं ब्रह्मबन्धुमनेन भुजंगकुटिलेनात्मनो दण्डकाष्ठेन स्तम्भान्तरिता भीषयामि ।

३. अर्हति किल कितव उपद्रवम् ।

४. अपि हा अपि हा । ननु दर्वीकरो ममोपरि पतितः ।

५. भर्तर्मा तावत्सहसा निष्क्रम । सर्प इति भणति ।

६. हा धिक् हा धिक् । भर्तैव एव धावति ।

---

1. A C D E इरावदीं.

3. E °कुडिलेण.—F om. "अत्तणो."—A °काट्ठेण.—E तम्भन्तरिअ; F थ्थम्भन्तरिआ.—A C भआआमि.

5. A उवद्दव्वस्स.

7. A B C D E omit "णं."

8. A C वडिदो.

10. E निक्कम.

12. A C धावई.

विदूषकः । सप्रहासम् । [1]कहं दण्डकट्ठं इदं । अहं उण जाणे जं मए केअइकण्डएहिं सप्पस्स विअ दंसो किदो तं फलिदंति ।

। प्रविश्य पटाक्षेपेण बकुलावलिका ।

बकुलावलिका । ससंभ्रमम् । [2]कहिं सप्पो । मा क्खु भट्टा पविस । इह कुडिलगइ सप्पो विअ दीसइ ।

इरावती । राजानमुपसृत्य । [3]अवि सिध्धा मणोरहा दिवासंकेदमिहुणस्स ।

सर्वे । इरावतीं दृष्ट्वा संभ्रान्ताः ।

राजा । अपूर्वोऽयमुपचारः ।

इरावती । [4]बउलावलिए दिट्ठिआ दोच्चाहिआरविसआ संपुण्णा दे पडिण्णा ।

बकुलावलिका । [5]पसीददु भट्टिणी । किं दद्दुरा वाहरन्तित्ति देव्वो पुडविं विसुमरदि ।

---

१. कथं दण्डकाष्ठमिदम् । अहं पुनर्जाने यन्मया केतकीकण्टकैः सर्पस्येव दंशः कृतस्तत्फलितमिति ।

२. क्व सर्पः । मा खलु भर्तः प्रविश । इह कुटिलगतिः सर्प इव दृश्यते ।

३. अपि सिद्धा मनोरथा दिवासकृतमिथुनस्य ।

४. बकुलावलिके दिष्ट्या दौत्याधिकारविषया संपूर्णा ते प्रतिज्ञा ।

५. प्रसीदतु भट्टिनी । किं दर्दुरा व्याहरन्तीति देवः पृथिवीं विस्मरति ।

---

1. A C D कधं.
2. A B C D वि for "विअ."—F तं एदं मे फलिदंति.
5. F सवो for "सप्पो."
6. D कुटिलगई.—D E दोसई.
11. A C D E दिठ्ठिया.
12. A C पडिणा.
13. A B C D E पसोद.—Our MSS. किं मए किदं । देवे पुच्छिदवो for "किं दद्दुरा" &c. We with G.

विदूषकः । [१]मा दाव । अत्तहोदीए दंसणमेत्तएण अत्तभवं पणिपादलङ्घणं विसुमरिदो । तुमं उण अज्जवि पसादं ण गेण्हेसि ।

इरावती । [२]कुविदावि दाणिं अहं किं करिस्सं ।

राजा । अस्थाने कोप इत्यनुपपन्नं त्वयि । तथा हि ।

कदा मुखं वरतनु कारणादृते
तवागतं क्षणमपि कोपपात्रताम् ।
अपर्वणि ग्रहकलुषेन्दुमण्डला
विभावरी कथय कथं भविष्यति ॥ १८ ॥

इरावती । [३]अट्ठाणेत्ति सुट्ठु भणिदं अज्जउत्तेण । अण्णसंक्कन्तेसु अम्हाणं भाअहेएसु जइ उण कुप्पिस्सं तदो हस्सा भविस्सं ।

राजा । त्वमन्यथा कल्पयसि । अहं पुनः सत्यमेव कोपस्थानं न पश्यामि । कुतः ।

नार्हति कृतापराधोप्युत्सवदिवसेषु परिजनो बन्धम् ।
इति मोचिते मयैते प्रणिपतितुं मामुपगते च ॥१६॥

---

१. मा तावत् । अत्रभवत्या दर्शनमात्रेणात्रभवान्प्रणिपातलङ्घनं विस्मृतः । त्वं पुनरद्यापि प्रसादं न गृह्णासि ।

२. कुपितापीदानीमहं किं करिष्ये ।

३. अस्थान इति सुष्ठु भणितमार्यपुत्रेण । अन्यसंक्रान्तेष्वस्माकं भागधेयेषु यदि पुनः कुप्ये ततो हास्या भविष्यामि ।

---

2. A B C D E omit "अज्जवि."
3. A गण्हसि ; C गेण्हसि.
4. A B C D E omit "°वि दाणिं."
10. D E F अ॰अ°.
11. A B C F भाअहेयेसु.—C जई.
13. B कलयसि for "कल्पयसि."
14. E omits "न" altogether.—Our MSS. गृह्णामि for "पश्यामि." We with G.
15. Our MSS. दण्डम्. We with G.

इरावती । [1]णिपुणिए देवीं विण्णवेहि । दिट्ठं भवदीए पक्खवादित्तणंति ।

निपुणिका । [2]तह ।

[इति निष्क्रान्ता ।

विदूषकः । आत्मगतम् । [3]अहो अणत्थो संपडिदो । बन्धणब्भट्ठो गिहकपोदो चिल्लाए मुहे पडिदो ।

। प्रविश्य निपुणिका ।

निपुणिका । [4]भट्टिणी जदिच्छादिट्ठाए माहविआए आचक्खिदं । एव्वं खु एदं णिव्वुत्तं । इति कर्णे कथयति ।

इरावती । आत्मगतम् । [5]उववण्णं । सअं एव्व बम्हबन्धुणा उब्भिण्णो दुग्गप्पओओ । विदूषकं विलोक्य । प्रकाशम् । इअं इमस्स कामतन्तसइवस्स णीई ।

विदूषकः । [6]होदी जदि णीइए एक्कंपि अक्खरं पढेअं तदो गाअत्तिंपि विसुमरेइं ।

---

१. निपुणिके देवीं विज्ञापय । दृष्टं भवत्याः पक्षपातित्वमिति ।

२. तथा ।

३. अहो अनर्थः संपतितः । बन्धनभ्रष्टो गृहकपोतश्चिल्लाया मुखे पतितः ।

४. भट्टिनि यदृच्छादृष्टया माधविकयाख्यातम् । एवं खल्वेतन्निर्वृत्तमिति ।

५. उपपन्नम् । स्वयमेव ब्रह्मबन्धुनोद्भिन्नो दुर्गप्रयोगः । इयमेतस्य कामतन्त्रसचिवस्य नीतिः ।

६. भवति यदि नीत्या एकमप्यक्षरं पठेयं ततो गायत्रीमपि विस्मरेयम् ।

---

1. A देवीए. — F विणवेहि. — F पक्खवादित्तणं अज्जेत्ति.

5. Our MSS. गन्दारलदालग्गो विभ for "बन्धणभट्ठो," which we read with Tullberg.

11. B C D दुग्गपआओ (=दुर्गप्रकाशः).

12. E णिइ ; A B C D णिई.

13. D E होदि.—A C D पढअं; E पठअं.

राजा । आत्मगतम् । कथं नु संकटादस्मादात्मानं मोक्ष्यामि ।

। प्रविश्य सावेगं जयसेना ।

जयसेना । [1]देव्व कुमारी वसुलच्छी कन्दुअं अणुधावन्ती पिङ्गलवाणरेण बलिअं उत्तासिदा अङ्कणिसण्णा देवीए पवादे किसलअं विअ वेवमाणा दाणिंपि पकिदिं ण पडिवज्जइ ।

राजा । कथं कातरो बालभावः ।

इरावती । सावेगम् । [2]तुवरेदु अज्जउत्तो णं समस्सासइदुं । मा से संदावजणिओ विआरो वड्ढदु ।

राजा । अहमेनां संज्ञापयामि । सत्वरं परिक्रामति ।

विदूषकः । आत्मगतम् । [3]साहु रे पिङ्गलवाणर साहु । परित्तादो तुए सपक्खो ।

[निष्क्रान्तो वयस्येन राजा इरावती प्रतीहारी च ।

---

१. देव कुमारी वसुलक्ष्मीः कन्दुकमनुधावन्ती पिङ्गलवानरेण बलवदुत्त्रासिताङ्कनिषण्णा देव्याः प्रवाते किसलय इव वेपमानेदानीमपि प्रकृतिं न प्रतिपद्यते ।

२. त्वरतामार्यपुत्र एनां समाश्वासयितुम् । मास्याः संतापजनितो विकारो वर्धताम् ।

३. साधु रे पिङ्गलवानर साधु । परित्रातस्त्वया सपक्षः ।

---

2. E सवेगं.

3. B °धावदी ; C D E °धावती; F धावन्दो.

4. A C °णिस्सण्णा ; F अङ्के णिसण्णा.

5. A C दाणीं°.—A पडिवज्जई.

7. F कहं for "कथं."

8. B D E तुवरदु.—D E अ-अ.°

9. A वड्ढदु ; E वड्ढदु.

10. C D E एतां.

11. We read "आत्मगतम्" with G.

मालविका । [1]हला देविं चिन्तअन्तीए वेवइ मे हिअअं । ण जाणे अदोवरं किं अणुहोदव्वंति ।

। नेपथ्ये ।

[2]अच्चरिअं अच्चरिअं । अपुण्णे एव्व पञ्चरत्ते दोहलस्स मुउलेहिं संणध्धो तवणीआसोओ । जाव देवीए णिवेदेमि ।

उभे । श्रुत्वा प्रहृष्टे ।

बकुलावलिका । [3]अस्ससदु पिअसही । सच्चप्पडिण्णा देवी ।

मालविका । [4]तेण हि पमदवणपालिआए पिठ्ठदो होम्म ।

बकुलावलिका । [5]तह ।

[इति निष्क्रान्ताः सर्वे ।

॥ इति चतुर्थोऽङ्कः ॥

---

१. हला देवीं चिन्तयन्त्या वेपते मे हृदयम् । न जानेऽतः परं किमनुभवितव्यमिति ।

२. आश्चर्यमाश्चर्यम् । अपूर्ण एव पञ्चरात्रे दोहदस्य मुकुलैः संनद्धस्तपनीयाशोकः । यावद्देव्यै निवेदयामि ।

३. आश्वसितु प्रियसखी । सत्यप्रतिज्ञा देवी ।

४. तेन हि प्रमदवनपालिकायाः पृष्ठतो भवावः ।

५. तथा ।

---

1. F देवीं चिन्दयन्दीए.

2. F inserts सत्वरं परिक्रामति after " अणुहोदव्वंति."

9. C पिट्ठदो.

। ततः प्रविशत्युद्यानपालिका ।

उद्यानपालिका । [1]उवक्खित्तो मए किदसक्कारविहिणो तवणीआसोअस्स भित्तिबन्धो । जाव अणुट्ठिअणिओअं अप्पाणं देवीए णिवेदेमि । परिक्रम्य । अहो देव्वस्स अणुकम्पणिज्जा मालविआ । तस्सिं तह चण्डिआ देवी इमिणा असोअकुसुमउत्तन्तेण पसादाहिमुही भविस्सदि । कहिं णु क्खु भवे देवी । विलोक्य । एसो देवीपरिअणब्भन्तरो किंवि जदुमुद्दालञ्छिअं चीरमञ्जूसं करे गेण्हिअ कुज्जो सारसओ चउस्सालादो णिक्कमेदि । पुच्छिस्सं दाव णं ।

। ततः प्रविशति यथानिर्दिष्टः कुब्जः ।

उद्यान० । उपसृत्य । [2]सारसअ कहिं पत्थिदोसि ।

---

१. उपक्षिप्तो मया कृतसंस्कारविधेस्तपनीयाशोकस्य भित्तिबन्धः । यावदनुष्ठितनियोगमात्मानं देव्यै निवेदयामि । अहो दैवस्यानुकम्पनीया मालविका । तस्यां तथा चण्डिका देव्यनेनाशोककुसुमवृत्तान्तेन प्रसादाभिमुखी भविष्यति । क नु खलु भवेद्देवी । एष देवीपरिजनाभ्यन्तरः कामपि जतुमुद्रालाञ्छितां चीरमञ्जूषां करे गृहीत्वा कुब्जः सारसकश्चतुःशालाया निष्क्रमति । प्रक्ष्यामि तावदेनम् ।

२. सारसक कुत्र प्रस्थितोसि ।

---

2. B D E तवणीया°.

6. F omits "इमिणा."—F °कुसुमश्श्रवएण.

7. F देवीए परि°. [वन्धनं.

8. A B C जतु°; F जउ°.—F चीर-

9. F सारओ (= सारकः), and retains the same form of the proper name in the succeeding speeches.—A B C पुच्छिसं.

सारसकः । [1]मधुअरिए विज्जापारआणं अणुचिट्ठन्ताणं बम्हणाणं इमा णिच्चदक्खिणा मासिआ दादव्वा । तं अज्जपुरोहिदस्स हत्थं पाविदुं ।

मधुकरिका । [2]किंणिमित्तं ।

सारसकः । [3]जदप्पहुदि सुदं सेणावइणा जण्णतुरअरक्खणे णिउत्तो भट्टिदारओ वसुमित्तओत्ति तदप्पहुदि तस्स आउसो णिमित्तं अट्ठादससुवण्णपरिमाणं दक्खिणं देवी दक्खिण्णेहिं पडिग्गाहेइ ।

मधुकरिका । [4]जुज्जइ । अह कहिं देवी ।

सारसकः । [5]मङ्गलघरए आसणत्था विदब्भविसआदो भादुणा वीरसेणेण पेसिदं लिविकरेहिं वाचिअमाणं लेहपत्तं सुणादि ।

---

१. मधुकरिके विद्यापारगाणामनुतिष्ठतां ब्राह्मणानामियं नित्यदक्षिणा मासिका दातव्या । तामार्यपुरोहितस्य हस्तं प्रापयितुम् ।

२. किंनिमित्तम् ।

३. यतःप्रभृति श्रुतं सेनापतिना यज्ञतुरगरक्षणे नियुक्तो भर्तृदारको वसुमित्र इति ततःप्रभृति तस्यायुषो निमित्तमष्टादशसुवर्णपरिमाणां दक्षिणां देवी दक्षिण्यैः परिग्राहयति ।

४. युज्यते । अथ क्व देवी ।

५. मङ्गलगृह आसनस्था विदर्भविषयाद्भ्रात्रा वीरसेनेन प्रेषितं लिपिकारैर्वाच्यमानं लेखपत्त्रं शृणोति ।

---

1. F महुअरिए.—A °पारअणां, C °पारआणां ; F विज्जापारअणं.

2. F इअं for "इमा."—D E F अ-अ°.

6. A C णिवुत्तो.

8. B D E दाक्खिणेहिं ; C दक्खिणेहिं. —F पडिग्गाहीअइ.

11. A E लिविंकरेहिं.

मधुकरिका । [1]को उण विदब्भराअवुत्तन्तो।

सारसकः । [2]वसीकिदो किल वीरसेणप्पमुहेहिं भट्टिणो विअअदण्डेहिं विदब्भणाहो । मोइदो से दाआदो माहवसेणो । तेण हि महासाराणि रअणवाहणाणि सिप्पिदारिआभूइट्ठं परिअणं अ उवाअणीकरिअ दूदो भट्टिणो सआसं पेसिदो । सुवो किल भट्टारं देक्खिस्सदित्ति ।

मधुकरिका । [3]गच्छ अणुचिट्ठ अत्तणो णिओअं । अहंवि देवीं पेक्खिस्सं ।

[निष्क्रान्तौ ।

॥ प्रवेशकः ॥

। ततः प्रविशति प्रतीहारी ।

प्रतीहारी । [4]आणत्तम्हि देवीए । विण्णवेहि अज्जउत्तं । इच्छामि अज्जउत्तेण सह असोअरुक्खपसूणलच्छीं पच्चक्खीकरेदुंति । जाव धम्मासणगदं देवं पडिवालेमि।

।इति परिक्रामति ।

---

१. कः पुनर्विदर्भराजवृत्तान्तः ।

२. वशीकृतः किल वीरसेनप्रमुखैर्भर्तुर्विजयदण्डैर्विदर्भनाथः । मोचितोस्य दायादो माधवसेनः । तेन हि महासाराणि रत्नवाहनानि शिल्पिदारिकाभूयिष्ठं परिजनं चोपायनीकृत्य दूतो भर्तुः सकाशं प्रेषितः । श्वः किल भर्तारं द्रक्ष्यतीति ।

३. गच्छानुतिष्ठात्मनो नियोगम् । अहमपि देवीं प्रेक्षिष्ये ।

४. आज्ञप्तास्मि देव्या । विज्ञापयार्यपुत्रम् । इच्छाम्यार्यपुत्रेण सहाशोकवृक्षप्रसूनलक्ष्मीं प्रत्यक्षीकर्तुमिति । यावद्धर्मासनगतं देवं प्रतिपालयामि ।

---

2. A C D E °पमुहेहिं.

5. Our MSS. परिअणं उवाअणीकरिअ दूदो अ. We with G.—B E °करीअ.

6. B सुत्रो.—F दक्खिस°.

8. B पेक्खीस्सं; F पक्खिस्सं.

12. E F अ-अ°.

13. DEFअ-अ°.—F °लच्छिं पच्चक्खीकरिदुंत्ति.

। नेपथ्ये वैतालिकौ ।

दिष्ट्या दण्डेनैवारिशिरःसु वर्तते देवः ।

प्रथमः ।

परभृतकलव्याहारेषु त्वमात्तरतिर्मधुं
नयसि विदिशातीरोद्यानेष्वनङ्ग इवाङ्गवान् ।
विजयकरिणामालानाङ्कैरुपोढबलस्य ते
वरद वरदारोधोवृक्षैः सहावनतो रिपुः ॥ १ ॥

द्वितीयः ।

विरचितपदं वीरप्रीत्या सुरोपमसूरिभिश्
चरितमुभयोर्मध्येकृत्य स्थितं क्रथकैशिकान् ।
तव हृतवतो दण्डानीकैर्विदर्भपतेः श्रियं
परिघगुरुभिर्दोर्भिः शौरेः प्रसह्य च रुक्मिणीम् ॥ २ ॥

प्रती० । [१]एसो जअसद्दसूइअपत्थाणो इदो एव्व आअच्छदि देवो । अहंवि दाव इमस्स पमुहादो किंवि ओसरिअ एदं मुहालिन्दतोरणं समस्सिदा होमि । एकान्ते स्थिता ।

। ततः प्रविशति सवयस्यो राजा ।

राजा ।

कान्तां विचिन्त्य सुलभेतरसंप्रयोगां
श्रुत्वा विदर्भपतिमानमितं बलैश्च ।
धाराभिरातप इवाभिहतं सरोजं
दुःखायते च हृदयं सुखमश्नुते च ॥ ३ ॥

---

१. एष जयशब्दसूचितप्रस्थान इत एवागच्छति देवः । अहमपि तावदस्य प्रमुखतः किंचिदपसृत्यैतन्मुखालिन्दतोरणं समाश्रिता भवामि ।

---

13. B जयसद्द°.— F आअच्छइ.

विदूषकः । [1]जह देक्खामि तह सव्वहा एक्कन्तसुहिदो भवं भविस्सदि ।

राजा । सखे कथमिव ।

विदूषकः । [2]अज्ज किल देवीए धारिणीए पण्डिदकोसिई भणिदा । भअवदि जइ तुमं पसाहणगव्वं वहेसि तं दंसेहि मालविआए सरीरे वेदब्भअं विवाहणेवथ्थंति । ता सविसेसालंकिदा मालविआ । तत्तहोदी कदाविब्भवदो मणोरहं पूरेइ ।

राजा । सखे मदपेक्षानुवृत्त्या निवृत्तेर्ष्याया धारिण्याः पूर्वचरितैः संभाव्यत एतत् ।

प्रती० । उपगम्य । [3]जेदु भट्टा । देवी विण्णवेदि तवणीआसोअस्स कुसुमसोहादंसणेण मह आरम्भो सफलो करीअदुत्ति ।

---

१. यथा पश्यामि तथा सर्वथैकान्तसुखितो भवान्भविष्यति ।

२. अद्य किल देव्या धारिण्या पण्डितकौशिकी भणिता । भगवति यदि त्वं प्रसाधनगर्वं वहसि तद्दर्शय मालविकायाः शरीरे वैदर्भकं विवाहनेपथ्यमिति । तत्सविशेषालंकृता मालविका । तत्रभवतो कदाचिद्भवतो मनोरथं पूरयेत् ।

३. जयतु भर्ता । देवी विज्ञापयति । तपनीयाशोकस्य कुसुमशोभादर्शनेन ममारम्भः सफलः क्रियतामिति ।

---

1. F दख्खामि.—Our MSS. do not give "तह." We according to G.—B °सुहितो.
2. A B C D E read त्ति after "भविस्सदि."
4. B E °कोसिइ.
5. A C D E F वहासि.
6. A D E °णेवछ्छं; F °णेपछ्छं.
7. D कदाचि for "कदाविभ्."
8. A B C D E पुराएइ.
11. A विणवेदि.
12. F सोहादस्सणेण.— A B C D E महारम्भो for "मह आरम्भो."—A B C D सफलं.

राजा । ननु तत्रैव देवी ।

प्रतीहारी ।[1]अह इं । जहारुहसंमाणसुहिदं अन्तेउरजणं विसज्जिअ मालविअपुरोगेण अत्तणो परिअणेण सह देवं पडिवालेदि ।

राजा । सहर्षम् । विदूषकं विलोक्य । जयसेने गच्छाग्रतः ।

प्रतीहारी ।[2]इदो इदो देवो ।

। सर्वे परिक्रामन्ति ।

विदूषकः । विलोक्य ।[3]भो वअस्स किंवि परिवुत्तजोव्वणो विअ वसन्दो पमदवणे लक्खीअदि ।

राजा । यथावृत्तं भवानाह ।

अग्रे विकीर्णकुरबकफलजालविभुज्यमानसहकारम् ।
परिणामाभिमुखमृतोरुत्सुकयति यौवनं चेतः ॥ ४ ॥

विदूषकः ।[4]भो अअं सो दिण्णणेवत्थो विअ कुसुमत्थबएहिं तवणीआसोओ । ओलोअदु भवं ।

---

१. अथ किम् । यथार्हसंमानसुखितमन्तःपुरजनं विसर्ज्य मालविकापुरोगेणात्मनः परिजनेन सह देवं प्रतिपालयति ।

२. इत इतो देवः ।

३. भो वयस्य किमपि परिवृत्तयौवन इव वसन्तः प्रमदवने लक्ष्यते ।

४. भो अयं स दत्तनेपथ्य इव कुसुमस्तबकैस्तपनीयाशोकः । आलोकयतु भवान् ।

---

2. F [2]सुहं for "सुहिदं."—B विसज्जीअ.
3. B C E F मालविआ°.
8. B वयस्य.—A C किंवि ; D E किंचि ; F किंचिप्परिवुत्त°. —A C E °जोवणो.
13. A D E °णेवच्छो.

राजा । स्थाने खल्वयं प्रसवमन्थरोभूत् । यदयमिदानीमनन्यसाधारणां शोभामुद्वहति । पश्य ।

सर्वाशोकतरूणां प्रथमं सूचितवसन्तविभवानाम् ।
निर्वृत्तदोहदेस्मिन्संक्रान्तानीव कुसुमानि ॥ ८ ॥

विदूषकः । [1]भो विस्सध्धो होहि । अम्हेसु उवगदेसु धारिणी पस्सपरिवट्टिणीं मालविअं अणुणेइ ।

राजा । सहर्षम् । पश्य सखे ।

मामियमभ्युत्तिष्ठति देवी विनयादुपस्थिता प्रियया ।
विस्मृतहस्तकमलया नरेन्द्रलक्ष्म्या वसुमतीव ॥ ९ ॥

। ततः प्रविशति परिव्राजिका देवी मालविका विभवतश्च परिवारः ।

मालविका । आत्मगतम् । [2]जाणामि णिमित्तं कोदुआलंकारस्स । तहवि मम हिअअं विसिणीपत्तगअं सलिलं विअ वेवदि । दक्खिणेदरंवि णअणं पफ्फुरइ ।

विदूषकः । [3]भो असंदेहं वेवाहिअणेवथ्थेण सविसेसं सोहइ अत्तहोदी मालविआ ।

---

१. भो विश्रब्धो भव । आवयोरुपगतयोर्धारिणी पार्श्वपरिवर्तिनीं मालविकामनुनयति ।

२. जानामि निमित्तं कौतुकालंकारस्य । तथापि मम हृदयं बिसिनीपत्रगतं सलिलमिव वेपते । दक्षिणेतरमपि नयनं प्रस्फुरति ।

३. भो असंदेहं वैवाहिकनेपथ्येन सविशेषं शोभतेत्रभवती मालविका ।

---

1. Our MSS. omit अयं after "खलु." We with G.

4. B C D F °दौहृदे (°दोर्हदे?).—

5. Our MSS. अम्हेसु उवगदेसु &c. as given above. G reads otherwise. See Notes.

8. F विनयादनु-[नू ?]-स्थिता प्रियया.

11. B D E परीवारः

13. B °पत्तगदं ; F बिसिणीपत्तगदं.

14. A C दक्खिणेदरं.

15. A D E °णेवच्छेण.

राजा । पश्याम्याभरणालंकृतामेनाम् ।

अनतिलम्बिदुकूलनिवासिनी
लघुभिराभरणैः प्रतिभाति मे ।
उडुगणैरुदयोन्मुखचन्द्रिका
गतहिमैरिव चैत्रविभावरी ॥ ७ ॥

देवी । उपेत्य । [1]जेदु अज्जउत्तो ।

विदूषकः । [2]वड्ढदु होदी ।

परिव्राजिका । विजयतां देवः ।

राजा । भगवत्यभिवादये ।

परिव्राजिका । अभिप्रेतसिद्धिरस्तु ।

देवी । सस्मितम् । [3]अज्जउत्त एस दे तरुणीजणसहाअस्स असोओ संकेदवरओ अम्हेहिं विसज्जिदो ।

विदूषकः । [4]भो तुमं आराहिदोसि ।

राजा । सव्रीडमशोकमभितः परिक्रामन् ।

नायं देव्या भाजनत्वं न नेयः
सत्काराणामीदृशानामशोकः ।
यः सावज्ञो माधवश्रीनियोगे
पुष्पैः शंसत्यादरं त्वत्प्रयत्ने ॥ ८ ॥

---

१. जयत्वार्यपुत्रः ।
२. वर्धतां भवती ।
३. आर्यपुत्र एष ते तरुणीजनसहायस्याशोकः संकेतगृहकोऽस्माभिर्विसर्जितः ।
४. भो त्वमाराधितोऽसि ।

---

6. B उपसृत्य.—E F अ-अ°.
11. D E F अ-अ°.
12. E संकेतघरए corrected from an original संकेतघरओ.—F सज्जिदो (= सज्जितः).
13. A C भराहिदो°.
17. B C D सापेक्षो; A E too so originally, but they afterwards correct it into सपेक्षो.

विदूषकः । [1]भो विस्सध्धो भविअ इमं जोव्वणवदिं पेख्ख ।

देवी । [2]कं ।

विदूषकः । [3]तवणीआसोअकुसुमसोहं ।

सर्वे । उपविशन्ति ।

राजा । मालविकां विलोक्यात्मगतम् । कष्टं खलु संनिधिवियोगो ममाद्य ।

अहं रथाङ्गनामेव प्रिया सहचरीव मे ।
अननुज्ञातसंपर्का धारिणी रजनीव नौ ॥ ९ ॥

। ततः प्रविशति कञ्चुकी ।

कञ्चुकी । जयतु जयतु देवः । अमात्यो विज्ञापयति । तस्मिन्विदर्भविषयोपायने द्वे शिल्पिदारिके मार्गपरिश्रमादलसशरीरे इति कृत्वा न प्रवेशिते । संप्रति देवोपस्थानयोग्ये । तदाज्ञां देवो दातुमर्हतीति ।

राजा । प्रवेशय ते ।

कञ्चुकी । यदाज्ञापयति देवः । इति निष्क्रम्य ताभ्यां सह पुनः प्रविश्य । इत इतो भवत्यौ ।

---

१. भो विश्रब्धो भूत्वेमां यौवनवतीं प्रेक्षस्व ।

२. काम् ।

३. तपनीयाशोककुसुमशोभाम् ।

---

1. B विस्सभो भवीअ.—Our MSS. तुमं for "इमं". We with G.

3. D °कुसूममोहं ; F तवणीआसोअस्स कुसुम°.

10. A C F do not repeat "जयतु."

11. A B C D E शिल्प°.—B C D E F °परिक्रमात्.

12. A देवोपस्थाने योग्ये.

13

प्रथमा । जनान्तिकम् । [1]हला रअणिए अपुव्वं इमं राअउलं पविसन्तीए पसीदइ मे अब्भन्दरगदो अप्पा ।

द्वितीया । [2]हञ्जे जोसणीए महवि एव्वं एव्व । अत्थि क्खु एसो लोअवादो आआमि सुहं वा दुक्खं वा हिअअसमवत्था कहेदित्ति ।

प्रथमा । [3]सो सच्चो दाणिं णो होदु ।

कञ्चुकी । एष देव्या सह देवस्तिष्ठति । तावदुपसर्पेतां भवत्यौ ।

। उभे उपसर्पतः ।

। मालविका परिव्राजिका च चेट्यौ दृष्ट्वा परस्परमवलोकयतः ।

उभे । प्रणिपत्य । [4]जेदु भट्टा जेदु भट्टा । जेदु भट्टिणी जेदु भट्टिणी ।

राजा । स्वागतम् । इतो निषीदतम् ।

उभे । उपविष्टे ।

---

१. हला रजनिके अपूर्वमिदं राजकुलं प्रविशन्त्याः प्रसीदति मेऽभ्यन्तरगत आत्मा ।

२. हञ्जे ज्योत्स्निके ममाप्येवमेव । अस्ति खल्वेष लोकवाद आगामि सुखं वा दुःखं वा हृदयसमवस्था कथयतीति ।

३. स सत्य इदानीमावयोर्भवतु ।

४. जयतु भर्ता जयतु भर्ता । जयतु भट्टिनी जयतु भट्टिनी ।

---

2. A C D E F अभ्भन्तरं.
3. A B C D E महवि अ एव्व.
7. F उपसर्पताम्.
11. A C D E F जेदु भट्टा । जेदु भट्टिणी.

राजा । कस्यां कलायामभियोगो भवत्योः ।

उभे । [1]संगीदए अब्भन्तरम्ह ।

राजा । देवि गृह्यतामनयोरन्यतरा ।

देवी । [2]मालविए इदो देक्ख कदरा संगीदसहाइणी रुच्चइ ।

उभे । मालविकां दृष्ट्वा । [3]अम्हो भट्टिदारिआ । प्रणिपत्य सह तया बाष्पं विसृजतः ।

। सर्वे सविस्मयमालोकयन्ति ।

राजा । के भवत्यौ का चेयम् ।

प्रथमा । [4]देव इअं अम्हाणं भट्टिदारिआ ।

राजा । कथमिव ।

उभे । [5]सुणादु भट्टा । जो सो भट्टिणा विअअदण्डेहिं विदब्भणाहं वसीकरिअ बन्धणादो मोइदो कुमारो माहवसेणो णाम तस्स इअं कणीअसी भइणी मालविआ णाम ।

---

१. संगीतकेऽभ्यन्तरे स्वः ।

२. मालविके इतः प्रेक्षस्व कतरा संगीतसखी रोचते ।

३. अहो भर्तृदारिका ।

४. देव इयमावयोर्भर्तृदारिका ।

५. शृणोतु भर्ता । योऽसौ भर्त्रा विजयदण्डैर्विदर्भनाथं वशीकृत्य बन्धनान्मोचितः कुमारो माधवसेनो नाम तस्येयं कनीयसी भगिनी मालविका नाम ।

---

2. D E संगीतए.

4. F दक्ख.—B संगीन°.— A C °सहायिणी.

5. A B C D E भट्टदारिआ.

9. A ईअं; D इयं.—A C भट्टार°; B D E भट्ट°.

12. B °करीअ.

देवी । [1]अम्हो राअदारिआ इअं । चन्दणं क्खु मए पादुआपरिभोएण दूसिदं ।

राजा । अथात्रभवती कथमिवेत्थंभूता ।

मालविका । निःश्वस्यात्मगतम् । [2]विहिणो णिओएण ।

द्वितीया । [3]भट्टा सुणादु । दाआदवसंगदे अम्हाणं भट्टदारए माहवसेणे तस्स अमच्चेण अज्जसुमइणा अम्हारिसं परिअणं उज्झिअ गूढं अवणीदा एसा ।

राजा । श्रुतपूर्वं मयैतत् । ततस्ततः ।

उभे । [4]एत्तिअं एव्व । अदो वरं ण आणीमो ।

परिव्राजिका । अतः परमहं मन्दभागिनी कथयिष्यामि ।

उभे । [5]भट्टिदारिए अज्जाए कोसिईए विअ सरओओ सुणीअदि ।

मालविका । [6]णं सा एव्व ।

---

१. अहो राजदारिकेयम् । चन्दनं खलु मया पादुकापरिभोगेण दूषितम् ।

२. विधेर्नियोगेन ।

३. भर्ता शृणोतु । दायादवशं गत आवयोर्भर्तृदारके माधवसेने तस्यामात्येनार्यसुमतिनास्मादृशं परिजनमुज्झित्वा गूढमपनीतैषा ।

४. एतावदेव । अतः परं न जानीवः ।

५. भर्तृदारिके आर्यायाः कौशिक्या इव स्वरयोगः श्रूयते ।

६. ननु सैव ।

---

1. A B C D E अहो for "अम्हो."
3. B अथ तत्र°.
4. D णीओएण.
6. B अमाच्चेण.—D E F अ-अ°.
7. B C D उज्झिआ.
8. B omits " ततस्ततः"
9. D E एत्तयं.
11. A B C भट्टार°; D E भट्ट°.—D E F अ-आए.—A C कोसीइए; B कोसिइए; D कोसीईए.—A सुरओओ; B C D सरिओओ.—F omits सुणीअदि.

उभे । [१] जइवेसधारिणी अज्जकोसिई दुख्खेण विभाविअदि। दुवेवि अम्हे भअवदिं वन्दामहे ।

परिव्राजिका । स्वस्ति भवतीभ्याम् ।

राजा । कथमाप्तवर्गोयं भवत्याः ।

परिव्राजिका । एवमेतत् ।

विदूषकः । [२] तेण हि कहेहि दाणिं अत्तहोदीए उत्तन्तावसेसं ।

परिव्राजिका । सवैक्लव्यम् । श्रूयतां तावत् । माधवसेनसचिवं सुमतिं ममाग्रजमवगच्छ ।

राजा । उपलब्धम् । ततस्ततः ।

परिव्राजिका । स इमां तथागतभ्रातृकां मया सार्धमपवाह्य भवत्संबन्धापेक्षया पथिकसार्थं वैदिशगामिनमनुप्रविष्टः ।

राजा । ततस्ततः ।

परिव्राजिका । स चाटव्यन्ते निविष्टो गताध्वा वणिग्जनोध्वश्रमार्तो विश्रमितुम् ।

---

१. यतिवेषधारिण्यार्यकौशिकी दुःखेन विभाव्यते । द्वे अप्यावां भगवतीं वन्दावहे ।

२. तेन हि कथयेदानीमत्रभवत्या वृत्तान्तावशेषम् ।

---

1. D E F अ-अ°.—A C °कोसिइ.
2. A दूवे°.—F भअवदीं.
4. E भगवत्याः.
6. F कहेहि २, *i. e.* कहेहि कहेहिं.—A C D E अत्तहोदिए.
8. F उपगच्छ for "अवगच्छ."
11. A, as an after-correction, वि-दिश°; F निदेश°.
14. B C D E F विश्रमितुम्.

राजा । ततस्ततः ।

परिव्राजिका । ततश्च

तूणीरबन्धपरिणद्धभुजान्तरालम्
आकर्णलम्बिशिखिपिच्छकलापधारि ।
कोदण्डपाणि निनदत्प्रतिरोधकानाम्
आपातदुष्प्रसहमाविरभूदनीकम् ॥ १० ॥

मालविका । भयं निरूपयति ।

विदूषकः । [१]मा भआहि । अदिक्कन्तं क्खु भअवदी कहेदि ।

राजा । ततस्ततः ।

परिव्राजिका । ततो मुहूर्तं बद्धयुद्धास्ते पराङ्मुखीकृतास्तस्करैः सार्थवाहयोद्धारः ।

राजा । भगवति अतः परमिदानीं कष्टं श्रोतव्यम ।

परिव्राजिका । ततः स मत्सोदर्यः

इमां परीप्सुर्दुर्जातेः पराभिभवकातराम् ।
भर्तृप्रियः प्रियैर्भर्तुरानृण्यमसुभिर्गतः ॥ ११ ॥

प्रथमा । [२]हंहो गदो तादो मरणं ।

---

१. मा भीः । अतिक्रान्तं खलु भगवती कथयति ।

२. हंहो गतस्तातो मरणम् ।

---

3. B C D तणीरबद्ध°; F तूणीरपट्ट°.
4. F आपार्ष्णि°.—F °शिखिबर्ह°.
8. B D E भयाहि. — E कहेइ; A C F कहेहि.
15. F भर्तुः प्रियः.
16. F तदो for "तादो."

द्वितीया । ¹अदो क्खु भट्टिदारिआए इअं समवत्था संवुत्ता ।

परिव्राजिका । बाष्पं विकिरति ।

राजा । तनुभृतामीदृशी लोकयात्रा । न शोचितव्यस्तत्रभवान्सफलीकृतभर्तृपिण्डः ।

परिव्राजिका । ततोहं मोहमुपागता यावत्संज्ञामुपलभे तावदियं दुर्लभदर्शना संवृत्ता ।

राजा । महत्खलु कष्टमनुभूतं भगवत्या ।

परिव्राजिका । ततो भ्रातृशरीरमग्निसात्कृत्वा पुनर्नवीकृतवैधव्यदुःखया मया त्वदीयं देशमवतीर्येमे काषाये गृहीते ।

राजा । युक्तः सज्जनस्यैष पन्थाः । ततस्ततः ।

परिव्राजिका । तत इयमप्याटविकेभ्यो वीरसेनं वीरसेनाद्देवीं गता देवीगृहे लब्धप्रवेशया मया पुनर्दृष्टा । इत्येतदवसानं कथायाः ।

मालविका । आत्मगतम् । ²किं णु क्खु संपदं भट्टा भणादि ।

राजा । अहो परिभवोपहारिणो विनिपाताः । कुतः ।

---

१. अतः खलु भर्तृदारिकाया इयं समवस्था संवृत्ता ।

२. किं नु खलु सांप्रतं भर्ता भणति ।

---

1. A B C D E भट्ट°.
3. Our MSS. तनुत्यजाम्. We according to G.
5. Our MSS. add अस्मि after "उपागता." We with G.
7. F कृच्छ्रम् for "कष्टम्."
9. A B C D E omit "मया."—F कषाये.
11. F omits "वीरसेनम्".
12. B °गृहलब्ध°.
14. A B C D E omit "खलु".
15. E परिभवप्रहारिणः, F परिभावोपनिपातिनो.

प्रेष्यभावेन नामेयं देवीशब्दक्षमा सती ।
स्नानीयवस्त्रक्रियया पत्त्रोर्णं वोपयुज्यते ॥ १२ ॥

धारिणी । [१]भअवदि तुए अभिजणवदिं मालविअं अणाचक्खन्तीए असंपदं किदं ।

परिव्राजिका । शान्तं पापं शान्तं पापम् । कारणेन खलु मया नैभृत्यमवलम्बितम् ।

धारिणी । [२]किं विअ अत्त कारणं ।

राजा । यदि वक्तव्यं कथ्यताम् ।

परिव्राजिका । इयं पितरि जीवति केनापि लोकयात्रागतेन सिद्धादेशेन साधुना मत्समक्षमादिष्टा संवत्सरमात्रं प्रेष्यभावमनुभूय ततः सदृशभर्तृगामिनी भविष्यतीति । तमवश्यं भाविनमादेशमस्यास्त्वत्पादशुश्रूषया परिणमन्तमवेक्ष्य कालप्रतीक्षया मया तत्साधु कृतमिति पश्यामि ।

राजा । युक्तोपेक्षा ।

। प्रविश्य कञ्चुकी ।

कञ्चुकी । देव कथान्तरेणान्तरितमिदममात्यो विज्ञापयति ।

---

१. भगवति त्वयाभिजनवतीं मालविकामनाचक्षाणयासांप्रतं कृतम् ।
२. किमिवात्र कारणम् ।

---

2. Our MSS. पत्त्रोर्णेवोपयुज्यते. We with Tullberg.
4. E omits "किदं."
6. A B C D E नैभृत्यम्.
10. A B C आदिष्टम्.
12. F omits "अवश्यम्."
16. B विज्ञापयामि for "निवेदयामि."

विदर्भगतमनुष्ठेयमवधारितमस्माभिः । देवस्य तावदभिमतं श्रोतुमिच्छामीति ।

राजा । मौद्गल्य तत्रभवतोर्भ्रात्रोर्यज्ञसेनमाधवसेनयोर्द्वैराज्यमवस्थापयितुकामोस्मि ।

तौ पृथग्वरदाकूले शिष्टामुत्तरदक्षिणे ।
नक्तं दिवं विभज्योभौ शीतोष्णकिरणाविव ॥ १३॥

कञ्चुकी । एवममात्यपरिषदे निवेदयामि ।

राजा । अङ्गुल्यानुमन्यते ।

[निष्क्रान्तः कञ्चुकी ।

प्रथमा । जनान्तिकम् । [1]भट्टिदारिए दिठ्ठिआ भट्टिदारओ अध्धरज्जे पइठ्ठं गमिस्सदि ।

मालविका । [2]एदं दाव बहु मन्तव्वं जं जीविदसंसआदो मुत्तो ।

।प्रविश्य कञ्चुकी ।

कञ्चुकी । विजयतां देवः । अमात्यो विज्ञापयति । कल्याणी देवस्य बुद्धिः । मन्त्रिपरिषदोप्येतदेव दर्शनम् ।

द्विधा विभक्तां श्रियमुद्वहन्तौ
धुरं रथाश्वाविव संग्रहीतुः ।
तौ स्थास्यतस्ते नृपतौ निदेशे
परस्परावग्रहनिर्विकारौ ॥ १४ ॥

---

१. भर्तृदारिके दिष्ट्या भर्तृदारकोर्धराज्ये प्रतिष्ठां गमिष्यति ।
२. एतत्तावद्बहु मन्तव्यं यज्जीवितसंशयान्मुक्तः ।

---

1. G's reading, अभिप्रेतं, for "अभिमतं" deserves attention.
9. A C insert इति before "निष्क्रान्तः."
10. A B C D E भट्टदारए.—D E द्विठ्ठिया.—A B C D E भट्टदारओ.
12. A B C D E एवं for "एदं."—E omits "जं."
17. Our MSS. "यथाश्वाविव." We with G.

राजा । तेन हि मन्त्रिपरिषदं ब्रूहि सेनापतये वीरसेनाय लिख्यतामेवं क्रियतामिति ।

कञ्चुकी । तथा । इति निष्क्रम्य सप्राभृतकं लेखं गृहीत्वा पुनः प्रविश्य । अनुष्ठिता प्रभोराज्ञा । अयं पुनरिदानीं देवस्य सेनापतेः पुष्पमित्रस्य सकाशात्सप्राभृतको लेखः प्राप्तः । प्रत्यक्षीकरोत्वेनं देवः ।

राजा । सहसोपसृत्य प्राभृतकं सोपचारकं शिरसि कृत्वा परिजनायार्पयति । लेखं च नाट्येनोद्वेष्टयति ।

देवी । [१]अम्हहे तदोमुहं एव्व णो हिअअं । सुणिस्सं दाव गुरुअणकुसलाणन्तरं वसमित्तस्स वुत्तन्तं । अहिआरे खु मे पुत्तओ सेणावइणा णिउत्तो ।

राजा । उपविश्य वाचयति । स्वस्ति । यज्ञशरणात्सेनापतिः पुष्पमित्रो वैदिशस्थं पुत्रमायुष्मन्तमग्निमित्रं स्नेहात्परिष्वज्यानुदर्शयति । विदितमस्तु । योऽसौ राजसूययज्ञे दीक्षितेन

---

१. अम्महे ततोमुखमेव नो हृदम् । श्रोष्यामि तावद्गुरुजनकुशलानन्तरं वसुमित्रस्य वृत्तान्तम् । अधिकारे खलु मे पुत्रकः सेनापतिना नियुक्तः ।

---

2. E omits "इति" after "क्रियताम्."
3. A B C D E सप्राभृतिकम्.
4. B inserts भो before "प्रभोः."
5. Our MSS. सोत्तरीयप्राभृतिक : [F °प्राभृतम्]. We with G.
6. B °करोत्वेतद्.
7. A C प्राभृतिकम्.
9. B तदोहमुहं (?) for "तदोमुहं"
10. B D उत्तन्तं.—G's reading is worth noticing, viz, अधिआरे खु सेणावइणो णिउत्तो.
11. B C णिवुत्तो.
13. B वैदेशस्थम्; E वैदिश्यम्.

मया राजपुत्रशतपरिवृतं वसुमित्रं गोप्तारमादिश्य संवत्सरोपावर्तनीयो निरर्गलस्तुरगो विसृष्टः स सिन्धोर्दक्षिणरोधसि चरन्नश्वानीकेन यवनानां प्रार्थितः। तत उभयोः सेनयोर्महानासीत्संमर्दः।

देवी। विषादं निरूपयति।

राजा। कथमीदृशं संवृत्तम्। शेषं पुनर्वाचयति।

ततः परान्पराजित्य वसुमित्रेण धन्विना।
प्रसह्य ह्रियमाणो मे वाजिराजो निवर्तितः॥ १५॥

देवी। [1]दाणिं अस्ससइ मे हिअअं।

राजा। लेखशेषं वाचयति। सोहमिदानीमंशुमतेव सगरः पौत्रेण प्रत्याहृताश्वो यक्ष्ये। तदिदानीं कालहीनं विगतरोषचेतसा भवता वधूजनेन सह यज्ञसंदर्शनायागन्तव्यमिति।

राजा। अनुगृहीतोस्मि।

परिव्राजिका। दिष्ट्या पुत्रविजयेन दंपती वर्धेते। देवीं विलोक्य।

भर्त्रासि वीरपत्नीनां श्लाघ्यायां स्थापिता धुरि।
वीरसूरिति शब्दोयं तनयात्त्वामुपस्थितः॥ १६॥

---

१. इदानीमाश्वसिति मे हृदयम्।

---

2. F तुरंगः.
4. F विमर्दः for "संमर्दः."
5. B रूपयति.
9. E आस्ससइ.
11. G reads अकालहीनम्.
12. We read "इाणि" here from G.

विदूषकः । [1]होदि परितुट्ठोम्हि जं पिदरं अणुगदो वच्छो ।

राजा । मौद्गल्य कलभेन खलु यूथपतिरनुकृतः ।

कञ्चुकी ।

नैतावता वीरविजृम्भितेन
चित्तस्य नो विस्मयमादधाति ।
यस्याप्रधृष्यः प्रभवस्त्वमुच्चैर्
वह्नेरपां दग्धुरिवोरुजन्मा ॥ १७ ॥

राजा । मौद्गल्य यज्ञसेनश्यालमुररीकृत्य मुच्यन्तां सर्वे बन्धनस्थाः ।

कञ्चुकी । तथा ।

[इति निष्क्रान्तः ।

देवी । [2]जअसेणे गच्छ । इरावदीप्पमुहाणं अन्तेउराणं पुत्तस्स विअअवुत्तन्तं णिवेदेहि ।

प्रतीहारी । [3]तह । इति प्रस्थिता ।

देवी । [4]एहि दाव ।

प्रतीहारी । प्रतिनिवृत्य । [5]इअंम्हि ।

---

१. भवति परितुष्टोऽस्मि यत्पितरमनुगतो वत्सः ।
२. जयसेने गच्छ । इरावतीप्रमुखाणामन्तःपुराणां पुत्रविजयवृत्तान्तं निवेदय ।
३. तथा ।
४. एहि तावत् ।
५. इयमस्मि ।

---

1. A होदी.
12. B इरावदिप्प°; C D इरावदिप°.
13. B D E विअयउ°.
16. Our MSS. उपसृत्य. We with G.—B इयम्हि.

देवी । जनान्तिकम् । [1]जं मए असोअदोहलणिओए पडिण्णादं मालविआए तं च से अभिअणं च णिवेदिअ मह वअणेण इरावदिं अणुणेहि । तुएहं सच्चादो ण परिब्भंसइदव्वेत्ति ।

प्रतीहारी । [2]तह । इति निष्क्रम्य पुनः प्रविश्य । भट्टिणी पुत्तविअएण दिण्णपारितोसिआणं अन्तेउराणं आभलणाणं रअणमञ्जूसिआ संवुत्तम्हि ।

देवी । [3]किं अथ्थ अच्चरिअं । णं साहारणो ताणं मम अ अअं अब्भूदओ ।

प्रतीहारी । जनान्तिकम् । [4]इरावदी उण विण्णवेदि । सरिसं खु देवी णिवेदेदि । पुढमं संकप्पिदं अण्णहा कादुं ण जुज्जइत्ति ।

---

१. यन्मयाशोकदोहदनियोगे प्रतिज्ञातं मालविकायै तच्चास्या अभिजनं च निवेद्य मम वचनेनेरावतीमनुनय । त्वयाहं सत्यान्न परिभ्रंशयितव्येति ।

२. तथा । भट्टिनि पुत्रविजयेन दत्तपारितोषिकाणामन्तःपुराणामाभरणानां रत्नमञ्जूषिका संवृत्तास्मि ।

३. किमत्राश्चर्यम् । ननु साधारणस्तासां मम चायमभ्युदयः ।

४. इरावती पुनर्विज्ञापयति । सदृशं खलु देवी निवेदयति । प्रथमं संकल्पितमन्यथा कर्तुं न युज्यत इति ।

---

2. A B तत्तं for " तं च."—A C D E F मम for " मह."

3. D परिभंस°.

6. C °पारितोसिअणं.—B अवलाजणाणं for " आभलणाणं "; F आभलणरअण°.

8. F एथ्थ for "अथ्थ".—A B C D E omit "णं."—F अन्तेउराणं for "ताणं".

10. A C सरोसं, E सरिस्सं.—A B C D E omit "खु."

11. B D देवि.—A संकल्पिदं.

देवी । [१]भअवदि तुए अणुमदं इच्छामि अज्जसुमदिणा पुढमदो संकप्पिदं अज्जउत्तस्स मालविअं पडिवादेदुं ।

परिव्राजिका । इदानीमपि त्वमेवास्याः प्रभवसि ।

देवी । मालविकां हस्ते गृहीत्वा । [२]अज्जउत्तो इमं पिआणिवेदणाणुरूवं पारितोसिअं मालविअं पडिच्छदु ।

राजा । सव्रीडं जोषमास्ते ।

देवी । सस्मितम् । [३]तं किं अवधीरेदि मं अज्जउत्तो ।

विदूषकः । [४]होदि एवं लोअप्पवादो सव्वोवि णववरो लज्जालुओ होदि ।

राजा । विदूषकमवेक्षते ।

विदूषकः । [५]अह वा इमं देवीए दिण्णदेवीसद्दं मालविअं अत्तभवं पडिग्गहीदुं इच्छदि ।

---

१. भगवति तवानुमतामिच्छाम्यार्यसुमतिना प्रथमतः संकल्पितामार्यपुत्रस्य मालविकां प्रतिपादयितुम् ।

२. आर्यपुत्र इमां प्रियनिवेदनानुरूपं पारितोषिकं मालविकां प्रतीच्छतु ।

३. तत्किमवधीरयति मामार्यपुत्रः ।

४. भवति एवं लोकप्रवादः सर्वोपि नववरो लज्जालुर्भवति ।

५. अथ वेमां देव्या दत्तदेवीशब्दां मालविकामत्रभवान्प्रतिग्रहीतुमिच्छति ।

---

1. D E F अ॰भ॰.
2. D E F अ॰भ॰.
4. D E F अ॰अ॰.
7. F अवधीरेहि = (अवधीरयसि).—E अवधारेदि.—D E F अ॰अ॰.
8. B लज्जलुओ.
11. Our MSS. do not give अह वा; and they read अरुहदि for इच्छदि in l. 12. We with G.—B इदं for "इमं."—B देवीसद्दं.—A B C D E तत्तभवं.
12. A B C D E पडिग्गहिदुं.

देवी । [1]जदा राअदारिआ इअं अभिअणेण एव्व तदा दिण्णो एव्व से देवीसद्दो । ता किं पुणरुत्तेण ।

परिव्राजिका । मा मैवम् ।

अप्याकरसमुत्पन्ना मणिजातिरसंस्कृता ।
जातरूपेण कल्याणि न हि संयोगमर्हति ॥ १८ ॥

देवी । [2]मरिसेदु भअवदी अब्भुदअकहाए मए लङ्घिदेत्ति । जअसेणे गच्छ तुमं दाव कोसेअपत्तोण्णं से सिग्घं उवणेहि ।

प्रतीहारी । [3]तह । इति निष्क्रम्य पत्त्रोर्णं गृहीत्वा प्रविश्य । देवि इदं तं ।

देवी । मालविकामवगुण्ठनवतीं कृत्वा । [4]दाणिं अज्जउत्तो पडिच्छदु ।

राजा । देवि त्वच्छासनादप्रत्युत्तरा वयम् ।

परिव्राजिका । हन्त प्रतिगृहीता ।

---

१. यदा राजदारिकेयमभिजनेनैव तदा दत्त एवास्या देवीशब्दः । तत्किं पुनरुक्तेन ।
२. मर्षयतु भगवती अभ्युदयकथया मया लङ्घितेति । जयसेने गच्छ त्वं तावत्कौशेयपत्त्रोर्णमस्याः शीघ्रमुपनय ।
३. तथा । इदं तत् ।
४. इदानीमार्यपुत्रः प्रतीच्छतु ।

---

2. B उणरुत्तेण.
6. A C अब्भूदअ°.—F लङ्घिदं for "लङ्घिदेत्ति."
7. B D E F कोसेअं पत्तोण्णं.
9. E omits "इति."—Our MSS. पत्त्रोर्णकौशेयम्. We with G.—A C D देवी इयं अम्हि, B E F इअं अम्हि, for "इदं तं." We with G.
11. D E F अ-अ°.

विदूषकः । [1]अहो देवीए अत्तहोदो अणुऊलदा ।

देवी । परिजनमवलोकयति ।

परिजनः । मालविकामुपेत्य । [2]जेदु भट्टिणी ।

देवी । परिव्राजिकामवेक्षते ।

परिव्राजिका । नैतच्चित्रं त्वयि । तथा हि ।

प्रतिपक्षेणापि पतिं सेवन्ते भर्तृवत्सलाः साध्व्यः ।
अन्यसरितां शतानि हि समुद्रगाः प्रापयन्त्यब्धिम् ॥१९॥

। प्रविश्य निपुणिका ।

निपुणिका । [3]जेदु भट्टा । इरावदी विण्णवेदि । उवआरादिक्कमेण तदा अहं अवरध्धा । संपदं पुण्णमणोरहो भट्टा । अहंवि भट्टिणा पसादमेत्तेण संभावइदव्वेत्ति ।

देवी । [4]णिउणिए अवस्सं ताए संदेसं अणुजाणिस्सदि अज्जउत्तो ।

निपुणिका । [5]जं देवी आणवेदि ।

[इति निष्क्रान्ता ।

---

१. अहो देव्या अत्रभवतोऽनुकूलता ।

२. जयतु भट्टिनी ।

३. जयतु भर्ता । इरावती विज्ञापयति । उपचारातिक्रमेण तदाहमपराद्धा । सांप्रतं पूर्णमनोरथो भर्ता । अहमपि भर्त्रा प्रसादमात्रेण संभावयितव्येति ।

४. निपुणिके अवश्यं तव: संदेशमनुज्ञास्यत्यार्यपुत्रः ।

५. यद्देव्याज्ञापयति ।

---

1. A C D देविए.—A B C अणुऊलदा.
2. F omits this and the following speech.
5. F omits "त्वयि."
7. F शतान्यपि for "शतानि हि".—F उदधिम् for "अब्धिम्."
9. A B C E F उअआरादि°.
11. "पसादमेत्तेण" taken from G.
12. F ताए सेविदुं जाणिस्सिदि अ॰अउत्तो, for "ताए संदेसं अणुजाणिस्सदि अज्जउत्तो."
13. D E अ॰अ°.
14. D E आणवेदि.

परिव्राजिका । देव अहममुना भवत्संबन्धेन चारितार्थं माधवसेनं सभाजयितुमिच्छामि यदि मयि तव प्रसादः ।

देवी । [१]अवसिदकज्जाए भअवदीए अम्हे परिच्चइदुं ण जुत्तं ।

राजा । भगवति मदीयेषु लेखेषु तत्रभवते त्वामुद्दिश्य सभाजनाक्षराणि पातयिष्यामि ।

परिव्राजिका । युवयोः स्नेहेन परवानयं जनः ।

देवी । [२]आणवेदु अज्जउत्तो भूओवि किं पिअं अणुचिट्ठामि ।

राजा । किमतः परम् । तथापि भवत्वेवं तावत् ।

त्वं मे प्रसादसुमुखी भव चण्डि नित्यम्
एतावदेव मृगये प्रतिपक्षहेतोः ।
आशास्यमीतिविगमप्रभृति प्रजानां
संपत्स्यते न खलु गोप्तरि नाग्निमित्रे ॥ २० ॥

[इति निष्क्रान्ताः सर्वे ।

॥ इति पञ्चमोऽङ्कः ॥

॥ इति कालिदासविरचितं मालविकाग्निमित्रं नाम नाटकं समाप्तम् ॥

---

१. अवसितकार्यया भगवत्या वयं परित्यक्तुं न युक्तम् ।

२. आज्ञापयत्वार्यपुत्रो भूयोऽपि किं प्रियमनुतिष्ठामि ।

---

1. B चरितार्थमा°.
2. F मे for "मयि."
3. B भवसोदक°.
7. D E F भ॰भ°.—B भूयोवि.
11. Our MSS. आशास्यमित्यधिगम°; G आशास्यमभ्यधिगम.° We with Tullberg.

NOTES.

ACT I.

P. 1, l. 1.—एकैश्वर्यस्थितोपि. The opposition shown by अपि between this epithet and प्रणतबहुफलः is merely verbal, the figure being an instance of what is called शब्दविरोध. एक, opposed to बहु in the other epithet, is used in a double sense, viz., that of 'supreme' and 'one.'

P. 1, l. 3.—अष्टाभिः. Cf. the introductory stanza of the S'âkuntala.

P. 1, l. 4.—सन्मार्गालोकनाय, 'to see the good paths' (of morality, religion &c.), *i.e., that we may see &c.*

P. 1, l. 7.—मारिषः. By this name the Sûtradhâra usually addresses his assistant (पारिपार्श्विकः), who in his turn uses भाव as a term of respect in addressing his master.

P. 1, l. 10.—वसन्तोत्सवे. The Vasanta Festival comes annually on the first day of the dark or second half of the month of Phâlguna, *i.e.*, on the first day of Spring, to welcome the advent of which was the original object of the festival. This holiday, now so much abused by the vulgar classes in the form of the *holi* enormities, appears to have been more soberly enjoyed in olden times. The observances enjoined for the Vasantotsava day are: 1, That a man shall touch a Mahâr, and shall then bathe, to secure freedom from all sin, from sorrows and diseases. 2, That he shall worship the *holi* spot, to secure the destruction of all pain, with this mantra: वन्दितासि सुरेन्द्रेण ब्रह्मणा शंकरेण च। अनस्तं पाहि नो देवि भूते भूतिप्रदा भव। 3, That he shall eat the blossom of the mango-tree mixed with sandal-wood, to secure the highest happiness, with this mantra: चूतमग्र्यं वसन्तस्य माकन्द

कुसुमं तव । सचन्दनं पिबाम्यद्य सर्वकामार्थसिद्धये. See *Nirṇayasindhu*, under 'Vasantotsava.' During the *holi* festival dramatic representations of all sorts are still very common. See also the opening of the first Act of Ratnâvalî.

P. 1, l. 12.—भास &c. Bhâsa and Saumilla were two dramatic writers, but nothing is known about them or the works they composed. None of our MSS. read धावक in place of भास. MS. G reads भाससौमिल्लकविपुत्रादीनां. See Preface.

P. 2, l. 14.—MS. G inserts the word उवदेसगाहणे after "अन्दरेण."

P. 2, l. 18.—धीरदा 'Whence this seriousness?' 'What are you contemplating so deeply?' The word signifies a pensive and contemplating mood of the mind when the person is so serious, and engaged so much in reflection, that he fails to mark what passes around or beside him.

P. 3, l. 3.—उवालम्भे, viz. "समीवेवि अदिक्कमन्दो इदो दिट्ठिं ण देसि."

P. 3, l. 7.—कहिं. Cf. note *infra* on p. 72, l. 14.

P. 3, l. 10.—ईदिस, referring to her studies in music and dancing.

P. 3, l. 12.—सो जणो, referring to Mâlavikâ.

P. 5, l. 2.—णिब्बन्धिदुं 'to press,' 'to importune.' Cf. Raghuvaṁs'a V. 21—वसुलच्छीए. Vasulakshmî was the younger sister of Dhâriṇî. MS. G.'s reading after पवुत्तो is worthy of note: जाव ण कहेदि देवी दाव कुमारिए &c.

P. 5, l. 11.—MS. G reads, very desirably, से after "जाव."

P. 5, l. 12.—गणदासः । प्रविश्य । The MSS. read प्रविश्य गणदासः in this place and similarly in almost every other place subsequently throughout the play, where the stage-direction, प्रविश्य So-and-So, occurs. But I have in all cases inverted the order, and given the name of the character first for the sake of uniformity.

P. 5, l. 13.—न पुनरस्माकं तु. With the use here of the two adversative particles, cf. S'âkuntala, Act VII., "किंतु अच्छरासंबन्धेण उण इमस्स बालअस्स जणणो इधज्जेव देवगुरुणो तवोवणे पसूदा," p. 176, l. 14, Calc. Ed. 1860.

P. 6, l. 2.—रुद्रेणेदमुमाकृतव्यतिकरे &c. The duality in unity of S'iva and his wife Pârvatî is represented as having but two sides between them, the left side of S'iva being the same as the person of Pârvatî, and *vice versa*, that is, S'iva and Pârvatî are one individual, the left portion of whose body is female (representing the goddess), and the right one male (representing the god). And as S'iva is fond of music and dancing, he is represented as dancing and singing with his consort thus united with him.

P. 6, l. 4.—बहुधा. Construe with भिन्नरुचेः.

P. 6, l. 9.—विज्ञाप्यताम्. 'Let (the Queen) be made to understand,' *i.e.* let her be informed, &c.

P. 7, l. 2.—मन्दायणीदीरे. Mandâkinî is a name that usually signifies 'the river of the air or heaven' (the Ganges or a feeder of it before it reaches the plains?); but it is also the name of an actual river flowing, according to the Vâyu Purâṇa, from the Riksha mountain. (See Vishṇu Purâṇa, p. 184. n. 70.) There is no doubt that the Mandâkinî of the present passage is a river of the Deccan. And further, it is probable that it may here stand for the *Narmadâ*, in conformity with a practice, still very common all over India, of designating any sacred river by the most sacred river-name, as Gangâ, &c. The apparent difficulty, however, would disappear by our reading with G, णम्मदा-[कूले] for "मन्दायणी"-[दीरे].

P. 7, l. 7.—जलमिव समुद्रशुक्तौ. Referring to the notion that drops of rain fallen under the auspices of the asterism or star *Arcturus* into the sea-shells produce pearls.

P. 7, l. 14.—लब्धक्षण:, 'who have obtained recess.' In क्षण the Marâṭhî reader will doubtless recognise his own word सण, a festival. For one of the secondary senses of क्षण is 'leisure,' 'vacation.' See note *infra* on p. 31, l. 1.

P. 8, l. 2.—किं प्रपद्यते वैदर्भ:, 'What is the king of the Vidarbhas about?' *i. e.* 'what does he mean?' प्रतिपद्यते, as read by G and also by Tullberg, would mean 'what does the Vidarbha say in reply?'

P. 8, l. 4.—MS. G reads लिखितम् in place of निदेशम्.

P. 8, l. 5.—पूज्येन. A term of respect applied to the person addressed, who is king Agnimitra in the present passage.

P. 8, l. 6.—प्रतिश्रुतसंबन्ध:, 'who had promised to become my relation.'

P. 8, l. 8.—मदपेक्षया, 'having regard to me,' *i. e.* 'if you do not wish to incur my displeasure.'—सकलत्रसोदर्य:, 'together with his wife and sister.'

P. 8, l. 14.—मौर्यसचिवं मम श्यालम्. The name of this brother-in-law of the king of the Vidarbhas is not known. As, however, he was the minister of the Maurya king of Pâṭaliputra, it seems probable that he was imprisoned by Agnimitra to prevent him from exciting the people to rebel against his (Agnimitra's) father, Pushpamitra, who had murdered the last of the Mauryas, Bṛihadratha, and usurped his throne in his son's favour. The imprisonment of Mâdhavasena, the intended brother-in-law of Agnimitra, by his cousin the king of the Vidarbhas, was only a retaliation for his brother-in-law's imprisonment by Agnimitra.

P. 9, l. 1.—अनात्मज्ञ:, 'foolish,' 'silly.' Cf. S'âkuntala Act VI., "प्रविश्य सक्रोधम् । मा तावदनात्मने! देवेन प्रतिषिद्धेपि मधूत्सवे चूतकलिकाभङ्गमारभसे."

P. 9, l. 3.—यातव्यपक्षे &c. The following is the natural order of the sentence: तत् यातव्यपक्षे स्थितस्य (वैदर्भस्य) उन्मूलनाय पूर्वसंकल्पितं वीरसेनप्रमुखं दण्डचक्रमाज्ञापय. यातव्यपक्षे स्थित: means 'standing under the category of those that make themselves liable to be attacked,' by provocation &c.

P. 9, l. 10.—तन्त्रकारवचनम्, viz. that quoted, or supposed to be quoted, by the minister in stanza 8. The *Tantras* do not usually teach politics, but they enjoin practices and ceremonies connected with the worship of S'akti. See Wilson's *Essays on the Religion of the Hindus*, Vol. I., pp. 247–250. It is perhaps possible, though by no means quite necessary, to understand तन्त्रकार in the present passage generally in the sense of शास्त्रकार.

P. 10, l. 10.—प्रभुः, predicated of सहायवानेव.

P. 10, l. 14.—व्यक्तिः. Cf. Raghuvaṁs'a, I. 10.

P. 10, l. 15.—त्वन्नीतिपादपस्य. The Nîti or intrigue here referred to is the creating of a feud between the two teachers of music as to their comparative merits, resulting in an actual exhibition of their powers of teaching by a dramatic representation, which gave the king an opportunity of seeing Mâlavikâ. Vidûshaka had also given the Parivrâjikâ her cue.

P. 11, l. 12.—पुरुषाधिकारमिदं ज्योतिः, equivalent to एतत्पुरुषाधिकारं ज्योतिः = एष पुरुषः अधिकारः अधिकरणं स्थानं यस्य तत्. None of our MSS. give the apparently easier reading 'पुरुषाकारं ज्योतिः,' as found in Tullberg's edition. On the contrary, cf. the following, as read by MS. G—'महत् खलु पुरुषाधिकरणमिदं ज्योतिः.'

P. 12, l. 2.—शिष्योपदेशकाले, 'at this time of the day, when you ought to be teaching your respective pupils.'

P. 12, l. 3.—तीर्थात्, 'गुरोः,' 'from my preceptor.' तीर्थ is another name for 'guru,' because he is 'one to whom honour is due.' It is not, I think, a proper name here, as Prof. Weber supposes.

P. 12, l. 4.—दत्तप्रयोगोस्मि, 'I have given lessons in the art of theatrical representation,' *i.e.* I am an experienced teacher of the art. प्रयोग has here the same sense as क्रिया in Act I., stanza 12.

P. 12, l. 6.—सोहम्, 'That I,' *i.e.*, and yet I, &c.

P. 12, l. 8.—अत्रभवत: किल. This is said ironically of Gaṇadâsa, who, we must suppose, used the simile at first to disparage his rival.

P. 12, l. 12.—समत्थं पडिण्णादं. 'Well challenged,' 'a good challenge that.' समत्थं is *reasonably.*

P. 12, l. 13.—प्रथम: कल्प:. 'That is the best course to follow.' Cf. S'akuntala पुढमो कप्पो Act IV., p. 75, l. 8; and प्रथम: कल्प: Act V., p. 114, l. 2; and Act. VII., p. 169, l. 11; Calc. Ed. 1860.

P. 12, l. 14.—तिष्ठतु तावत्. 'Let it be (lit. *stand*) a little while,' *i.e. wait a moment.* मन्यते for मन्येत, as very often.

P. 12, l. 18.—अमुं प्रस्तावं निवेद्य, 'mentioning this subject.' प्रस्ताव is उपस्थितं वस्तु. प्रस्तु is 'to put forth.' Cf. *infra,* p. 51, l. 10. Also Ratnâvalî, Act IV., "भद्र प्रस्तूयतां बहुविधमिन्द्रजालम्" p. 55, l. 10, Calc. Ed. Sam. 1921.

P. 13, l. 6.—G's reading प्रतिद्वन्द्विनो for केनचित् is certainly worthy of attention.

P. 13, l. 8.—राज्ञीशब्दभाजनम्, agreeing with आत्मानम्, which is always masculine singular, whatever the gender and number of the noun it refers to.

P. 13, l. 10.—भानो: परिग्रहादनल:. It is easy to see that this alludes to the supposed interest of the king in the cause of Haradatta, and the words चन्द्रोपि निशापरिगृहीत: to the queen's interest in the success of Gaṇadâsa.

P. 13, l. 12.—पीठमर्दिकम्. पीठमर्द means one who assists the Nâyaka, or lover, to obtain his mistress. And accordingly पीठमर्दिका means a woman who assists the Nâyikâ, or the mistress, in her endeavours to gain her lover. The Pratâparudra says, तत्सहाया: (= नायकस्य सहाया:) पीठमर्दविटचेटविदूषका: नायिकानुकूलने. And it defines पीठमर्द as being किंचिदून:, 'somewhat short of stature.' See *Pratâparudra,* Nâyaka Prakaraṇa, 40. In the present instance, also, the term पीठमर्दिका, as applied to the female ascetic, has the same sense that the Pratâparudra attaches to it. Having been previously taught by Vidûshaka what part she was to play in deciding the case of the two professors of music and dancing, the Parivrâjikâ is sent for by the King (p. 12, l. 18). She tells the Queen Dhâriṇî, when questioned by her, that Gaṇadâsa may safely venture on a competition with his rival (अलं स्वपक्षावसादशङ्कया &c. p. 13, l. 5). Further, she declares that it will be no sufficient criterion to examine the teachers orally, but that they must be judged by the performances of their respective pupils also (प्रयोगप्रधानं हि नाट्यशास्त्रम् किमत्र वाग्व्यवहारेण &c., p. 14, l. 18, and शिष्टा क्रिया &c., p. 15, l. 12, *et seq*). Again when the Queen says the teachers might make their pupils perform before the Parivrâjikâ alone, the latter replies that it would be unjust to make the decision of the case dependent upon a single individual's judgment (नैतन्न्याय्यम् &c., p. 17, l. 13). Having thus prevailed upon the Queen that she should allow Gaṇadâsa to prove his abilities by making Mâlavikâ, his pupil, perform before an assembly where the King should be present, she orders, taking as good care to avoid suspicion as an interested party could, that the teachers should bring forward their pupils unencumbered by their stage-dresses (निर्णयाधिकारे ब्रवीमि &c., p. 20, ll. 8, 9), thus contriving that the King should see Mâlavikâ in a state that would impress him most favourably. Further the Parivrâjikâ, to avoid any mischance, decides, doubtless somewhat partially, that so far as knowledge was concerned the teachers being equally old—though this was the very matter in dispute—Gaṇadâsa deserved precedence on the ground of his seniority by years (ननु समानेऽपि ज्ञानवृद्धभावे &c., p. 22, l. 5), and gives him the opportunity of presenting Mâlavikâ first. And lastly the ascetic, being questioned as to what she thought of the performance of Mâlavikâ, pronounces it to be a complete success (अङ्गैरन्तर्निहितवचनैः &c., p. 26, ll. 2—5). Having thus far contributed to the development of the King's passion for Mâlavikâ, she subsequently comes to the assistance of the girl by informing Vidûshaka of the consignment to a dark room of Mâlavikâ and her friend Bakulâvalikâ, and thus causing them to be liberated. It is on account of these her services to Mâlavikâ that the ascetic Kaus'ikî is called पीठमर्दिका.

P. 13, l. 15.—मङ्गलालंकृता, 'decorated with such dress and ornaments as she must wear as the wife of a living husband.' Cf. Vikramorvas'î, Act III., "सितांशुका मङ्गलमात्रभूषणा."

P. 13, l. 16.—अध्यात्मविद्यया, *i. e.* by the Upanishads, which abound in disquisitions on the nature &c. of the soul; *i.e.* 'like stern Simplicity accompanied by Wisdom.'

P. 14, l. 4.—धारिणीभूतधारिण्योः, 'of Dhâriṇî the queen, and of the earth, the supporter of the creation.'

P. 14, l. 15.—परिच्छेत्तुम् 'to distinguish,' (lit. *to measure*).

P. 14, l. 19.—वाग्व्यवहारेण. Cf. above, p. 12, l. 15.

P. 14, l. 20.—कथं वा देवी मन्यते. MS. G makes these words a part of the preceding speech of the Parivrâjikâ, an arrangement which has certainly something to recommend it.

P. 15, l. 2.—अनुमन्तुमर्हति &c. 'I pray that you may not allow or cause me to be beaten by one who is only my equal.' Gaṇadâsa means that, if the queen should not permit him to accept the challenge of Haradatta, he would be considered as inferior to his rival, whom he considers, at the most, his equal. मन्तुम् as read by MS. G, gives an equally good sense. समानविद्यतः परिभवनीयं मन्तुं नार्हति, 'Your Majesty ought not to be afraid lest I should be defeated by my rival.'

P. 15, l. 8.—उभयोः स्वाङ्गसौष्ठवाभिनयम्; *i. e.* उभयकर्तृकम् &c., exhibited by the teachers themselves in their own persons.

P. 15, l. 12.—श्लिष्टा क्रिया कस्यचिदात्मसंस्था. 'Of some the acting is excellent in their own persons,' *i. e.*, some excel as actors when they act personally, but they cannot teach others how to act well.

P. 16, l. 1.—णिण्डिदत्थो, *i. e.* गर्भितार्थः, 'her real sense.'

P. 16, l. 5.—अमेहाविणी. 'मन्दमेधाविणी,' G's reading, deserves attention.

P. 16, l. 8.—अद्रव्यपरिग्रहः. One of our MSS., E, has on its margin: सूक्ष्मबुद्धिः शिष्यो द्रव्यम् । तद्भिन्नो जडबुद्धिरद्रव्यम्.

P. 16, l. 9.—This speech is made quite intelligible by our reading it as follows with G :—जनान्तिकम् । गणदासं विलोक्य । कहं दाणिं । अलं अज्जउत्तस्स उच्छाहकालणं मणोरहं पूरिअ । प्रकाशम् । विरम णिरत्थआदो आरम्भादो. This is doubtless the true reading. The existence as well as the position of the direction प्रकाशम् is of vital importance to the proper understanding of the passage, and its connection with what follows. The absence of प्रकाशम् would make it impossible to explain how Vidûshaka comes to hear what the Queen whispers to Gaṇadâsa. Nor are the words "कहं दाणिं । अलं अज्जउत्तस्स उच्छाहकालणं मणोरहं पूरिअ," embodying a suspicion of Dhâriṇî as to the King's motives, intended to be heard by the latter. It is also evident that कहं दाणिं forms part of the whisper, and ought to follow the stage-direction जनान्तिकम् । गणदासं विलोक्य ।

P. 17, l. 2.—सरस्सईउवाअणमोदआइं. The 'modaka,' a dishful of which is offered as a present to the goddess Sarasvatî, and which is in reality given to the teacher, the minister of the goddess, is a round ball of a slightly conical shape at the top, made of rice or wheat flour stuffed with sugar, thin slices of the kernel of the cocoanut, together with spices, and then either boiled over steam, or fried in clarified butter. Such presents are not only made when the ceremony of giving the first lessons in an art is performed, but on many subsequent occasions when the goddess may be worshipped.

P. 17, l. 6.—परेण. Supply कृताम्.

P. 17, l. 9.—अइरोवणीदा, 'but lately made over to the preceptor for instruction.' उपनयनम् is lit. '*bringing up to*' (the tutor), 'initiation,' the beginning of a course of study.—All our MSS. except F, corroborated as they are by MS. G, assign this speech to the Queen (देवी). Attributed to Vidûshaka it must be taken to be ironical.

P. 17, l. 11.—अत एव, *i. e.* 'in order the more creditably to show my skill in teaching.'—On निर्बन्धः, cf. *infra*, p. 62, l. 13. Also S'âkuntala, Act III., "साहि अदो ज्जेव णिब्बन्धो" &c., p. 52, l. 13, Calc. Ed. 1860.

P. 18, l. 6.—प्रभवन्त्योपि, 'even when governing, even when allowed to domineer over their husbands.' The Parivrâjikâ does not mean that Dhâriṇî is not such a प्रभवन्ती, but that she should not abuse her privilege to such an extent as to be offended without cause.

P. 18, l. 11.—क्रियासंक्रान्तिम्, 'my ability to pass over to my pupil my skill in representation.'

P. 18, l. 13.—आसनादुत्तिष्ठति. Quite characteristic of the irascibility of the Brâhmaṇ character.

P. 18, l. 14.—अज्जो, said of Gaṇadâsa.

P. 19, l. 6.—एपहविस्सं &c. 'I shall be still mistress of my attendant.' That is, propose freely anything you like: if it be any way objectionable, I would still be able to check it, as Mâlavikâ is my servant.

P. 19, l. 7.—मम चेति ब्रूहि. A fine stroke of gallantry.

P. 19, l. 11.—उपदेशान्तरम्. MS. G reads उपदेशानारतम्यम्.

P. 20, l. 4.—ण हि &c. Translate: 'No, I am not hostile to your success, Gaṇadâsa,' *i. e.* 'Go, I wish you all success, Gaṇadâsa.' MS. G has a shorter and simpler reading: "देवी । विजअप्पत्थिणो अहं आअरिअस्स."

P. 20, l. 8.—निर्णयाधिकारे ब्रवीमि. This is said to avoid being misunderstood by the suspicious Queen.—सर्वाङ्ग &c. 'Let your pupils appear without their stage dresses, to enable us to discern more clearly the comparative excellences of their limbs' motions.' The reading of MS. G is perhaps an easier one, viz. "सर्वाङ्गाभिनयसौष्ठवाभिव्यक्तये विरलनैपथ्ययोः पात्रयोः प्रवेशोऽस्तु."

P. 20, l. 12.—जइ इदरेसु &c. Though this reading is quite intelligible, that found in G is certainly preferable, viz., "जइ ईरिसेसु विअ राजकज्जेसुवि ईरिसो उवाअणिउणदा अज्जउत्तस्स णं सोहणं हवे."

P. 20, l. 16.—परस्परयशःपुरोभागाः. This is equivalent to परस्परस्य यशसि (= यशोविषये) पुरोभागो येषां तैः *i. e.* परस्परस्य यशसि पुरोभागिनः 'not brooking the renown of each other,' or 'jealous of each other's fame.'

P. 21, l. 4.—उपहितमध्यमस्वरोत्था. It is difficult to say what उपहित means in this compound. May it mean 'highly-pitched' (scil. मध्यम)?

P. 21, l. 9.—भो &c. 'I say, do not be impatient, put on a grave mood and walk slowly; lest the Queen Dhâriṇî should find (or let not the Queen find) you inconsistent with yourself,' *i.e.* lest she should discover, by your impatience to go to the Sangîtas'âlâ, that the indifference you showed as to the result of the contest of the two masters of dancing and music was merely assumed, and that an intrigue lay at the bottom of the affair.* But adopting this

---

* Ms. G reads "विसंवारइस्सदि," but that reading may have arisen from writing र for द, as the two letters are so similar to each other in Telugu, especially in the Manuscripts: (ర and ద).

interpretation, we must read, with MSS. A B D E, "तुमं" in the passage as object to विसंवादइस्सदि. Another interpretation, however, is possible, and supported by one or two parallel passages from Kâlidâsa himself. It is this: 'walk slowly, lest the Queen Dhâriṇî should cause you to be disappointed;' *i.e.* 'having unwillingly given permission to Gaṇadâsa to bring Mâlavikâ before the King, she may yet withdraw her permission, seeing that you are so impatient to go to the music saloon as if you were interested in the matter of the examination.' In this case we must supply गणदासेन as the direct agent of the disappointment (विसंवाद) विसंवादइस्सदि is the causal of विसंवद्, to fail in fulfilling one's promise: *fidem fallere*, to promise and then not to do the thing promised. Cf. S'âkuntala, Act VI. "रमणोओ खु अवहो विहिणा विसंवदिदो" scil. रण्णा (p. 143, l. 11, Calc. Ed. 1860.) Also Vikramorvas'î, Act II., "तदो किं दाणिं तथ्थभोदी उव्वसी भवदो मणोरहकुसुमं दंसिअ फले विसंवददि." On the use of मा with the future, cf. S'âkuntala, p. 39, l. 14; p. 67, l. 5; p. 92, l. 10, Calc. Ed. 1860.

P. 21, l. 13.—स्वमनोरथस्येव शब्दः, 'as the sound of my desire that is going to be fulfilled.' In मनोरथ lurks a little pun, as the word literally means 'the chariot of (*i.e.* consisting of) the mind,' and as thus only can मनोरथ have a sound.

ACT II.

P. 22, l. 1.—MS. B has the following note in its margin on the opening of this Act:—

एष उत्तराङ्कस्य पूर्वाङ्कानुसंगतत्वादङ्कावतारः प्रवेशकविष्कम्भकादिशून्यः। प्रथमाङ्के विदू° । तेण हीत्यारभ्य अह वा मिभङ्गसद्दो ज्जेव्व उड्डावइस्सदोत्युपक्रमे मृदङ्गशब्दश्रवणानन्तरं सर्वाण्येव पात्राणि प्रथमाङ्कप्रक्रान्तानि पात्रसंक्रान्तदर्शनं द्वितीयाङ्कादावारम्भः। अङ्कावतारलक्षणं प्रतापरुद्रे।

यत्र स्यादुत्तराङ्कार्थः पूर्वाङ्कार्थानुसंगतः।
अमूच्चिताङ्कपात्रं तदङ्कावतरणं मनम्॥

P. 22, l. 7.—तेन हि, 'well then,' 'if so.' तेन हि corresponds here exactly with the Marâṭhî वरें तर मग.

P. 22, l. 7.—अत्रभवतोः, scil. आचार्ययोः.—एवमावेद्य स्वनियोगमशून्यं कुरु, 'tell them so, and go thou about thy business.' Lit. 'execute the command given to thee.' अशून्यं कुरु = अनुतिष्ठ. This means that he is to deliver the message to the teachers, and is not to return again to the king. No particular command (नियोग) is referred to. For similar instances of स्वनियोगमशून्यं कुरु, cf. S'âkuntala, p. 36, l. 19; p. 46, l. 13; p. 136, l. 7, Calc. Ed. 1860.

P. 22, l. 12.—तस्याश्चतुर्थवस्तुकप्रयोगं श्रोतुम्, 'to hear one-fourth of the whole piece performed with the gestures belonging to it.' MS. G reads चतुर्थवस्तुकं प्रयोगम्, which perhaps is a clearer reading than ours.

P. 22, l. 19.—MS. F, having given मक्षिकं as the Sanskrit of मक्खिअं, very properly remarks: "मक्षिकाशब्देन भारिणो कथ्यते."—अप्पमत्तो 'being cautious,' *i.e.* cautiously.

P. 23, l. 6.—सुस्वस्था भव. 'Be well composed,' 'do not be bashful.'

P. 23, l. 9.—प्रमृष्ट इव, 'as if they were planed off,' like boards that are thinned off by the plane, *i.e.* that were so smooth.

P. 23, l. 10.—मध्यः पाणिमितः, 'Her waist so narrow as that it may be *measured* (*i. e.* encompassed) by the fingers of the hand.'—G reads तुक्षदे पिए तरिसं.

P. 24, l. 9.—प्रणयगतिमदृष्ट्वा, 'not seeing how to tell me that she loves me.'

P. 24, l. 10.—इव, 'it seems as if.'

P. 25, l. 1.—अहो &c. Cf. S'âkuntala, Act VI. "अहो सर्वास्ववस्थासु रमणीयत्वमाकृतिविशेषाणाम्," p. 134, l. 16, Calc. Ed. 1860.

P. 25, l. 3.—संश्रितमितवलयम्, 'with the bangles collected round the wrist.'

P. 25, l. 4.—श्यामाविटपसदृशम्, 'like a branch of the s'yâmâ.' The s'yâmâ is commonly identified in this part of India with the वावांटी. On the simile cf. Ritusamhâra, III. 18:—

"श्यामा लताः कुसुमभारनतप्रवालाः
स्त्रीणां हरन्ति धृतभूषणबाहुकान्तिम् ।"

Cf. also S'âkuntala, p. 68, l. 8, Calc. Ed. 1860.

P. 25, l. 6.—ऋज्वायतार्धम्, = ऋजुः आयतार्धं यस्य तत्, 'in which the middle or the trunk is straight.' For आयतार्ध seems here to be applied to the trunk of the body from the neck to the waist.

P. 25, l. 7.—अज्जो. Referring to Gaṇadâsa.

P. 25, l. 11.—पङ्कच्छिद्, also called कतक, is what is known in Marâṭhi by the name of निवळी, whose dry fruit, reduced to powder, is still mixed with muddy water, when this is required to be freed from its impurities.

P. 26, l. 1.—MS. G reads यथादर्शनम् in place of यथाशास्त्रम्.

P. 26, l. 10.—श्यामायते. Cf. Raghuvams'a, I. 8. Also S'âkuntala, Act I., "आ परितोषाद्विदुषां न साधु मन्ये प्रयोगविज्ञानम्" &c., p. 2, l. 6, Calc. Ed. 1860.

P. 26, l. 12.—वृद्धिहेतुः, 'the cause of my success.' Lit. 'of my prosperity.'

P. 27, l. 1.—MS. G. has अहो प्रयोगाभ्यान्तरप्रश्नः. The same MS. has the following speech of Vidûshaka, in answer to the ridicule of the ascetic: *अयि पण्डितमण्णे किं अण्णं । मोदअखण्डणेवि ण समत्थासुमं, किं जाणासि । पसण्णचन्दपादसरिसेहिं केसपासेहिं एदाणं भोसिआसि ।

P. 28, l. 2.—परकीअंति करिअ, 'why, because it belongs to another,' Because it is not mine. The other reading noticed in our critical foot-notes "परकेरंति करिअ," is also what G reads. Adopting this latter version, we must, I think, supply some such word as 'करणिज्जं.' 'Why, because I have to do another person's work,' Vidûshaka referring to the Parivrâjikâ, who should give the reward to Mâlavikâ. It is not improbable that a covert allusion to the King might lurk in पर, and to his love to Mâlavikâ in केर.

P. 28, l. 7.—एत्तिओ मे विहवो भवन्तं सेविदुं, 'thus far, and no more can my genius go to serve you,' *i. e.* this is all I can do for you, for the rest you must shift for yourself. Cf. Vikramorvas'î, Act II., "भो णं भणामि चिन्तिदो मए दुल्लहजणसमागमोवाओ...... सिविणअसमागमकारिणं णिद्दं सेवदु भवं......एत्तिओ मे मदिविहवो."

P. 28, l. 9.—अलमलं परिच्छेदेन. That is, 'away with the supposition that what you have done already is all that you can do'; your ingenuity is not to stop here, but has to be exercised still further.

P. 28, l. 11.—द्वारपिधानमिव भृतेः, 'like a shutter of the entrance to pleasure.' On भृति, cf. *infrá*, p. 56, l. 7, 'भृतिपुष्पमयम्' &c.

P. 29, l. 8.—सौधानि अत्यर्थतापात् वलभिपरिचयद्वेषिपारावतानि. That is, अत्यर्थतापात् वलभिपरिचये द्वेषशीलाः पारावताः येषां तादृशानि सौधानि (वर्तन्ते). This means, that the sun had so much heated the sloping roofs of the palaces that the pigeons had left them, the place where, when the sun is not hot, they gather (परिचय) in large numbers. वलभि is the sloping roof of a house (especially that part of

* That is, अयि पण्डितमन्ये किमन्यत् । मोदकखण्डनेपि न समर्था त्वं किं जानासि । प्रसन्नचन्द्रपादसदृशैः केशपाशैरेतान्भीषयसि ।

it which is near the eaves) on which, there is nothing more common than to see large flocks of the green pigeons collected in the cool hours of the morning and evening in this country. Cf. Vikramorvas'î, Act III., "धूपैर्जालविनिःसृतैर्वडभ्यः संदिग्धपारावताः." सौध in this passage is any large house, a palace. In *valabhi* the Marâṭhâ will recognise the origin of his word पडवी.

P. 29, l. 9.—बिन्दूत्क्षेपान्पिपासुः, 'desirous of drinking the small drops of water,' thrown out by the wheel. For the भ्राम्निमद् वारियन्त्रम् (= भ्राम्यत् or भ्रमणं कुर्वत् वारियन्त्रम्) here referred to is doubtless the Persian wheel.

P. 30, l. 2.—होदि &c. It is also possible to render this speech thus: भवतो विशेषेण पानभोजनं त्वरयतु, 'May your Majesty be pleased to order that the dinner be quickly served.' This, however, though favoured by the form तुवरदु, would hardly be a suitable request to the Queen.

P. 31, l. 1.—गहीदक्खणोम्हि 'I have pledged my word, and will of course strive to redeem it at all hazards, and will not do any thing else till I have done so.' The word क्षण originally means 'a moment,' hence 'leisure,' 'vacation,' in which last sense our own Marâṭhî word सण, a festival, is derived from it. The phrase गहीदक्खणोम्हि has its origin in the following formula addressed to a Brahman, who, having been invited to a *s'râddha*, has come and is seated ceremoniously near the dish in which he is to dine at the end of the rite. The formula is:—

गृहीत्वामुकसंज्ञस्यामुकगोत्रस्य चामुके ।
श्राद्धे तु वैश्वदेवार्थे करणीयः क्षणस्त्वया ।
इत्येवं श्राद्धकृद् ब्रूयात्तं प्राप्नोतु भवानिति ।
स वदेत्प्राप्नवानीति इतरस्तं प्रति द्विजः ।
पित्रादेरप्यनेनैव वृणीत विधिना द्विजान् ।

S'aunakasmṛiti, 96, 11—

where the commentator observes: गृहीत्वेत्यत्र दक्षिणं जानु इति शेषः.

दक्षिणं जानुमालभ्येति स्पृशन्नरानुरोधात्, and where I think, we have to translate क्रियतां क्षणस्त्वया by 'May it please you to be at leisure for the s'râddha of' &c. (*i.e.* to be freed from every engagement,* *and attend to the S'râddha* &c.). The same formula is thus given by Gâlava, as quoted by Hemâdri :—

ॐ तथेति द्विजा ब्रूयुस्ते प्राप्नोतु भवानिति ।
कर्ता ब्रूयात्ततो विप्रः प्राप्नवानीति वै वदेत् ॥

After the formula is addressed, the Brahman is not to leave his seat or attend to any thing else, but is to remain seated and attentive to the S'râddha ceremony until it is finished. The person who addresses in the words of the formula (the श्राद्धकृत्) is said *to give the* क्षण, and the Brahman to whom it is addressed to *take the* क्षण, in the language of ignorant priests. Hence, because the word क्षण is so often used in the formula, so it has come, in the common parlance of Brâhmaṇs, who subsist mostly upon such occasional dinners at s'râddhas, and to which class our Vidûshaka belonged, to signify 'an engagement at a s'râddha, which, when once begun, must be carried out, on pain of incurring a sin.' It may be observed that Vidûshaka's way of expressing his obligation to accomplish what he has undertaken is perfectly in keeping with his character. क्षण घेणें, however, is still used in Marâṭhî in the sense of 'pledging one's self for the performance of a thing.' As, त्या कामाविषयीं आह्मीं क्षण घेतला आहे. *I have pledged myself to do that work, and am bound to do it at all hazards.* Cf. also S'âkuntala, Act II., p. 33, Calc. Ed. 1860.

P. 31, l. 2.—सुणोपरिचरो विअ विहंगमो, 'like a bird hovering over the shop of a butcher.'

---

* On this meaning of क्षण, cf. Dakshasmṛiti, *v.* 16, उदयास्तमयं यावन्न विप्रः क्षणिको भवेत्, on which passage Nâgoji Bhaṭṭa (Âhnikas'ekhara, II. *ad init.*) observes : "क्षणो निर्व्यापारः स्थितिः तद्युक्तो न भवेत्." Cf. also *supra*, p. 7, l. 14.

ACT III.

P. 32, l. 6.—संभाविमि, 'I will greet her,' 'ask her how she is doing.' संभावय् is what we mean by our समाचार घेणें. Cf. p. 71, l. 12.

P. 33, l. 5.—G reads "गणदासो उण्णमिदो उवदेसे."

P. 33, l. 6.—"किं" as read by G in place of our किंति is a good reading.

P. 34, l. 8.—तवणीआसोअस्स. This seems to mean an As'oka tree bearing flowers of golden colour. It was this As'oka only that had held off its blossom, as the red As'oka had already burst into flowers. See p. 38, l. 8, "रक्ताशोकरुचाविशेषित°." &c. Cf. also Ratnâvalî, Act I., "मअरन्दुड्डाणं गदुअ रत्तासोअपाअवतलसंट्ठाविदस्स भअदो कुसुमाऊहस्स पूआ णिव्वत्तिदव्वा" &c., p. 7. l, 22, Calc. Ed. Sam. 1921. Also Act I., "दाणिं सो रत्तासोअपादवो" &c., p. 9, l. 7, Id. Also p. 9, ll. 12, 16.

P. 35, l. 6.—प्रसक्ते निर्वाणे. 'The object of thy greatest desires being in thy embraces.'

P. 35, l. 7.—अलं भवदो धीरदं उज्झिअ परिदेविएण. Cf. Vikramorvas'î, Act II., "अलं भवदो परिदेविएण । अइरेण" &c.

P. 35, l. 12.—तवस्सिणी. Used simply as a word of pity, applied to Mâlavikâ in the present instance. It corresponds to the English 'poor' and the Latin 'miser.' Cf. also below, p. 53, l. 12.

P. 35, l. 13.—मणी &c. This refers to the notion that the cobra has a gem in his head. णिभो as read by G is a very good reading.

P. 36 l. 2.—कालान्तरक्षम:, 'able to bear delay.'

P. 36, l. 4.—ते विश्वसनीयमायुधम्, 'thy weapon apparently so harmless, being made of flowers.' Lit. विश्वसनीयम्, 'deserving to be trusted,' 'safe.' As a parallel passage, cf. S'âkuntala, कुतस्ते कुसुमायुधस्य सततेऽणम्" &c., p. 48, l. 5, Calc. Ed. 1860.

P. 36, l. 7.—ता पज्जवत्थावेदु अत्ताणं तत्तभवं. 'Be pleased, Sir, to have patience,' 'Pray compose yourself.' Cf. Vikramorvas'î, Act I., हला उव्वसी पज्जुवत्थावेहि अत्ताणअं" &c.

P. 36, l. 10.—वसन्तपुढमावदारसूअभाणि &c., 'indicative of the first manifestation (on earth) of spring.' पुढम, 'first,' in the year. Cf. Vikramorvas'î, Act II. "वसन्तावदारसूइदस्स अहिरामत्तं पमदवणस्स."

P. 37, l. 6.—विहन्तुम्. Used passively.—बहवः खण्डनहेतवो हि दृष्टाः, 'Many are the pretexts under which I can disappoint her.'—उपचारविधिर्मनस्विनीनां न तु पूर्वाभ्यधिकोपि भावशून्यः. On this passage, cf. Vikramorvas'î, Act II., "प्रियवचनकृतोपि योषितां दयितजनानुनयो रसादृते प्रविशति हृदयं न तद्विदाम्" &c.—मनस्विनीनाम्. Objective genitive.

P. 37, l. 7.—न तु......भावशून्यः. Supply वरं as predicate from the preceding line.

P. 37, l. 9.—G reads चित्तप्पाडिट्ठिदं for our "अन्तेउरपाडिट्ठिदं."

P. 38, l. 1.—अभिजातः, 'nobly sympathising.' On the meaning of this word compare also the following from the Kuvalayânanda :—

प्रदानं प्रच्छन्नं,गृहमुपगते संभ्रमविधिः,
निरुत्सेको लक्ष्म्यामनभिभवगन्धाः परकथाः ।
प्रियं कृत्वा मौनं,सदसि कथनं चाप्युपकृतेः
श्रुतेत्यन्तासक्तिः,पुरुषमभिजातं कथयति ॥

P. 38, l. 5.—दक्षिणो मारुतः. 'the south wind.' Cf. Vikramorvas'î, Act II., "भणालविभ....भगन्तुकेण दक्खिणमारुएण."

P. 38, l. 13.—रक्ताशोकरुचाविशेषितगुणो बिम्बाधरालक्तकः = बिम्बसदृशोधरो यस्याः सा बिम्बाधरा स्त्री । बिम्बसदृशोधरो वा बिम्बाधरः । तस्यास्तस्य वा अलक्तकः बिम्बाधरालक्तकः । स रक्ताशोकस्य रुचा रक्तिम्ना अविशेषितगुणः अविशेषितः नीचीकृतः जितो वा गुणो रक्तत्वरूपो यस्य सः । 'By the beauty of the (flowers of the) red-flowered As'oka the red dye of women's lips is defeated.' अविशेषितगुणः is the predicate here, and बिम्बाधरालक्तकः the subject. It is also possible, though not so good, to read रक्ताशोकरुचा विशेषितगुणो बिम्बाधरालक्तकः, 'The red colour of the bimba-lip of the Vernal Beauty is heightened in quality (विशेषितगुणः) by that of the red-flowered As′oka.' In this case बिम्बाधरालक्तकः must be considered to mean बिम्बमेव बिम्बरूपो वा माधव्याः श्रियः योधरस्तस्य अलक्तकः रक्तिमा. But, as suggested above, this latter interpretation is not so good. बिम्बाधरालक्तकः must refer to the red lac women apply to their lips, as do विशेषक and तिलकक्रिया in the following lines to the marks on the forehead and on the intervening space between the brows, respectively.

P. 38, l. 14.—Vis′eshaka is the mark on the forehead.—कुरबकं &c. Cf. Vikramorvas′î, Act II., "कुरबकं श्यामं द्वयोर्भागयोः" &c.

P. 38, l. 15.—Tilaka signifies the Tila-like mark between the brows.

P. 38, l. 16.—श्रीमाधवी. On this personification of the Vernal Beauty, cf. Vikramorvas′î, Act II., "निषिञ्चन्माधवीं लक्ष्मीं लतां कौन्दीं च लासयन्." Also many other passages *passim* in Raghuvaṁs′a and Ritusaṁhâra.

P. 40, l. 2.—सीधुपाणुव्वेज्जिअस्स &c. Vidûshaka seems to mean that the King, who is already maddened by his passion for Mâlavikâ, will be still more so, when he sees her alone, just as a man that is already intoxicated by drink and is helpless under its influence is rendered still more helpless by drinking or eating anything that is sweet. On Vidûshaka's simile, see S′âkuntala, Act II., "भो जधा पिण्डीखज्जूरेहिं" &c., p. 38, Calc. Ed. 1860.

P. 41, l. 1.—नितम्बबिम्बे. Cf. p. 49, l. 10.

P. 41, l. 4.—शरकाण्डपाण्डुगण्डस्थला, 'with her cheeks turned pale white like the inner part of the S′ara grass.'

P. 41, l. 8.—एवम्, scil. 'मअणवाहिणा परिमिट्ठा' इति.

P. 41, l. 9.—ललिअदोहलापेक्खी. See p. 54, l. 5.

P. 41, l. 15.—किसलयपुटभेदसीकरानुगतः, 'किसलयपुटभेदेभ्यो निर्गतैः सीकरैरन्वितः.'

P. 42, l. 3.—अवेक्षते, 'cares for,' 'gives heed to.' Lit. 'sees,' 'looks at.' On the fondness of the elephant for the lotus, cf. the following from the Kuvalayânanda:—

रात्रिर्गमिष्यति भविष्यति सुप्रभातं
भास्वानुदेष्यति हसिष्यति पङ्कजश्रीः।
इत्थं विचिन्तयति कोशगते द्विरेफे
हा हन्त हन्त नलिनीं गज उज्जहार ॥

Also—

रवितप्तो गजः पद्मांस्तद्गृह्यान्त्राधितं ध्रुवम्।
सरो विशति न स्नातुं गजस्नानं हि निष्फलम्॥

G's reading deserves notice: "न हि कमलिनीं सरितं दृष्ट्वा ग्राहं गणयति मत्तगजः"

P. 42, l. 10.—तत्त्वावबोधैकरसो न तर्कः, 'Nor does conjecture like to acquaint me with that only which is true;' *i.e.* it is no use to try my skill in conjecture, as this may as probably lead me to what is not the truth.

P. 42, l, 14.—अप्पिअमअणसंदेसा, 'अर्पितो मदनसंदेशो यस्यै सा.' 'Charged with your message of love.' She had not yet delivered the message to Mâlavikâ, and so we cannot say, अर्पितो मदनसंदेशो यया.

P. 43, l. 2.—अहंवि दाणिं एदं ण विसुमरेमि. 'Even *I* have not forgotten it.' It is easy to see the ludicrousness of the remark.

P. 43, l. 7.—G reads, not perhaps undesirably, simply "जोग्गदाए," and not दोहलकरणजोग्गदाए.

P. 43, l. 8.—सालत्तअं. It was not only the sole of the foot that was to be besmeared with the red dye, but the whole foot up to the ankle. See p. 49, l. 7, "आर्द्रालक्तकं चरणं." Cf. also Ratnâvalî, Act III., "आत्मानमपनयामि विलक्ष एष लाक्षाकृतां चरणयोस्तव देवि मूर्ध्ना," p. 42, ll. 9, 10, Calc. Ed. Sam. 1921.

P. 43, l. 10.—अलं सुहिददाए. 'Do not consider thyself happy that,' &c. सुहिददाए is the reading of all our MSS. corroborated by G. सुखितता would seem to be the same as सुखिना. On the latter, cf. S'âkuntala, Act VII., "अनेन कस्यापि कुलाङ्कुरेण स्पृष्टस्य गात्रे सुखिना मन्येवम्" &c., p. 175, l. 11, Calc. Ed. 1860.

P. 43, l. 11.—कहं दाणिं अत्ताणं मोएअं? 'How shall I now free myself?' Mâlavikâ means that she feels her life to be a burden, from which she would fain be free.—अह वा &c. 'Or why should I devise a means of putting an end to this life? Death is soon to follow of its own accord; and this decoration is only like that which a *Satî* or any other devoted woman undergoes as a preparation for death.'

P. 44, l. 13.—G has "अलंकारो" in place of our अहिआरो.

P. 45, l. 4.—आर्द्रापराधम्. This can either mean, 'who has committed a gentle fault,' *i.e.* who has tripped in the matter of some delicate subject; or 'whose fault is fresh,' *i. e.* not yet forgotten. I prefer the latter.

P. 45, l. 5.—पारइस्ससि &c. That is, 'You will marry her, so as one day or other to be able to ask her forgiveness' for a fault; an opportunity so much coveted by lovers. G reads very differently; *i.e.*, पसादइस्ससि अत्तभोदोए अवरध्धं अत्ताणं (= प्रसादयिष्यसि अत्रभवत्याः अपराद्धमात्मानम्). But प्रसादयिष्यसि आत्मानम् in the sense of 'you will appease her' is hardly satisfactory. पारय् in the sense of 'being able,' is a word of very frequent occurrence in Prâkrit. Cf. S'âkuntala, p. 62, l. 9; p. 81, l. 14; p. 140, l. 13; Calc. Ed. 1860. Also Ratnâvalî, p. 33, l. 11; p. 46, l. 24; p. 51, l. 3; Calc. Ed. Sam. 1921.

P. 45, l. 6.—परिगृहीतम् &c. This does not refer to any knowledge that Vidúshaka possessed of the art of foretelling, but simply to the notion that a blessing given by a Brahman is fulfilled by the gods. Cf. Vikramorvas'î, Act II., "प्रतिगृहीतं ब्राह्मणवचनम्."

P. 45, l. 7.—G reads मुक्तमदा instead of उन्मत्तवेषा.

P. 46, l. 1.—वसन्दोवआअणलोल्लेण. See note on सोथ्थिवाअणमोदएहिं, p. 82, l. 11.

P. 47, l. 3.—पिपीलिआदंसणं. It is doubtless the red ants living on trees that are meant here. They are known in Konkaṇ by the name of हुमले. The mango-tree is a very favourite abode of them. They configure its leaves into hollow globular nests for themselves.

P. 47, l. 13.—महदो खु से संभावणा. 'This is indeed a great honour conferred upon her by Dhâriṇî.' संभावय् is 'to honour,' 'to pay regard to,' 'to attend to,' 'to visit.' Cf. S'âkuntala, Act II., "अहे संभावइदव्वम्हि," p. 45, l. 5; Act VI., "अनुगृहीतास्मि अनया मघवत: संभावनया," p. 163, l. 13; Calc. Ed. 1860. Also Ratnâvalî, p. 3, l. 22; p. 60, l. 21; Calc. Ed. Sam. 1921. Raghuvaṁs'a V. 11.

P. 48, l. 4.—ठाणे, because she is struck with Mâlavikâ's beauty.

P. 49, l. 2.—सिध्धं मे दोच्चं, 'I have done my work,' referring to her commission of painting Mâlavikâ's feet. G reads णेवच्छं for our "दोच्चं."

P. 49, l. 8.—प्रतिपन्न: &c. The king means that the present were a very fit opportunity for him to serve the lady Mâlavikâ, but that he regrets he cannot avail himself of it, as he does not yet know whether she loves him. G has किं नावकाश: for सेवावकाश:.

P. 49, l. 9.—कुदो दे अणुसओ &c. 'Why do you regret that you could not use this occasion and show yourself ready to serve her? You will be able shortly to do all this, and will then continue to do so for a long time.' Unless we suppose that Vidûshaka is not very classical in the use of his words, अनुशय does not seem here to be used in its usual sense. It properly means the regret felt at having done or having omitted to do something that a person might not or might have done. (See S'âkuntala, e.g., p. 137, l. 1; p. 145, l. 1; p. 182, l. 17: Calc. Ed. 1860.) In the present passage, however, the King might not, with any propriety, have presented himself before, and made himself serviceable to, Mâlavikâ.

P. 49, l. 15.—अवचणीअं मन्तेसि, 'You talk nonsense.' मन्त्रय् is properly 'to mutter in a low voice,' as a mantra, from which word the verb is derived. But in the present passage, as also very often in Prâkrit, मन्त्रय् means simply 'to speak.' When Bakulâvalikâ says, in answer to Mâlavikâ's remark, मन्तिदव्वं एव्व मए मन्तिदं, she plays upon the word मन्तिदव्वं, which means both 'that which deserves to be said,' and also 'that which one has to say,' *i. e.* is commissioned to say. As for Bakulâvalikâ's commission on the present occasion, see p. 35, l. 8 *et seqq.*

P. 50, l. 8.—पुढमं भणिदं विअ हदासाए उत्तरं. 'The wench has her answers, as it were, learned by rote.' Nipuṇikâ means that Bakulâvalikâ's answers to the questions of Mâlavikâ are given in such a ready way, as if she had been taught by some one previously what answers to give if such and such questions should be asked, and such and such difficulties started, by Mâlavikâ. गुणिदं as read by MS. G, as well as by Tullberg in place of our "भणिदं," has the same meaning, 'repeated,' 'got or learned by rote, by repetition.'—हदासा is a slang word corresponding to the Marâṭhî मेलो, so often used by our illiterate women.

P. 51, l. 1.—अप्पणो छन्देण. Cf. Vikramorvas'î, Act III., "विज्ञाप्यतां देवी यस्तव छन्द इति."

P. 51, l. 7.—दुब्जादा. An abusive word of endearment (though not always), like हदासा.—अच्चन्तसहाइणी. अच्चन्त, because the enterprise is so difficult.

P. 51, l, 8.—विमद्दसुरही, 'giving more and more fragrance the closer it comes in contact with us.' Bakulâvalikâ puns upon her own name, which literally means a garland of Bakula flowers. And she means, that as such a garland gives more and more fragrance the longer it is worn in close contact with the body, so her serviceableness will be known by degrees, as Mâlavikâ comes more and more in contact with her, *i. e.*, becomes better acquainted with her. On विमर्द cf. S'âkuntala, p. 178, l. 8, Calc. Ed. 1860.

P. 51, l, 10.—प्रस्तुतेन (वाक्येन) 'putting forth her errand.' Literally, 'with her words put forth.' Cf. note on p. 12, l. 18, *suprá.*

P. 51, l. 11.—प्रत्याख्याने, such as " अवचणोअं मन्तेसि," " एदं एव्व मइ णत्थि' &c.

P. 51, l. 12.—स्थापिता स्वे निदेशे, *i.e.* 'वशीकृता.' G. has नियोगे in place of our " निदेशे."

P. 52, l. 1.—कारिदं एव्व &c. 'Bakulâvalikâ has already induced Mâlavikâ to enter upon the enterprise of trying to become the King's bride.' पदं कृ is 'to set foot upon,' 'to enter.' And so in the present passage कारिदं पदं means 'has induced her to go with her to do as she (Bakulâvalika) would direct.' See S'âkuntala, p. 81, ll. 8, 9, Calc. Ed., for a similar though not quite parallel passage. The Banglaore MS. G has quite a different reading in this place ; इज्जे पेख्ख असंपेख्खिअकारित्तणं वउलावलिआए एदं पदं मालविआए ।

P. 53, l. 5.—एतावता, scil. सादरोत्कण्ठितयुक्तेन " किं भट्टा" इति प्रश्नेन. On पर्याप्तम्, cf. Vikramorvas'î, Act II., " सुदं ण उण पज्जत्तं हिअअस्स."

P. 53, l. 6.—अनादरोत्कण्ठितयो: &c. The King means, that now that he has learned that Mâlavikâ is as anxious and love-sick as he himself, and that he is himself the object of her passion, he would not care even if he and his mistress should die without ever being joined in actual wedlock. For he had rather that two persons loving each other equally should never be able to marry, than that, if they are not really passionate of each other, but one of them indifferent (अनादर), and the other panting with love, they should come in contact and be married. G reads अनातुरोत्कण्ठितयो: for अनादरोत्कण्ठितयो:.

P. 53, l. 10.—सलीलम्, 'playfully,' 'gracefully.'

P. 53, l. 12.—अत्र चरणमर्पयति. 'Blesses him with her foot,' *i.e.* touches or kicks him with her foot. Here अत्र = अस्मिन्.

P. 53, l. 13.—सदृशविनिमयात्. सदृश, because both were red.—आत्मानं वञ्चितं मन्ये. 'I consider myself as the only unfortunate one.' The King means, that both the As'oka and the lady Mâlavikâ have honoured each the other, the As'oka having been favoured by the latter with the graceful touch of her lovely foot, and the lady having received in return a bud or sprout of young leaves to make a pendant of for her ear; but that he (the King) himself has unfortunately exchanged nothing as yet with the object of his love. वञ्चित means 'passed over' or 'disregarded in distribution,' 'void of,' 'wanting in.' Cf. Raghuvaṁs'a, VII. 8, "तद्वञ्चितवामनेत्रा." Cf. also S'âkuntala, p. 17, stanza 1, "चलापाङ्गां" &c., Calc. Ed. 1860.

P. 54, l. 3.—संभावित: 'honoured.' See note on p. 47, l. 13.

P. 54, l. 5.—दोहलं ललितकामिसाधारणम् 'a desire common with persons fond of the graceful actions of young women,' viz., the desire to be kicked by them. ललितकामी, 'स्त्रीविलासितकामी' 'विलसनशील: कामी' वा. Cf. also stanza 12, above.

P. 54, l. 6.—प्रवेष्टुमिच्छामि. Cf. the very similar scene in S'âkuntala, Act. III., "अवसर: खल्वयमात्मानं दर्शयितुम्." &c., p. 58, l. 4, Calc. Ed. 1860.

P. 54, l. 14.—गहीदत्थाए, 'who knewest the fact, namely, that the As'oka belongs to His Majesty the King.' गहीदत्था means 'informed,' 'made aware of.' It is used absolutely, however, and does not always require to be joined, like the Latin 'certior factus,' to its object. Lit. it signifies, 'one who has taken the sense.' See above p. 52, l. 15. Also S'âkuntala, p. 132, l. 3, Calc. Ed. 1860. Also Vikramorvas'î, Act II., "णं गहीदत्था होहि."

P. 55, l. 10.—संप्रति बाधा. Supply अस्ति किम्.

P. 56, l. 7.—भृतिपुष्पम्, 'यादृशं [= पादताडनानुभवसुखानन्तरम्] पुष्पमशोके बद्धा तादृशं भृतिपुष्पं [पादताडनाद्यनुभवसुखरूपं पुष्पम्]. The पुष्प as referred to the King is the gratification he will feel after Mâlavikâ should comply with his entreaty.

P. 56. l. 9.—णं असोओ &c. We have here adopted the reading of G, as being probably more correct than that of our MSS., which read: "णं असोओ कुसुमं ण दंसेदि | अअं उण ण केवलं फुल्लइ फलइ एव."

P. 56, l. 10.—फलइ अ. This refers to the children that Mâlavikâ would bear to the King. The coarseness of the allusion is in keeping with the character of Irâvatî.

P. 56, l. 12.—प्रतिपत्तिः. Cf. Raghuvams'a, III. 45, "विषादलुप्तप्रतिपत्ति" &c.

P. 56, l. 13.—जङ्घाबलं एव्व. 'No other way of getting out of this scrape but by taking to our heels.'

P. 57, l. 9.—संधिच्छेअसिक्खको, 'One that punishes or wants to punish a crime of house-breaking.' With संधिच्छेद. cf. संधिचौर, a house-breaker. शिक्षक, properly a teacher, is used here in its modern sense, 'a chastiser,' or 'punisher.' G. reads "संधिच्छेअसिक्खी होमि" &c. On the simile, cf. Vikramorvas'î, Act II., "लोत्तेण सूइदअस्स कुम्भीलअस्स णत्थि वाआ पलिविधाणं."

P. 57, l. 11.—मया. This is to be construed with विनोदितः, and not with चिरायसि.

P. 58, l. 2.—अण्णहा दुःखतरं एव्वं ण करेमि. 'Otherwise (*i.e.* had I known that you have obtained such a thing to while away your time with), I would not have been the cause of so much annoyance to you' by intruding upon your privacy. दुक्खतरं एव्वं ण करेमि seems to be rather a difficult passage. This is, however, the reading of all our MSS.* If the reading is not corrupt, the poet appears to have intended that Irâvatî's words should express the sense of the easier speech of Queen Aus'înarî in Vikramorvas'î, Act II., "दुरागदं दाणिं मे संवुत्त."

P. 58, l. 5.—समापत्तिदिट्ठेण, 'यदृच्छया दृष्टेन.'

P. 58, l. 6.—एत्थ तुमं एव्व प्पमाणं. 'You only are an authority for such a doctrine.' Or 'do as you like, we must obey.'

---

* G reads दुक्खरं &c.

P. 59, l. 3.—परिचयवति मयि. 'Against me, who am so familiar with you.' He means that the entreaties of the zone in his favour, being not an ordinary intercession, should be minded by Irâvatî. The pun upon the word चरणपतित is apparent. To read परिचयवतो, and construe it with अवधीरणा, would be to suppose, that the King was always similarly upbraided by Irâvatî for his intrigues.

P. 59, l. 10.—अभ्यपेक्षाच्युतेन. 'fallen or dropped unexpectedly.'

P. 59, l. 14.—आलम्बते, 'holds up as if to strike the King with it.' G reads "रशनां हस्तमालम्बते."

P. 60, l. 4.—किदप्पसादोसि. Ironical.

P. 60, l. 7.—जाव अङ्गारओ रासिं विअ सा अणुवक्कं ण करेइ, 'as long as she does not return with vengeance like the planet *Mars*,' which, when it turns back retrogressively to any sign of the zodiac, exercises a malignant influence upon the fortunes of any one that may have been born under the auspices of that sign. It is not only *Mars* that performs such a retrogressive journey in the zodiac, but all the planets except the Sun and the Moon. But why *Mars* in particular is mentioned by the author is uncertain.

P. 60, l. 10.—प्रियाहृतमनाः. This alludes to the King's passion for Mâlavikâ.—प्रणिपातलङ्घनं सेवासु, because Irâvatî thereby affords him a pretext for neglecting her. Cf. Vikramorvas'î, Act II. *ad fin.* "किं तु प्रणिपातलङ्घनादहमपि तस्यां धैर्यमवलम्बिष्ये."

ACT IV.

P. 61, l. 3.—तामाश्रित्य &c. That is, श्रुतिपथगतायां तस्यां विषये या आस्था तया करणेन लब्धं मूलं येन सः = श्रुतिपथगतमालविकासंबन्धिनी या आस्था तदेव मूलं यस्य सः. The agent to आश्रित्य is आस्थया.

P. 61, l. 4.—रूढरागप्रवालः i.e., रूढो रागः प्रीतिरेव प्रवालो येन सः.

P. 61, l. 5.—हस्तस्पर्शे मुकुलित इव &c. Cf. Vikramorvas'i, Act I. "स्पृष्टं सरोमकण्टकमङ्कुरितं मनसिजेनेव." MS. G has "हस्तस्पर्शैर्मुकुलित इव."

P. 61, l. 16.—विडालगहीदाए परहुदिआए. This must probably refer to a tame cuckoo kept in a cage, as it is otherwise difficult to see how a cat can catch a wild one.

P. 62, l. 1.—पिङ्गलच्छीए (= पिङ्गलाक्ष्या). This refers to Queen Dhâriṇî.

P. 62, l. 1.—सारभण्डभूमिघरए. A भूमिघर is a cellar, or a compartment under ground. सारभण्डभूमिघर seems to mean a cellar which was used as a storehouse, or as a room to keep provisions in. The cellars are of course dark.

P. 62, l. 3.—मत्संपर्कम् &c. MS. G reads, "मत्संबन्धमुपलक्ष्य."

P. 62, l. 7.—देविं सुहं पुच्छिदुं, 'inquire after the Queen's health,' as she was suffering from the fall. MS. G has "सुहपुच्छिआ."

P. 62, l. 8.—किं ण लक्खिदो &c. This is a somewhat difficult passage, if not corrupt. The meaning, however, is pretty clear. Translate: 'Why is it I have not seen lately our dear one?' referring to the King. The other said, 'Little is the regard he pays you now, since he is no longer *your* beloved, but of your maid-servant. Do you not know that?' मन्दो वो उवआरो literally means, 'scanty is his salutation to you,' *i. e.* he does not care to come and pay his respects to you. परिजणस्स वल्लहत्तणं does not mean परिजणो रण्णो वल्लहो जादो, but is equivalent to 'राआ परिजणस्स वल्लहो, ण उण

नुह.' MS. G's reading is worthy of attention, as throwing some light on our interpretation of the passage: "तदो देवीए [सा] पुच्छिदा किं आलिक्खिदो वल्लहोत्ति। ताए उत्तं जं देवि -[दे ?]- परिअणस्स वल्लहत्तणं ण जाणिअ पुच्छुसित्ति," where "किं आलिक्खदो वल्लहो" = 'Did you see the dear one?'

P. 62, l. 11.—शङ्कयति, scil. शृण्वन्तं जनं, राज्ञोसदृशम्.

P. 62, l. 13.—अविणअं अन्तरेण = 'अविनयविषये,' 'with reference to your fault or misconduct.' The अविनय here referred to is the conversation between the King and Mâlavikâ in the last preceding Act. See pp. 55, 56 *suprâ.* On अन्तरेण cf. S'âkuntala, Act V., "देवीं हंसवतीमन्तरेण" &c., p. 104, l. 4, Calc. Ed. 1860.

P. 62, l. 14.—परिगहीदत्था. See note on p. 54, l. 14, *suprâ.*

P. 63, l. 1.—तत्रभवत्याः, referring to Iravatî.

P. 63, l. 3.—पादालवासं, humourously applied to the cellar.—णाअकण्णआ विअ, 'like the daughters of the Nâgas,' a race of fabled beings, distinguished for their beauty, and supposed to live in the nether regions (पातालं).

P. 63, l. 7.—प्रबलपुरोवाता, 'accompanied by a violent gale.' Cf. Vikramorvas'î, Act IV., "प्रबलपुरोवातनर्तितशिखण्डः."

P. 63, l. 11.—G has, very desirably, "मालविआ बउलावलिएत्ति."

P. 64, l. 1.—सुणादि (= शृणोति), for शृणुयान्.

P. 64, l. 4.—रत्तचन्दणधारिणा. The रक्तचन्दन or red sandal is devoid of any fragrance. Slight wounds and bruises are supposed to be healed when besmeared with it. The principal effect said to be secured by the use of the red sandal, however, is the relief it gives to the inflamed part. See p. 69, l. 7, शीतक्रिया चास्य प्रशस्ता.

P. 64, l. 8.—अरित्तपाणि &c. 'Shall get some flowers to present the Queen with.'

P. 64, l. 10.—जयसेनायाः संवेद्य. Jayasenâ's assistance was to be used in putting into practice the dodge for bringing the Queen's ring, and thereby liberating Mâlavikâ and her friend Bakulâvalikâ.

P. 65, l. 2.—अतः परं पुनः कथयिष्यामि. 'From this point I will resume it afterwards.'

P. 65, l. 7.—मां च पीडयितुम्. See note on p. 19, l. 7.

P. 65, l. 11.—दाणिं विसेसो. 'It is a little better now.' Literally विसेसो or विशेषः means 'difference,' 'a change,' viz. for the better. See an exactly similar passage in S'âkuntala, Act III., "अम्मो अत्थि विसेसो," p. 71, l. 6, Calc. Ed. 1860. MS. G omits दाणिं altogether.

P. 66, l. 1.—आआरपुप्फ° &c. With this compound compare आचारलाजाः &c., so often occurring in Raghuvaṁs'a and elsewhere. Raghuvaṁs'a, II. 10, "आचारपुष्पाणि," 'flowers which it is required by the custom of the good (आचार = शिष्टाचार) to take with one's self when on a visit to a god or great personage.'

P. 66, l, 3.—जीविदसंसए, 'to this danger to his life.' जीविदसंसओ would literally mean, 'doubt whether the life will be preserved or no.' Cf. *infrâ* p. 79, l. 14, and p. 105, l. 12. See also Ratnâvalî, p. 41, l. 20; p. 60, l. 16, Calc. Ed. Sam. 1921.

P. 67, l, 2.—सिमिसिमाअन्ति. This is an imitative verb, expressive of a tremulous and aching sensation, probably convulsive. Probably our Marâṭhî शिवशिवणें may owe its origin to this word.

P. 67, l. 6.—प्रकृतिभीरुस्तपस्वी. 'The poor Brahman is naturally timid. On 'तपस्वी,' see note on p. 35, l. 12 above.—ध्रुवसिद्धेरपि &c 'He has no confidence in the success of even Dhruvasiddhi, blessed as the latter always is with success.' For Dhruvasiddhi literally means, *one who is always successful* (ध्रुवा सिद्धिर्यस्य सः).

P. 67, l. 8.—ओअरक्खेमं वहेहि, 'take upon yourself the care of the welfare of my old mother.' मुद्धा, 'simple,' 'silly,' and therefore unable to support herself. MS. G reads थविराए for "मुद्धाए."

P. 68, l. 8.—उदकुम्भविहाणे सप्पमुद्दिअं कंपि अण्णेसोअदुत्ति. This seems to mean, that Dhruvasiddhi was to take a ring having the image of a snake engraved on it, and put it upon the lid of a pitcher full of water, and then having encharmed the pitcher with his mantras, was to use the water as a specific to effect the cure of the snake-bite. The use of encharmed water for curing a snake-bite is a well known recipe. But I have found the particular mode, here referred to as followed by Dhruvasiddhi, noticed nowhere else. MS. G reads the passage somewhat differently: "धुवसिध्धी विण्णेवदि उदकुम्भपिहाणे सप्पमुद्दिअं कप्पिइदव्वं [कप्पइदव्वं ?] । तं अण्णेसिअदुत्ति." If our interpretation is correct, this reading seems to be easier than our own. Prof. Weber, I do not know on what authority, considers उदकुम्भ as a proper noun.

P. 68, l. 12.—कर्मसिद्धौ. 'After the business is done.' That is, as soon as Gautama is cured of the snake-bite.

P. 69, l. 2.—पकिदिथ्थो, 'प्रकृतिं प्रतिपन्नः.' That is, 'he is made as sound as he was before the accident.' Cf. p. 87, ll. 5, 6. Cf. also S'âkuntala, p. 176, l. 1; p. 179, l. 15: Calc. Ed. 1860.

P. 69, l. 4.—एसो अमच्चो &c. A contrivance for the King to bring his interview to an end. G very properly inserts 'उण' after एसो.—अणुग्गहीदुं. Used passively.

P. 69, l. 14.—समाप्तकृत्यो गौतमः. Alluding to the liberation of Mâlavikâ and her friend by means of the Queen's ring.

P. 70, l. 3.—प्रयोगम्. Referring to the contrivance by which the Queen was made to give the ring.

P. 70, l. 6.—मङ्गलकज्जाइं. A *mangala kârya* is any religious work, the performance of which is associated with joy and prosperity; *e.g.*, the marriage ceremony, the thread ceremony, &c. All precautions are taken that no obstacle of any kind should interrupt the progress of such ceremonies or works. Vidûshaka by applying the term to what he has done means, that he has fortunately performed his great mission without any let or hindrance. Works that are not *mangalakâryâṇi* are such as the funeral ceremonies.

P. 70, l. 7.—नियोगमशून्यं कुरु, 'thou, go about thy business.' Cf. note. on p. 22, l. 7.

P. 70, l. 13.—देव्याः. MS. G reads "देव्या," more correctly, perhaps, than our MSS.

P. 71, l. 4.—इरावदीचित्तं रक्खन्तीए, who had put the girls into confinement only to please Irâvatî, and not because she herself wanted to punish them. For it was at the instance of Irâvatî that the Queen had confined them.—राआ किल मोएदित्ति &c. Vidûshaka was to say to Mâdhavikâ, that the Queen was requested (lit. caused) by the King to set Mâlavikâ at liberty. And when delivering the message, he added that the Queen easily complied with the King's desire, because that she had put the girls into confinement only to please Irâvatî.—राआ किल &c. G reads, "राआ किल मोचेदि मालविअंति."

P. 71, l. 10.—समुद्दघरए. This refers to a pleasure-house, probably so called from some ponds of water being attached to it. All manner of names are given to pleasure-houses by the poets. The student will recollect the मणिहर्म्य of King Purûravas in the Vikramorvas'î.

P. 71, l. 12.—संभावयामि, *i. e.* 'सत्करोमि,' 'go to receive her.' Cf. note on p. 47, l. 13.

P. 71, l. 13.—MS. G inserts "परिक्रम्य" after "एदु भवं."

P. 72, l. 4.—पलिहलणीआ चन्दिआ. Vidûshaka, true to his character, puns upon the word चन्द्रिका, which, while the King uses it as a proper noun, he takes to mean *the moonlight*. One of our MSS. (E) has the following on its margin opposite the present line :— "विटचोरतमश्चक्रपद्मान्याश्चन्द्रशत्रवः."

P. 72, l. 11.—पस्सदो पिट्ठदो देक्खिअदि, 'whom you see at your side behind you.' Bakulâvalikâ refers to a likeness of the King painted on the wall with his harem.

P. 72, l. 14.—कहिं. This is merely the locative कस्मिन्, used to signify 'rest where,' analogously to the ablative कस्मात् or कुतः, which shows 'motion whence.' The form कहिं, like many others belonging to pure Sanskrit and the Prâkṛit, is still preserved in the Konkaṇî dialect, spoken about Malvan, in the word खईं or खैं, 'where.'

P. 73, l. 2.—या. Supply समवस्था.

P. 73, l. 6.—हला तदा &c. This also appears to be a passage that has not been preserved to us in its original purity, especially the last part of it. I would translate thus :—'Being then in the presence of the King, I had not the boldness to take a full view of him so as to satisfy myself; to-day, however, I am fully satisfied. For I have now looked on him attentively, though this look of him is obtained only as he stands in the picture.' विभाविदो चित्तगददंसणो एव्व भट्टा is added to explain why she was not वितृष्ण, when she had seen him actually. एव्व. The force of this is, 'ण उण पच्चक्खदंसणो (भट्टा विभाविदो).' विभावय् usually means 'to recognise,' 'to perceive.' Cf., *e.g.*, S'âkuntala, p. 14, l. 3; p. 79, l. 5: Calc. Ed. 1860. Vikramorvas'î, Act IV., "स्पर्शाविभावितप्रियः," Act V. "वर्णविभावनसहा दृष्टि :." In the present passage it appears to be used in the sense of 'considering,' 'contemplating.' MS. G omits एव्व.

P. 73, l. 10.—सुषा दाणिं &c. Vidûshaka means, that whatever might be the beauty of the King's person and his youth, it did not at least impress Mâlavikâ favourably, and if he should be proud of his beauty and his youth, a casket might be equally proud of the lustre of the gems it contains. MS. G reads "रअणं" simply, for रअणभण्डं.

P. 74, l. 2.—कास्स्न्येन &c. 'Though they (women) desire to take a full view of the appearance of their lovers that meet them for the first time, still their looks do not fall fully upon them, possessed as they are of large eyes.' This means that though women do desire to have a full glance of their lovers who come within their view for the first time, yet they will not look such persons full in the face and satisfy themselves. Such is their modesty.—च.... च means 'though—yet.'

P. 74, l. 10.—MS. G has अन्तेउरजणं" for देवीजणं.

P. 75, l. 4.—कान्तापराधकुपितेषु *i. e.* 'कान्तेन कृते अपराधे आगतेषु कोपेषु.'—विनेतुः, 'of her teacher.' To be construed with शिक्षा, and not with संदर्शिता. विनेतुः शिक्षा, subjective genitive. 'The lesson she had received from her preceptor.'

P. 75, l. 10.—पच्चाणेआदि *i. e.* त्यज्यते. प्रति has here the sense of '*undoing*.' प्रति आनी, lit. 'to send back.'

P. 75, l. 13.—किमेवमयि. It were also possible to divide this into किमेव मयि, and construe एव with चित्रार्पितचेष्टया.

P. 76. l. 6.—MS. G reads "स्थित्वा स्थित्वा" for स्थित्वा स्वप्ने.

P. 76, l. 7.—अबला सती. These are both common epithets of a woman. In the present passage the pun in अबला सती, 'though she is an *abalá*' (= weak), is apparent enough.

P. 76, l. 8.—समागममायया, 'by the delusion of a meeting.'

P. 77, l. 6.—लङ्घिदुं, 'to bite,' 'to browse the sprouts of.' Cf. S'ákuntala, p. 172, l. 14, Calc. Ed. 1860. On the poet's artifice of withdrawing any character when no longer wanted on the stage, cf. S'ákuntala, p. 62, ll. 5—8, Calc. Ed. 1860.

P. 77, l. 9.—एवम्, viz. बालाशोकस्य पल्लवानां हरिणलङ्घनाद्रक्षणे यथा.

P. 77, l. 10.—MS. G altogether omits the two speeches एवमस्मद्रक्षणे &c. and एदंवि &c.

P. 78, l. 3.—सिलाविसेसस्स, 'of this excellent stone.' On this meaning of विशेष at the end of compounds, see Vikramorvas'í, Act IV., अक्किदिविसेसा चिरं दुक्खभाइणो &c.

P. 78, l. 9.—अतिमुक्तलता. This plant is identified with what is known in Marâṭhî by the name of Kusarî or Kastûrî Mogarâ. The act of the Kusarî (अतिमुक्तलताचरितम्) that the poet alludes to is the coiling itself by the plant round, or grasping with its tendrils, the mango tree, on which it is propped up.

P. 78, l. 13.—जो ण भाएदि &c. Malavika refers to such passages as those at p. 17, l. 15; p. 56, l. 12, *et seqq.*

P. 78, l. 16.—बैम्बिकानाम्, 'धूर्तानाम्,' 'of lovers,' 'of persons versed in love matters.' बैम्बिक is derived from बिम्ब which is, though not by itself, used to signify the loins. Cf. श्रोणीबिम्ब &c. above Act III. St. 20.—कुलव्रतम्. A *kulavrata* is a family custom inherited from generation to generation, such as the celebration, for instance, of a festival in honour of any deity on a particular day, annually. A *kulavrata* is observed by every member of a family when divided, whereas a common *vrata* does not descend from father to son and need not be taken up by the members of a divided family. By calling दाक्षिण्य a *kulavrata* the king means that it is common to all lovers and must necessarily be observed by them.

P. 79, l. 5.—रशनाव्यापार, viz. that of unclasping it.—पातुम् &c. Construe: पक्ष्मलचक्षुः आननं पातुम्, [तद् आननम्] उन्नमयतः मम सतः, [तद्] साचीकरोति.—व्याजेनापि. 'Though all this is but pretended.' The king means that Mâlavikâ's opposition was not real, but merely a playful excuse.

P. 79, l. 11.—हञ्जे सच्चं तुह &c. Compare with these two speeches a similar dialogue between Queen Aus'înarî and her maid in Vikramorvas'î, Act II., "हञ्जे णिउणिए सच्चं लदाघरं वीसन्तो अज्जमाणवसहाओ दिट्ठो महाराओत्ति" &c.

P. 79, l. 14.—संसआदो णिम्मुत्तं, 'just rescued from the jaws of death,' referring to Vidûshaka's late escape from death from the snakebite.

संशय is used here in the sense of जीवितसंशय, 'a peril.' Compare the passages referred to in the note on p. 66, l. 3, *suprâ.*—ताहिं. Cf. the Konkaṇi थईं or थैं. See also note above on p. 72, l. 14.

P. 80, l. 2.—चित्तगदं अज्जउत्तं, referring to the king's picture in the *Samudragṛiha.* Cf. note on p. 72, l. 11. Irâvatî did not know that the king was there in person.

P. 80, l. 5.—उवआरादिक्कमं. Irâvatî refers to her haughty behaviour towards the king at the end of the third Act, the particular act, that formed the उपचारातिक्रमं, being that she went angrily away unreconciled with the king, with the words ण हु इमे मालविआए चलणा &c. (p. 60, l. 1), even though he had prostrated himself at her feet.

P. 80. l. 9.—एस ण मे &c. Dhariṇî means that her act of putting Mâlavikâ and her friend in irons was simply to show how much she honoured Irâvatî, and not because she herself was jealous of Mâlavikâ. But if Iravatî would like to join her in obliging the king, who, as we must suppose, had requested permission to set the two poor girls at liberty on the ground of there being a holiday, she (Dhâriṇî) would free them. Of course, when Dhâriṇî sent this message she did not know, any more than Irâvatî, that Mâlavikâ and her friend had already been rescued from their confinement by the designing Vidûshaka. MS. G reads the passage thus: "जइ अणुमण्णेसि अ—अउत्तंवि तव किदे विण्णावइस्संति."

P. 81, l. 11.—MS. G has "दुवारदेसे" for 'दुवारुच्छङ्गे.'

P. 82, l. 2.—जं मए केअइकण्डएहिं सप्पस्स विअ दंसो किदो. This refers to his pretended snake-bite at the commencement of this Act.

P. 82, l. 5.—असङ्कणीअं पावं, 'nothing evil need be suspected.' पाप here is 'अमङ्गलम्,' 'अनिष्टम्,' 'a misfortune,' 'evil.' Cf. S'âkuntala, p. 97, l. 1, Calc. Ed. 1860.

P. 82, l. 7.—अत्तणोणो, answering to our बेटा or साला used abusively. For आत्मनीनः means both, 'a son' and 'a brother-in-law.'—अब्भवहारसंवादापेक्खी, 'eagerly catching any talk about eating.' On this and the other epithet, ओदरिओ, cf. Vikramorvas'î, Act I., "पञ्चविहस्स अब्भवहारस्स" &c. Also Ratnâvalî, p. 20, l. 22, Calc. Ed. Sam. 1921.—सोत्थिवाअणमोदएहिं. On मोदक see note on p. 17, l. 2. स्वस्तिवायन is a present of sweetmeats, such as that given to Vidûshaka by Queen Aus'înarî in Vikramorvas'î, Act III., or that given by Queen Vâsavadattâ in Ratnâvalî, Act I. (see p. 12, Calc. Ed. Sam. 1921).

P. 83, l. 2.—अच्चाहिदं, 'Alas ! O misfortune.' Cf. S'âkuntala, Act I., "अज्ज ण किंपि अच्चाहिदं &c." p. 18, l. 7, Calc. Ed. 1860.

P. 83, l. 3.—भुअंगमकुडिलेण. Cf. Ratnâvalî Act, II., "पिसुणहिअअकुडिलेण दण्डभट्टेण" &c., p. 20, l. 15, Calc. Ed. Sam. 1921.

P. 83, l. 7.—दव्वीकरो मे उवार पडिदो. Kâlidâsa everywhere represents his Vidûshaka as being afraid of snakes. Cf. Vikramorvas'î, Act II., "भो किंणदं भुअंगणिमोअअं किं मं खादिदुं णिवडिदं."

P. 84, l. 1.—अहं उण जाणे &c. जाणे is here used for the past tense. 'I thought the pretended snake-bite was going to be followed by a true one.' Vidûshaka refers to the common notion, that a person who falsely assumes an evil is visited by the fates with a reality of it in retribution.

P. 84, l. 7.—दिवासंकेद &c. It is the unguarded words of Vidûshaka above ("होदि मालविए," "इरावदिं अदिक्कमन्दी होहि"), and the appearance of Mâlavikâ with the words भट्टा मा दाव सहसा णिक्कम &c., said while Irâvatî was observing all, without herself being observed,—that give rise to this question of Irâvatî. Before that she had even no suspicion that Mâlavikâ was in the Samudragriha with the king. MS. G's reading of the passage is अणिव्विग्घमणोरहो दिवासंकेदो णिहुणस्स.

P. 84, l. 10.—अपूर्वोयमुपचारः. This should be construed as an answer to Irâvatî's sarcastic congratulation, अवि सिध्धा &c., and be translated 'This is an extraordinary manner of salutation.'

P. 84, l. 13.—किं दद्दुरा वाहरन्तित्ति &c. Bakulâvalikâ means, that whatever she and her poor friend Mâlavikâ might have said (see pp. 49—55) about the King, that talk would have no more effect on the king's love to Irâvatî, than the croaking of the frogs on the desire of the cloud to refresh the earth.

P. 85, l. 2.—विसुमरिदो, as shown by his giving her an answer in the words "अपूर्वोयमुपचारः" to her cutting and bitter salutation.

P. 85, l. 2.—पसादं ण गेण्हेसि, 'are not yet reconciled,' 'प्रसन्ना न भवसि.' अनुनयं ग्रह् is used in the same sense. Cf. S'âkuntala, p. 77, l. 15, Calc. Ed. 1860.

P. 85, l. 8.—ग्रह, scil. Râhu.

P. 85, l. 11.—G has "कक्कसा" for हस्सा.

P. 86, l. 1.—णिउणिए.... दिट्ठं भवदोए पक्खवादित्तणं. This is of course ironical. Irâvatî now suspects, that the Queen Dhâriṇî had really liberated Mâlavikâ and her friend, not to oblige the King, who was alleged to desire their freedom on the ground of the day being a festive occasion, but that she had done so designedly to aid the King's intrigue with her. पक्खवादित्तणं, as shown at first by the confinement of Mâlavikâ and her friend.

P. 86, l. 6.—चिल्लाए मुहे पडिदो &c. Vidûshaka alludes to what may probably befal poor Mâlavikâ when the Queen Dhâriṇî comes to learn through Irâvatî's message of what took place in the Samudragṛiha. He expects some such punishment to be inflicted upon Mâlavikâ with her friend and upon himself, as that awarded by Queen Vâsavadattâ to Sâgarikâ and Vasantaka. Cf. Ratnâvali, Act III. *ad fin.* "वासवदत्ता। सक्रोधम्। हञ्जे कञ्चणमाले एदेण एव

लदापासेण वन्धिअ गेण्ह एणं बम्हणं दुव्विणीदकण्णआ अ अग्गदो करेहि" &c. (P. 46, l. 19 *et seqq.* Calc. Ed. Sam. 1921.)—कपोदो. This word is still preserved in the Konkaṇî कौडो or कवडो, the spotted dove.

P. 86, l. 10.—उब्भिण्णो दुग्गप्पओओ. This seems to mean: 'this rogue of a Brahman himself concocted and carried out the design of taking the fortress,' *i.e.*, of liberating Mâlavikâ and her friend from the safe custody of Mâdhavikâ. All our MSS., and also G, have दुग्ग. G reads, however, ओच्छिण्णो for उब्भिण्णो.

P. 86, l. 13.—G has "णं मए अत्तभवं पवेसिदो हवे," for तदो णाअत्तिपि &c.

P. 87, l. 12.—सपक्खो, 'your friend,' 'your caste-fellow.' Vidûshaka means, that the storm which was going to burst on his own head was averted by the monkey, who, by frightening the girl Vasulakshmî, made Irâvatî to forget her revenge and to tell the king to depart, and thus to give him an opportunity of leaving the place without further trouble. Vidûshaka is not only regarded by others as belonging to the fraternity of animals, but even he himself does so in keeping with his character as a buffoon. Cf. Vikramorvas'î, Act V., "किंति मे सङ्कदि। भस्समं परिदो परिचिदा एदस्स साहामिआ."—परित्तादो. See above note on p. 86, l. 6.

P. 88, l. 4.—दोहलस्स. Construe with पञ्चरत्ते.

P. 88, l. 8.—सच्चप्पडिण्णा. See p. 39, ll. 11, 12.

ACT V.

P. 89, l. 3.—उवक्खित्तो....भित्तिबन्धो, 'I have thrown up a wall round. It was this short wall erected round the As'oka that made that tree संकेदघरओ (see p. 96, l. 12). MS. G reads वेदिआबन्धो for "भित्तिबन्धो."

P. 89, l. 6.—पसादाहिमुही. G has पसादसुमुही.

· P. 89, l. 8.—चीरमञ्जूसं, 'a leather box.' G reads simply मञ्जूसं.

P. 90, l. 1.—अणुचिठन्ताणं (अनुतिष्ठनाम्) *i.e.* 'अनुष्ठानं कुर्वाणानाम्.' अनुष्ठानं 'जपहोमपारायणादि करणम्.' Among other things the word means the recital of certain Vedic verses for a certain number of times within a definite period. For instance, the muttering of the couplet त्र्यम्बकं यजामहे सुगन्धिं पुष्टिवर्धनम् । उर्वारुकमिव बन्धनान्मृत्योर्मुक्षीय मामृतात्, which is known by the name of मृत्युंजयमन्त्र, Rigveda VII., 4, 59, 12, accompanied by three nights' fast and a hundred oblations of cooked rice in honour of S'iva, makes a man live for one full century. Such an observance would be an अनुष्ठान. The word is also applied to the chanting of texts other than those of the Vedas. Thus the recitation of the chapter called *S'ivakavacha Adhyâya* (Skanda Purâṇa, Brahmottara Khaṇḍa, Adhyâya 12) is enjoined as an observance for the prolongation of life (आयुर्वृद्ध्यर्थमनुष्ठानम्). The performance of an अनुष्ठान is supposed to lead to many supernatural results. To avert an imminent calamity or danger, to restore a sick man to health, to make the heavens send down showers of rain, are among purposes for which an अनुष्ठान may be, or may be ordered to be, performed.

P. 90, l. 2.—णिच्चदक्खिणा मासिआ दादव्वा, 'the daily dakshiṇâ accumulated for a month,' or 'for one month in advance.' MS. G has this speech very differently: महुअरिए विज्जापारगामीणं बम्हणाणं इमाणि दक्खिणाणिक्काणि । ता पुरोहिदस्स हत्थे पावइस्सं.

P. 90, l. 5.—सेणावइणा, *i.e.* पुष्पमित्रेण. He is called सेनापति, not because he was Agnimitra's general, but because he still retained his title of Senâpati of the Maurya kings, the last of whom he had deposed, and usurping his throne, put his own son Agnimitra on it. See note on p. 8, l. 14. This retention of the old title by Pushpamitra is analogous to that of 'Peshvâ' by the late Brahman rulers of the Deccan, who, instead of being the Peshvâs or ministers of the descendants of S'ivâji, were in reality their masters.

P. 90, l 10.—मङ्गलघरए. This refers to a part of the palace set apart for sacred purposes, the apartment, most likely, where the gods were worshipped. With मङ्गलगृह cf. मध्यगृह, 'the middle hall,' and not 'the middle house,' as the word would literally signify.

P. 90, l. 11.—लेहपत्तं. G has simply लेहं.

P. 91, l. 4.—तेण, viz. by Mâdhavasena, and not by Yajñasena.—सिप्पि-दारिआ°. G has सिप्पिकारिआ°.

P. 91, l. 12.—देवीए. MS. G has an adjective, असोअसक्कारव्वावुदाए (=अ-शोकसत्कारव्यापृतया) after "देवीए."

P. 92, l. 4.—आत्तरतिः, 'आत्तप्रीतिः,' 'delightfully,' pleasantly.' In रति there lurks an allusion to the wife of the god of love ('अनङ्ग').

P. 92, l. 5.—विदिशातीरोद्यानेषु. 'In the gardens situate on the banks of the Vidis'â.' This river is in Malva, and Professor Wilson identified it with the Bess, a small stream that joins the Betwa where the modern Bhilsa (identified by some with the ancient city of the name of Vidis'â) is situated. Vidis'â, the city, is supposed by some to have been the capital of Agnimitra. But there does not seem to be any other authority for that opinion than the fact of Vidis'â being made by Kâlidâsa the scene of this play. The Purâṇas do not mention that the S'ungas, after their usurpation of the throne of the Mauryas, transferred the capital of their empire from Pâṭaliputra in Magadha to Vidis'â in Mâlava.

P. 92, l. 7.—वरदारोधोवृक्षैः. The Varadâ is the modern Wurda, a tributary of the Godâvarî. The whole verse means, that while the king was enjoying the spring on the banks of the Vidis'â, his armies, encamped on the banks of the Varadâ, subjected the chief of the Vidarbhas to his dominion.

P. 92, l. 9.—विरचितपदं &c. It is also possible to take सुरोपम and सूरिभिः as separate words and refer the former to the king.—चरितम् &c. Construe: क्रथकैशिकान् मध्येकृत्य स्थितं (यद्) उभयोश्चरितं (तद्) विरचितपदम् (अस्ति): where विरचितपदं is the predicate. विरचितपदं means, 'is celebrated by song,' 'is made the subject of panegyric,' 'विरचितानि पदानि पद्यानि यस्मिंस्तत्.' It is, perhaps, equally correct to take स्थितं with विरचितपदं, and to consider it as a mere copula.—क्रथकैशिकान् मध्येकृत्य, 'making the Krathakais'ikas the middle;' *i. e.*, putting them as it were in the middle, and the two heroes, Krishṇa and Agnimitra, on the two sides, they sing of their exploits, which were both achieved over the Krathakais'ikas. Shortly we may render क्रथकैशिकान्मध्येकृत्य by, 'over the Krathakais'ikas.' The Krathakais'ikas are the same as Vidarbhas. See our note on Raghuvaṁs'a V., stanza 39.—तव and शौरेः are together exegetical of उभयोः. Supply इतवतः after शौरेः. On the seizure of Rukmiṇî by Krishṇa, here alluded to, see Vishṇu Purâṇa, Cap. XXVI.

P. 92, l. 12.—शौरेः. MS. G reads विष्णोः.

P. 92, l. 13.—जअसद्दसूइदपथ्थाणो. The जअसद्द, here referred to, is the customary formula 'इत इतो देवः.' We may, however, as well take 'जअसद्द' to refer to the panegyric stanzas "परभृत०" &c. and "विरचितपदं" &c., sung by the bards as the King left his throne.

P. 92, l. 15.—मुहालिन्दतोरणं समस्सिदा होमि. 'Let me put myself under this arch of the terrace.' मुहालिन्द is the terrace or veranda at the first entrance of the palace, and the मुहालिन्दतोरण is an arch cut into the wall adjoining such a terrace.

P. 92, l. 19.—सुलभेतरसंप्रयोगां *i.e.* 'दुर्लभसंगमाम्.'

P. 93, l. 5.—पसाहणगव्वं. G reads पसाहणणेउणं (= प्रसाधननैपुण्यम्).

P. 93, l. 12.—मह आरम्भो, 'my labours,' viz. of causing the *dohada* to be made by Mâlavikâ upon the As'oka, that it might put forth flowers.

P. 94, l. 2.—जहारूहसंमाणसुहिदं &c. The Queen Dhâriṇî had invited also the other ladies of the King's harem to come and see the As'oka which had just burst into flowers. Having shown them the tree with its flowers, she had just dismissed them, says the Pratîhârî, and they had gone home highly pleased with the courteous reception which the Queen gave them severally according to their merits (जहारूहसंमाणसुहिदं).

P. 94, l. 8.—परिवुत्तजोव्वणो, 'to whom his youth has come back', *i.e.* renovated, restored to youth.

P. 94, l. 11.—MS. G reads विकीर्णकुरवकफलजालकभज्यमानसहकारम्.

P. 94, l. 13.—दिण्णणेवथ्थो विअ, 'as if adorned with so many ornaments.' Lit. 'to whom ornaments are given,' or, 'who is made to wear them.'

P. 95, l. 6.—पस्सपरिवट्टिणीं मालविअं, 'Mâlavikâ, who stands by.' Cf. S'âkuntala, p. 15, ll. 20, 21; p. 26, l. 10; p. 58, l. 15: Calc. Ed. 1860.

P. 95, l. 6.—मालविअं अणुणेइ, 'is instructing Mâlavikâ,' 'is getting her consent.' Cf. *infra*, p. 109, l. 3. MS. G reads, अम्हेसु दूरगदेसुचि धारिणी पस्सपरिवत्तिणिं मालविअं अणुमण्णेदि.

P. 95, l. 9.—विस्मृतहस्तकमलया. This means, that nothing was wanting to make Mâlavikâ completely resemble Lakshmî, except that she had no lotus in her hand. Lakshmî, when she was churned out of the ocean, is supposed to have come out with a lotus in her hand. Cf. Mâgha, VIII. 64:—

दीव्यानामपि कृतविस्मयां पुरस्ताद्
अभ्यस्तः स्फुरदरविन्दचारुहस्ताम् ।
उद्वीक्ष्य श्रियमिव काचिदुत्तरन्तीम्
अस्मार्षीज्जलनिधिमन्थनस्य शौरिः ॥

On Lakshmî attending upon a king with the lotus in her hand, cf. Raghuvaṁs'a, IV. 5, "छायामण्डललक्ष्येण" &c.

P. 96, l. 11.—तरुणीजणसहाअस्स. No direct reference is made hereby to Mâlavikâ. Dhâriṇî is delighted that her application of the *dohada* has been successful, and presents the As'oka to the king, that he may resort thither to pass his time with his young wives. तरुणीजण refers ostensibly to such young ladies of the harem as Irâvatî, but there is also an occult reference to Mâlavikâ, of whom she is about to make a present to the king.

P. 96, l. 12.—संकेदघरओ, 'serving as a rendezvous.' संकेतगृह is, lit., 'a *house* that is a rendezvous of a secret meeting;' and संकेदघरओ is 'having a house for a rendezvous,' which house consisted in the present instance of a simple enclosure. Cf. note on p. 89, l. 2. MS. G reads: अ-अउत्त एसो दे अम्हेहिं तरुणीजणसहाअस्स असोओ संगेदघरअं सज्जिदो । पविसदु भवं ।

P. 97, l. 1.—इमं जोव्वणवदिं. This alludes really to Mâlavikâ, though not ostensibly, which latter fact allows Vidûshaka to make a shift to the तवणीआसोअकुसुमसोहा.

P. 97, l. 2.—कं. The Queen puts the question, because she has not yet made a declaration of her wish to present Mâlavikâ to the king.

P. 97, l. 7.—रथाङ्गनामेव, 'like him who is called by the name that is borne by a member of a chariot,' *i.e.* the *chakra* or *chakravâka* bird. The poets say, that the chakravâka, though having his mate all night beside him, can never, as long as the night lasts, come in close contact with her.

P. 97, l. 11.—विदर्भविषयोपायने, 'in the present from the country of the Vidarbhas.'—शिल्पिदारिके, 'शिल्पिन्यौ च ते दारिके च शिल्पिदारिके.' Cf. Pâṇini, VI., 3, 42. MS. G reads शिल्पकारिके.

P. 98, l. 4.—आआमि &c. MS. G has: आआमि सुहं वा दुक्खं वा हिअअं सम-त्थीकरेदि.

P. 98, l. 10.—मालविका परिव्राजिका च &c. It is not correct to read this stage-direction thus: मालविकां परिव्राजिकां च चेट्यौ दृष्ट्वा परस्परमवलो-कयतः. Though we have not yet been told by the author that Mâlavikâ and the Parivrâjikâ knew each other, as they really did (cf. p. 100, l. 13), we must still read the words as they are given in the present edition, on the authority of all our MSS.* For if the चेट्यौ looked at each other to imply, that they recognised Mâlavikâ and Parivrâjikâ, they would rather burst into surprise immediately than subsequently, when the Queen calls Mâlavikâ by her name.

P. 99, l. 1.—G has अभिविनीते भवत्यौ for "अभियोगो भवत्योः;" and it reads the following answer thus: भट्टा संगीदे अभिविणीदेम्ह.

P. 100, l. 1.—पादुआरम्भोएण दूसिदं, 'defiled by being made into shoes.' G reads पादुपयोगेण.

P. 100, l. 11.—सरओओ, 'voice.' Lit. 'a harmony of several sounds or notes.' G reads सरजोओ. Cf. S'âkuntala, Act V. "वीणाए सलसं-जोओ सुणिअदि," p. 103, l. 5, Calc. Ed. 1860.

P. 101, l. 6.—भत्तहोदीए, *i.e.* of Mâlavikâ.

P. 101, l. 11.—वैदिशगामिनम्, 'going to the Vaidis'a country. Vaidis'a means the country in which Vidis'â was a city. See above, note on page 67, l. 3.

P. 101, l. 14.—स चाटव्यन्ते, 'encamped in a forest.' Cf. Raghuvaṃs'a II., 58, "वृत्तः स नौ संगतयोर्वनान्ते" &c., and our note *ad loc.* MS. G, however, reads स चाटव्यन्तरे.

---

* G, however, reads "मालविकां परिव्राजिकां च" &c.

P. 102, l. 6.—आपातदुष्प्रसहम् ‘terrifying by its very first appearance.’

P. 102, l. 14.—G reads दुर्जाते for “दुर्जातेः,” and भर्तृप्रिया for भर्तृप्रियः.

P. 102, l. 14.—इमां परीप्सुः, ‘desirous of defending this girl.’—दुर्जातेः, ‘प्रतिरोधकानामनीकात्.’

P. 103, l. 4.—सफलीकृतभर्तृपिण्डः, ‘who showed that he had not in vain eaten his master's salt.’ Lit. पिण्डः, ‘food,’ ‘a morsel of rice.’ MS. G reads सफलीकृतभर्तृप्रतिज्ञः.

P. 103, l. 10.—MS. G reads युक्तः सुजनस्यैवं पन्थाः.

P. 104, l. 2.—स्नानीयवस्त्रक्रियया उपयुज्यते, ‘is used as a bathing-cloth.’ A स्नानीयवस्त्र is any piece of old and worn out cloth tied round the waist (the Hindus never bathe naked) at the time of bathing. It may likewise refer to such a cloth used to wipe the body with after bath.

P. 104, l. 3.—भणाचखखन्तीए &c. Cf. Ratnâvalî, Act IV., “भो भणाचखिखदोवि एदस्स अभिप्पाओ मए जाणिदो” &c., p. 64, l. 22, Cal. Ed. Sam. 1921.

P. 104, l. 9.—चिनरि जीवति. MS. G has परिदीव्यन्ती for “चितरि जीवति.”—लोकयात्रागतेन सिद्धादेशेन साधुना, ‘by a certain divine personage of infallible preternatural powers, who had assumed the human form.’ सिद्धादेश means, ‘whose order is *effectual*,’ *i.e.* prosperous, ‘one whose word, whether conveying a prediction, command, or wish, is infallibly fulfilled.’ A Sâdhu is one who, by holy works and abstinence from all worldly concerns, has acquired supernatural powers to work miracles. One, in short, who is a divine person. Persons like Kabîra, Râmadâsa, Tukârâma, and others of more modern ages, are popularly called Sâdhus. लोकयात्रागतेन, ‘while living in this mortal world.’ Lit. लोकयात्रा is the ‘fair or show of this life.’ Cf. *supra* p. 103, l. 3. On सिद्धादेश and आदिष्ट, cf. Ratnâvalî, Act IV. (pp. 58, 64, Calc. Ed. Sam. 1921); where the whole scene seems to be borrowed from the present one of our play.

P. 104, l. 16.—कथान्तरेणान्तरितम्, 'this which I was going to say, but which I could not say on account of the introduction of another subject'. Lit. कथान्तरेणान्तरितम्, 'separated or put off by a different story.'

P. 105, l. 1.—विदर्भगतम्, 'the matter concerning the Vidarbha.'

P. 105, l. 8.—MS. G has मौद्गल्यमनुमन्यते.

P. 105, l. 12.—जीविदसंसभादो. Cf. note on p. 66, l. 3.

P. 105, l. 18.—MS. G reads नृपते: for "नृपतौ."

P. 106, l. 4.—देवस्य सेनापते:. Cf. note on p. 90, l. 5. Mark the addition of देवस्य to the name of सेनापतिः पुष्पमित्रः, whereas वीरसेन in l. 1 is styled simply सेनापतिः

P. 106, l. 7.—सोपचारकम्. An adverb. G has सोपचारम्.

P. 106, l. 9.—अम्हहे तदोमुहं एव्व णो हिअअं. 'My heart has already been eagerly expecting to hear some news about my son' तदोमुहम्, lit. 'looking towards that,' 'with face turned towards that.' तदो, scil., the affairs of her son.

P. 106, l. 12.—यज्ञशरणात्. Construe with "अनुदर्शयति." यज्ञशरणात्, 'from the sacrificial compound,' 'यज्ञस्थानात्' 'यज्ञमण्डपाद्वा.' This marks the place whence the epistle was despatched. Cf. "अग्निशरणम्" S'âkuntala, p. 105, l. 17, Calc. Ed. 1860. Also "अग्निशरणाद्गच्छता महेन्द्रमन्दिरम्," Vikramorvas'î, Act III.

P. 106, l. 13.—वैदिशस्थम्. See note on p. 92, l. 5.

P. 107, l. 2.—सिन्धोः. G's reading, सिद्धार्थो for "सिन्धोः," is, if correct, deserving of particular attention.

P. 107, l. 10.—अंशुमतेव सगरः See Wilson's Vishṇu Purâṇa, p. 377 *et seqq*.

P. 107, l. 11.—कालहीनम्, 'without delay.' Lit. *without time*.

P. 107, l. 11.—विगतरोषचेतसा. It is not known whether there was any misunderstanding or quarrel between Agnimitra and his father. We can only understand the propriety of विगतरोषचेतसा by supposing that Agnimitra had disapproved of his father's having sent out the boy Vasumitra as champion of the courser. And in support of this supposition, it may be added, that the words, योसौ.... वसुमित्रं गोप्तारमादिश्य...... तुरगो विसृष्टः, clearly imply that Agnimitra knew already of young Vasumitra's mission. See also p. 90, ll. 5, 6.

P. 108, l. 1.—होदि, referring to the Parivrajika.

P. 108, l. 4.—वीरविजृम्भितेन, 'अनया वीरचेष्टया.'

P. 108 l. 7.—वह्नेरपां दग्धुरिवोरुजन्मा, 'as the Thigh-born of that fire, the consumer of the waters.' For the myth of Aurva's birth from his mother's thigh, and for the destructive flame which afterwards proceeded from him and was made to abide in the waters of the ocean, with the mouth of a horse, see Wils. V. P. p. 290, Note 1.

P. 108, l. 8.—यज्ञसेनश्यालमुररीकृत्य, 'पुरस्कृत्य,' यज्ञसेनश्यालादय इत्यर्थः.

P. 109, l. 3.—मह वअणेण. MS. G has मह अणुणएण.—अणुणेहि. See note on p. 95, l. 6.

P. 109, l. 10.—सरिसं, 'right,' 'proper.' MS. G reads: सरिसं खु देवीए पहवदीए पुढमं संकप्पिदं &c.

P. 110, l. 3.—इदानीमपि, *i.e.*, as hitherto.

P. 110, l. 4.—पिअणिवेदणाणुरूवं. The पिअं, here referred to, is the good news of Vasumitra's success.

P. 110, l. 11.—देवीए दिण्णदेवीसद्दं. Cf. Ratnâvali, Act IV., "रत्नावलीमङ्गुल्या देवीशब्देन प्रसादं करोति," p. 65, l. 23, Calc. Ed. Sam. 1921.

P. 111, l. 4.—अप्याकर° &c. Construe अपि with 'मणिजातिः.'

P. 111, l. 6.—लङ्घिज्जन्ति. MS. G reads ण लङ्घिअदं instead.

P. 112, l. 6.—प्रतिपक्षेणापि, 'even by giving new brides to their husbands who thereby become their rivals.'

P. 112, l. 11.—अहंवि भट्टिणा पसादमत्तेण सभावइदव्वोत्ति, 'that I also should be honoured by reconciliation and pardon;' *i.e.* the king should pardon her haughty conduct. See p. 60. MS. G reads thus: इरावदी विण्णवेदि । जं उवआरादिक्कमेण तदा अहं अवरद्धा भट्टिणो ता अणुरूवं मए आअरिदं । संपदं संपुण्णमणोरहेण भट्टिणा अहंवि पसादमेत्तेण संभावइदव्वत्ति.

P. 113, l. 1.—चरितार्थम्, 'who has got what he wanted,' *i.e.* happy.

P. 113, l. 2.—सभाजयितुमिच्छामि.', 'I wish to salute him,' 'I wish to pay him my respects.' Cf. S'âkuntala, Act V., "इसीओ देवं सभाजइदुं आअदेत्ति," p. 106, l. 8, Calc. Ed. 1860.

BOMBAY: PRINTED AT THE EDUCATION SOCIETY'S PRESS, BYCULLA.

Bombay Sanskrit Series;

EDITED UNDER THE SUPERINTENDENCE OF

G. BÜHLER, Ph.D., Prof. of Oriental Languages, Elphinstone College,

AND

F. KIELHORN, Ph.D., Superintendent of Sanskṛit Studies, Deccan College.

Already published.

No. I. PANCHATANTRA IV. AND V.,—Edited with Notes by G. BÜHLER, Ph.D.

No. II. NÂGOJÎBHAṬṬA'S PARIBHÂSHENDUS'EKHARA,—Edited and explained by F. KIELHORN, Ph.D.; Part I., the Sanskṛit Text and Various Readings.

No. III. PANCHATANTRA II. AND III.,—Edited with Notes by G. BÜHLER, Ph.D.

No. IV. PANCHATANTRA I.,—Edited with Notes by F. KIELHORN, Ph.D.

No. V. KÂLIDÂSA'S RAGHUVAṀS'A, with the Commentary of Mallinâtha,—Edited with Notes by SHANKAR P. PAṆḌIT M.A.; Part I., Cantos I.—VI.

No. VI. KÂLIDÂSA'S MÂLAVIKÂGNIMITRA,—Edited with Notes by SHANKAR P. PAṆḌIT, M.A.

In the Press.

NÂGOJÎBHAṬṬA'S PARIBHÂSHENDUS'EKHARA,—Edited and explained by F. KIELHORN, Ph.D., Part II., Translation and Commentary.

KÂLIDÂSA'S RAGHUVAṀS'A, with the Commentary of Mallinâtha.—Edited with Notes by SHANKAR P. PAṆḌIT, M.A., Part II.

In Preparation.

PANCHATANTRA, Part IV.,—containing an Introduction, Critical Notes, &c., by Drs. G. BÜHLER and F. KIELHORN.

DAS'AKUMÂRACHARITA, with extracts from a Sanskṛit Commentary,—Edited with Notes by G. BUHLER, Ph.D.

KÂDAMBARÎ,—with extracts from a Sanskṛit Commentary,—Edited with Notes by G. R. BHÂGVAT, M.A.

MÂLATÎMÂDHAVA, with extracts from a Sanskrit Commentary,—Edited with Notes by R. G. BHÂNDÂRKAR, M.A.